Human Life and the Natural World

Readings in the History of Western Philosophy

Human Life and the Natural World

Readings in the
History of Western Philosophy

edited by Owen Goldin and Patricia Kilroe

broadview press

Canadian Cataloguing in Publication Data

Main entry under title:
  Human life and the natural world : readings in the history of western
  philosophy

ISBN 1-55111-107-1

1. Environmental ethics - History. 2. Human ecology -
Philosophy. I. Goldin, Owen, 1957– . II. Kilroe, Patricia.

GE12.H85 1997   179'.1'09   C97-930431-8

broadview press
P.O. Box 1243
Peterborough, Ontario
K9J 7H5   Canada

B.R.A.D. Book Representation
& Distribution Ltd.
244a, London Road
Hadleigh, Essex
SS7 2DE United Kingdon

broadview press
3576 California Road
Orchard Park, NY
14127   USA

Bruce Watson,
St. Clair Press
P.O. Box 287
Rozelle, NSW
2039 Australia

printed in Canada

To our children

Table of Contents

Preface

Environmental philosophy is, in one sense, an emerging field. Only in recent decades has there been widespread recognition of the gravity of environmental problems, leading to much thought concerning their nature and their possible solutions. Sustained philosophical analysis has helped to clarify these problems. For how can we morally condemn certain acts of injury to plants, animals, or ecosystems, unless we are clear on what constitutes morality? On the one hand, the basis of our ethical obligation to the natural world can be found in its significance *to us*, that is, to the physical, intellectual, and spiritual well-being of human beings. On the other hand, one might explain this ethical obligation on the basis of some value that natural things possess in themselves, regardless of the attitudes that human beings happen to take toward them. One who argues that natural things have such intrinsic value owes an explanation of what it is about these things that gives them this value. So, as is so often the case, ethical questions lead to metaphysical questions: What is a natural thing? Is there a significant metaphysical difference between human beings and other sorts of natural beings? Does this difference carry any ethical weight? Sometimes ethical significance is attributed to species or ecosystems: do these have any ontological standing?

Not surprisingly, many philosophers in the West have turned to established philosophical theories to answer these questions. For, although the environmental problems that have rekindled interest in these issues have only recently taken center stage in Western intellectual and political discourse, the general issues to which philosophical reflection on these issues leads are not new. Indeed, they are among the oldest of philosophical questions, questions to which philosophers must continually return. For what more basic philosophical questions can there be than "What am I?", "What sort of place is the world?", and "What sort of things are in the world?" And, although philosophical fashions come and go, two general truths stand. First, the most effective way to understand philosophical issues and problems is to work through the history of debate and discussion of these issues. Those who have been the first to argue for a certain point or philosophical strategy are usually those who see most clearly what their new idea amounts to. For them, their position is not a received teaching, being carried along once again; rather, it is a new proposal meant to address certain issues that the author has in mind. Second, key thinkers in the history of philosophy are usually those with the greatest influence. In many cases, the understanding of later thinkers can be appreciated only by turning to those who most profoundly shaped their thought. This is certainly true in the case of Western environmental philosophy.

The main goal of this book is to provide the general reader and the student of environmental philosophy with key texts in the history of Western philosophy (ancient times to 1900) that form the historical and conceptual foundation for current environmental philosophy. No slight is here intended toward the teachings of Eastern and aboriginal traditions, which are increasingly influencing Western philosophical ideas on environmental matters. But because there is a great wealth of important, influential material within the Western intellectual tradition alone, we decided to begin with that. Perhaps a future volume, containing key texts from outside the Western tradition, shall complement the work presented here.

We have selected texts that bear on the following issues:

1. What is it to be a natural being? What is the ontological composition of a living natural being? How do human beings differ from other living beings? Are soul and body two different sorts of things, or merely different ways of regarding the same thing? The above questions necessarily lead to a consideration of teleology: Are living beings such as they are for the sake of some end or goal? If so, what is this?
2. Do living things, other than human beings, have ethical standing in their own right? If they do, how can one account for this? If not, why not?
3. In what ways is the natural world as a whole important for human well-being? No one would deny that the natural world provides the raw materials for satisfying human physical needs and desires, but does it have other significance for us as well? How might unspoiled nature be important for a highly developed intellectual, moral, and spiritual life?
4. How is human power over the nonhuman natural environment to be understood? To what extent is this to be celebrated, to what extent regretted? In each case, on what grounds can such an attitude be justified?

Even given our exclusive emphasis on the West, many significant texts that bear on these issues could not be included. No doubt there will be readers whose favorite philosophical author does not appear here. To this we plead the space constraints of a single volume, which do not permit inclusion of all worthy texts. We have also been guided by a policy of giving priority to those texts that have had the greatest impact historically, and those that most concisely and clearly express important theories or points of view. Thus, for example, Mill was chosen to represent the traditions of British empiricism and utilitarianism; and, at the expense of Muir, Thoreau was selected to represent the North American defense of the value of wilderness.

These goals have led us to include both familiar names in the pantheon of Western philosophy and biology and lesser known authors whose writings succinctly express important and influential points of view.

The following additional principles have guided us in compiling the present volume:

1. To the greatest extent possible, selections have been provided with minimal abridgement.
2. For each selection, we have provided an introduction and notes, to allow the texts to be approached and studied by those with little or no background in philosophy. (The notes for St. Augustine, Sermon 241 are by the editors and David Church. Some selections contain notes written by the authors of the texts themselves; these have been labeled as such. Otherwise, all explanatory notes are the editors'.)
3. Accurate, up-to-date translations have been used. All translations of Greek and French texts were done by the editors, except for Rousseau's *Reveries*, which is P. Kilroe's revision of J.G. Fletcher's translation. In our own translations, we have striven to uphold strict standards of scholarship, but, because this book is intended for a general readership, we have not included notes concerning editions and textual difficulties.
4. Selections that are in the public domain have undergone only minimal editing of spelling and punctuation.

We would like to thank Don LePan of Broadview Press for his support and guidance of this project as it progressed through its various stages, and Eileen Eckert for her careful editing of the manuscript. Others who have offered generous help and advice of various kinds include Vernon Bourke, Andrew Brennan, Kim Chaloner, David Church, Richard Davis, Fr. William Dooley, Lloyd Gerson, Stan Godlovitch, Brad Inwood, Robert Kirkman, Patricia Marquardt, Joseph O'Malley, Mark Peterson, Mary Rousseau, Ann Shteir, Eddy Souffrant, Fr. Roland Teske, Michael Vater, and Holyn Wilson. We are grateful to the Marquette University Department of Philosophy, which assigned the able and conscientious Silas Langley as a Research Assistant to Owen Goldin.

This book is dedicated to our children, Woody and Camille, and to the future they will inherit.

Acknowledgments

St. Bonaventure, *Major Life of St. Francis,* and Celano, *The First Life of St. Francis,* from *St. Francis of Assisi: Writings and Early Biographies. English Omnibus of the Sources for the Life of St. Francis,* ed. Marion A. Habig. Chicago, IL: Franciscan Herald Press, © 1973. Reprinted by permission of Franciscan Press.

Cicero, *On the Nature of the Gods,* from *Hellenistic Philosophy: Introductory Readings,* tr. with introduction and notes by Brad Inwood and L.P. Gerson. Indianapolis: Hackett Pub. Co., © 1988. Reprinted by permission of the publisher.

Engels, "The Part Played by Labor in the Transition from Ape to Man," from *Dialectics of Nature,* Frederick Engels; tr. and ed. Clemens Dutt with a preface and notes by J. B. S. Haldane. New York: International Pub., © 1940. Reprinted by permission of the publisher.

Genesis, from *The Holy Scriptures According to the Masoretic Text. A new translation with the aid of previous versions and with constant consultation of Jewish authorities.* Philadelphia: Jewish Publication Society of America, 1973, © 1955. Reprinted by permission of the publisher.

Hildegard of Bingen, *The Book of Divine Works,* from *Hildegard of Bingen's Book of Divine Works with Letters and Songs,* ed. and introduced by Matthew Fox. Santa Fe, NM: Bear & Co., © 1987. Reprinted by permission of the publisher.

Hildegard of Bingen, *The Book of the Rewards of Life,* from *Hildegard of Bingen: the Book of the Rewards of Life (Liber Vitae Meritorum),* tr. Bruce W. Hozeski. New York: Garland Pub., © 1994. Reprinted by permission of Bruce W. Hozeski.

Kant, *Critique of Judgment,* Immanuel Kant; tr., with an introduction, by Werner S. Pluhar; with a foreword by Mary J. Gregor. Indianapolis, IN: Hackett Pub. Co., © 1987. Reprinted by permission of the publisher.

Spinoza, Letter 32, from *A Spinoza Reader: The Ethics and Other Works,* Benedict de Spinoza; ed. and tr. Edwin Curley. Princeton, NJ: Princeton University Press, © 1994. Reprinted by permission of the publisher.

St. Thomas Aquinas, *Summa Contra Gentiles,* from *On the Truth of the Catholic Faith* by St. Thomas Aquinas. Copyright © 1955 by Doubleday, a division of Bantam Doubleday Dell Publishing Group, Inc. Used by permission of Doubleday, a division of Bantam Doubleday Dell Publishing Group, Inc.

St. Thomas Aquinas, *Summa Theologica,* from *Summa Theologica: 1st complete American ed. Literally tr. by Fathers of the English Dominican Province; with synoptical charts.* New York: Benziger Bros., © 1948. Reprinted by permission of Benziger Publishing Company.

Introduction

A rather widely held view maintains that the Western intellectual tradition is hostile or at best indifferent to the integrity and inherent value of the natural world. Indeed, there is no doubt that within Western intellectual history there have been important figures who have taken a hostile, indifferent, or exploitative stance toward nature, and whose writings have had an important influence on Western society. But the Western intellectual tradition is by no means monolithic. For almost every view that has been introduced by one eminent philosopher, there has been an opposing view put forward by another. Cicero's assertion that there is no position so ridiculous that it has not been held by some philosopher[1] is as true today as when it was written two thousand years ago. One especially sees a wide variety of approaches in philosophical accounts of the natural world. Within the history of Western philosophy, there is a kaleidoscopic array of accounts concerning the metaphysics of natural beings and whether this has ethical implications for how human beings relate to other natural beings.

That is not to say that the history of philosophy in the West is a chaotic tale of diverse positions being bandied about by a motley philosophical crew in a game without rules. Philosophical thought on nature and its moral status follows a certain story line, with opposing voices eliciting reasoned responses to one another. These responses in turn lead to the clarification and development of the philosophical views that are put forward. Although it is true that the Western philosophical community differs from the natural science community in not following a single set of fundamental principles and theories, continuing dialogue has nevertheless served to clarify the advantages and disadvantages of various philosophical strategies, despite disagreement on how these are to be weighed. Helping to shape the dialogue as it unfolds is the development of scientific thought, which on the one hand is partially determined by preceding philosophical speculation and on the other provides philosophers with new empirical evidence to consider and new problems to solve.

The history of Western philosophy, a slowly shifting web of opposing positions and supporting arguments, provides much of the theoretical basis for current environmental philosophy. To understand the stance taken toward nature by this tradition as a whole, we must examine a number of ideas and arguments on their own terms, appreciating how they are intended to respond to one another, and how each makes its own distinctive contribution. This book is intended to help the reader do just that.

A brief introduction precedes each selection in this volume. These introductions are meant to alert the reader to features of each extract that are relevant to environmental philosophy, and to point out how the author of each selection is responding to views expressed by other authors, including those represented in the present anthology. We here provide an overview of a different sort, distinguishing the central issues and the positions taken in regard to them by the authors we have included. We are necessarily oversimplifying here; the full complexities and subtleties of these positions will be discovered by carefully working through the relevant texts.

1. What is nature? What is life?

What makes a thing "natural"? In *Physics* 2.1, Aristotle defines nature as an internal metaphysical principle that makes a body a whole, able to do certain things on its own, in a way that cannot be adequately explained on the basis of the kinds of material stuff that constitute the body. Every artificial thing is what it is on account of the external agency of human beings. Ultimately, even artificial things have the abilities they have on account of the natures of the stuffs or parts that make them up. To call something "natural" is to say that its unity and integrity are somehow basic. On the other hand, John Stuart Mill, in *Nature*, argues that a thing's nature is simply the laws governing its behavior. To call something "natural" for Mill is not to grant to it any inherent unity or integrity.

An environmental philosophy will necessarily need to focus attention on a certain kind of natural being: a living being. How are we to understand life and living things? In *On the Soul*, Aristotle says that a living being is a certain kind of natural being, one marked by the natural ability to perform certain special kinds of actions. He is followed in this by the metaphysical analysis of St. Thomas Aquinas. Both philosophers hold that a living thing, like any natural thing, cannot be adequately explained by the stuffs that make it up. But for the Stoics and Bacon, living things are merely complex aggregates of material stuffs. It would follow from this that they can be put to human use like any material stuff. This is reflected in the Stoic arguments contained in Cicero's *On the Nature of the Gods* and Porphyry's *On Abstinence from Animal Food*, and in Bacon's *The New Organon*. In *Discourse on Method*, Descartes argues that a living being that is sentient or conscious has a soul, which is of a metaphysically different order than material bodies. But Descartes argues that animals other than human beings are not in fact sentient or conscious.

According to Plato's *Timaeus*, *any* living being has life on account of soul, a principle that can exist apart from its association with bodies. Further, for Plato all soul is rational. Hence human beings are not metaphysically unique. Plato is followed in this by Porphyry, St. Augustine (Sermon 241), Ray (*The Wisdom of God*

Manifested in the Creation), Emerson (*Nature*), and Wakefield (*Instinct Displayed*). The Platonic view lends itself to the conclusion that living beings other than people deserve moral consideration, for there are no *basic* relevant differences between what it is to be a human being and what it is to be another sort of living being. This conclusion is drawn, in different ways, in the texts by Porphyry, Ray, and Wakefield.

As noted above, Aristotle and his followers, such as St. Thomas Aquinas, agree with Plato that life cannot be understood entirely on the basis of the interactions among the material constituents of the body. They disagree, however, in two key respects. First, they deny that all soul is rational. Second, because they hold that soul is a formal principle that exists insofar as it imparts structure and various abilities to organized bodies, they deny that soul is capable of separate existence, at least in the case of living things other than human beings. Each of these two views has implications for environmental philosophy. First, if human beings are the only living beings on earth that have a rational soul, then they have a kind of metaphysical privilege that could be appealed to in order to justify their exploitation of other living beings. This conclusion is clearly drawn by St. Thomas Aquinas in the *Summa Theologica*. (There is a precedent for this view in Aristotle's *Politics*.) Second, the view that the soul and body together make up an organic unity is conducive to the view that each living thing—considered as an organic, material whole—has a dignity and value of its own that must be respected. Neither Aristotle nor St. Thomas Aquinas draws this conclusion, as have some contemporary environmental philosophers.

In his metaphysical writings, including the letter to Oldenburg included in the present volume, Spinoza argues that there is no real distinction between the soul, which is the seat of consciousness, and the body, which is that which takes up space; they are simply two ways of considering the same thing. This view, like that of Plato, narrows or eliminates the gap between human beings and other living beings. Holding such a view may well lead one to grant moral standing to these other organisms.

A related question concerns how we are to conceive the world, or system of living beings, as a whole. Plato (*Timaeus*), the Stoics (as reported by Cicero), St. Thomas Aquinas (in *Summa Theologica*), and Spinoza (in the letter to Oldenburg) clearly regard the world as a single living organism. One possible implication of such a view is the granting of moral status to the earth or the universe as a whole. Linnaeus (in *The Economy of Nature*) and Darwin (in *On the Origin of Species*) do not go so far, but both are pioneers in regarding the world as made up of networks of interdependent living things. For Linnaeus, each network is established by God and is stable. For Darwin, these networks come about through the process of natural selection, and their balance and health can be disturbed.

2. Are we ethically required to take into account the effects that our actions have on living things other than human beings?

One common view is that other living beings are here for our sake; this view is put forward by Xenophon (*Memorabilia* 4.3), the Stoics, St. Thomas Aquinas (*Summa Contra Gentiles*), Bacon (*The New Organon*), Locke (*Second Treatise of Government*), and Linnaeus. (Kant's position is complex. On the one hand, in the *Critique of Judgment* he denies that biology can legitimately conclude that other living beings are such as they are for our sake. On the other hand, in the *Lectures on Ethics* he argues that only rational beings are ends in themselves; so we are justified in regarding other living beings as to be put to the service of human beings.) From the legitimacy of regarding other organisms as existing for the sake of human beings, one may conclude that we are not obliged to care for the welfare of living things other than people. Such a conclusion is explicitly drawn by the Stoics (as reported by Porphyry in *On Abstaining from Animals*), St. Thomas Aquinas (*Summa Contra Gentiles*), and Kant (*Lectures on Ethics*). (Aquinas and Kant discourage cruelty to animals, however, on the grounds that it can lead to cruel treatment of people.) An alternative view is that we are indeed obligated to care for other living beings, but only because hurting them can have unexpected effects that are disastrous for human beings. Marsh (*Man and Nature*) and Engels ("The Part Played by Labor in the Transition from Ape to Man") clearly express this view.

On the other hand, there have been important figures in the history of Western thought who have taken organisms other than human beings to be worthy of moral consideration on account of their being like human beings in some crucial respect. Biographical stories of St. Francis of Assisi are evidence that St. Francis held that such organisms are capable of praising God, and hence are worthy of human charity. For Porphyry and Wakefield, animals other than human beings have a share of reason, and this fact obligates us to take ethical account of their interests. For Mill, an action is ethical insofar as it maximizes the pleasure in the world and minimizes pain. In *Whewell on Moral Philosophy*, Mill argues that we are ethically obligated to consider the effects that our actions have on animals other than human beings, because they can feel pleasure and pain.

3. What is the importance of our being aware of the natural world?

For the ancients, such knowledge was a good in and of itself, because all knowledge is intrinsically a good for human beings. For Bacon and Mill (*Nature*), scientific knowledge of nature is valuable insofar as it allows us to alter the natural workings of the world to human advantage. St. Augustine, St. Francis, and Hildegard of Bingen (*The Book of Divine Works* and *The Book of the Rewards of Life*) hold that the natural world symbolizes aspects of God's activity or attributes, and therefore has an important role to play in the spiritual lives of human beings. For Kant (*Critique of Judgment*) and Emerson ("Nature"), paying attention to the workings of nature can lead human beings to a better awareness of the moral dimension of their own existence. Rousseau (*The Reveries of a Solitary Walker*), Emerson, and Thoreau ("Walking") value the study of the natural world, and the very living of a life close to natural things and processes, as a cure for the evils brought to human life by human society and civilization.

4. To what extent is the enormous power human beings exercise over the natural world a good thing? To what extent is it a bad thing?

The alteration of the environment through human activity is celebrated by Bacon, Locke, Mill, and Godwin (*On Population*). Godwin's book was written in response to the dire predictions of Malthus (*An Essay on Population as It Affects the Future Improvement of Society*), who asserts that there are insuperable limits to sustaining growth in population and consumption. An early warning of the danger that human interference with the environment poses to human beings themselves can be detected in Plato's *Critias*; more explicit warnings are found in Darwin, Marsh, and Engels.

Current debates in the field of environmental philosophy contain echoes, developments, and distortions of all of the above positions. In order to better understand the roots of these critical debates, we must turn to the study of their historical sources.

Notes

1 Cicero, *De divinatione* 2.119.

I

The Ancient World

CHAPTER ONE

Xenophon

SOCRATES (469–399 BC) was a charismatic, idiosyncratic, and revolutionary thinker whose relentless questioning of conventional Athenian views of religion and morality earned him the enmity of conservatives. At age 70, he was charged with impiety and corrupting the morals of the youth, convicted, and executed.

Though a number of his associates wrote dialogues representing the style and substance of his teaching, only those of Plato and Xenophon (c. 427/8– c. 354 BC) survive. The *Memorabilia* of Xenophon is a collection of dialogues in which the author tries to show that Socrates was greatly misunderstood by his accusers. Xenophon portrays Socrates as a reverent man who, in his philosophical discussions, encouraged his associates to lead the moral life. Nonetheless, Xenophon's Socrates relies on the use of rational argument, not appeal to convention, to determine how one's life ought to be led.

The present selection belongs to a group of dialogues in which Xenophon portrays Socrates' manner of moral education. Socrates is shown to have been a good influence on his companions not only by the example of his own actions, but by means of arguments showing that it is rational to act morally. The present selection portrays a discussion between Socrates and Euthydemus that has the effect of making the latter more reverent.

Socrates points to the natural world, and to how it is perfectly suited to human life, in order to show that the gods take good care of humans. He asserts that the whole natural world has been designed for the benefit of human beings. This extremely anthropocentric view, which here receives its first explicit formulation, helped to shape the Stoic account of the relation between nature and human beings, which in turn was a guiding force in the development of Christian thought on these matters.

✝═══✝

XENOPHON
Memorabilia 4.3
TR. OWEN GOLDIN

He was in no hurry for his companions to become skilled at speaking, taking action, and devising schemes;[1] rather, he thought that they ought to acquire good sense[2] before acquiring these other things. For he believed that those who have these abilities without having good sense are more unjust and more likely to do evil.

First, he tried to make his companions have good sense concerning the gods. I grant that others who were in his company while he was talking to other people about these things have told all about this.[3] But *I* was present when he and Euthydemus had a conversation like this:

"Tell me, Euthydemus," he said, "has it ever occurred to you to reflect on how considerate the gods have been in furnishing people with what they need?"

"No, by Zeus," he replied. "That has never occurred to me."

Socrates said, "You know this, at any rate. The first thing we need is light, and the gods provide us with it."

"By Zeus," he agreed, "if we didn't have *that*, as far as our eyes are concerned, we would be just like blind people."

"But since we also need rest, the gods have also provided us with the sweet resting time of night."

"Most true," he said, "and for this too they deserve thanks."

"Then don't you agree that the sun, through its shining, marks for us the time of day and everything else? But, on account of its darkness, nothing is revealed in the night. This is why they lit up the stars at nighttime, which mark the time of night for us. This allows us to do many things that we need to do."

"That's how it is," he said.

"But the moon does not only show us the divisions of the night. It also shows the divisions of the month."[4]

"Absolutely," he agreed.

"Think about this. Since we need nourishment, they offered it to us from the earth, and they gave us the seasons that are well adapted for this, which furnish us with all kinds of things, which we not only need, but also enjoy."

"In this," he said, "they have shown their great love for human beings."[5]

"And consider that they likewise provided us with precious water, with the result that it works with the earth and the seasons to allow everything of use to us to sprout and grow, and helps to nourish us, too, and, when our food is moistened with it, makes it both easier to digest, more beneficial, and tastier. Since we need so much of this, they provided us with it in great abundance."

He replied, "This too shows forethought."

"And consider how they brought us fire, which protects us from the cold and from darkness, and cooperates with us in every craft, and to produce everything helpful which people acquire for themselves. In a word, of the things that people acquire for themselves that are useful for life, there is nothing worth mentioning that is acquired without fire."[6]

"This too," he said, "shows a superabundance of love for human beings."

"Notice how, following the winter solstice, the sun advances, ripening some things and drying up others whose time has passed. Once it has brought these things about, it advances no further, but turns back, so that we are protected from any injury on account of too much heat. Further, when in its retreat it comes to the point where it is clear to us that, if it were to retreat any further, we would freeze on account of the cold, think of how it again turns around and approaches, and maintains its orbit where it helps us the most."

"Yes, by Zeus," he replied. "These things really do seem like things that come about for sake of human beings."

"Notice this as well. Since it is clear that we cannot bear sudden onslaughts of heat or cold, the sun advances little by little, so that we don't notice when we are brought to either extreme condition."

Euthydemus declared, "As for me, I'm beginning to wonder if the gods' only task is to take care of human beings. But this alone bothers me: the other kinds of animals also share in these things."

Socrates answered, "But isn't it also clear that the other animals are born and are nourished for the sake of human beings? For what other animal enjoys as many good things as those which human beings enjoy from goats, sheep, cows, horses, asses, and the other animals? For it seems to me that there are more of these good things than there are good things we enjoy from plants. At any rate, people get nourishment and profit from animals no less than from plants. There is a large group of people who do not get food from the things that grow out of the earth,[7] but live off the milk, cheese, and meat that they get from livestock. All peoples tame and subdue useful animals, and enlist their help in war and in many other enterprises."

"I'm in agreement on this, too," he responded. "For I see that some of these animals that are quite a bit stronger than us come to be under the power of human beings, so that humans make use of them as they please."

"And notice this. Since there are things that are both beautiful and beneficial, yet are distinct from each other, the gods gave human beings sense organs suited to each of these things. It is by means of these sense organs that we enjoy all good things. We are also born with the ability to reason. When we reason about or remember the things we perceive, our reason allows us to learn the advantage of each. It also allows us to devise many means for enjoying good things and for keeping bad things away from us. And see how they gave us the ability to communicate, by which we share all good things with one another through teaching, and by which we have dealings with one another, and lay down laws, and take part in political life."

"Socrates, it really does seem that the gods take very good care of human beings."

"And notice how, since we cannot foresee what things will be to our advantage, they cooperate with us on this. By means of divination they tell the future to those who ask and teach them how things might turn out for the best."

He said, "They seem to deal more lovingly with you than with others, if it is true that, without being questioned, they give you signs in advance concerning what you ought and ought not do."[8]

"Even you would know that I am speaking the truth, if seeing the works of the gods were enough to lead you to worship and honor them, without your waiting until you had seen their bodily form. Notice that the gods themselves suggest as much. They never become visible when they give us good things. The god who orders and sustains[9] the whole cosmos,[10] in which all things are beautiful and good, is seen to be doing the most tremendous things. He always provides things to those who use them, in a pristine, healthy, and ageless condition, and they faithfully serve him more quickly than thought itself. Yet, though it is he who puts these things in order,[11] he is invisible to us.

"And notice that Helios,[12] who is apparently visible to everyone, does not allow people to get a good look at him; rather, anyone who shamelessly tries to behold him has his sense of sight destroyed. Further, you will discover that the servants of the gods are invisible. For while it is obvious that lightning is hurled from on high, and that it prevails[13] over anything it encounters, it is seen neither as it advances, nor as it strikes, nor as it returns. The winds, too, are not themselves seen; rather, what is evident to us is what they do, and we see their approach. For that matter, the human soul, which partakes of the divine if anything human does, is not itself seen, though it is obvious that it is the monarch within us. If you understand these things you should not disdain what cannot be seen. Rather, once the things that occur lead you to appreciate the power of what is not seen, you must honor what is divine."

"Socrates," said Euthydemus, "I clearly see that I will by no means disregard the divine. But this is discouraging. It seems to me that no human being could ever repay the gods for their good works with the gratitude that they deserve."

"Euthydemus, do not be discouraged," he answered. "For you see that the god in Delphos,[14] when he was asked how one could show gratitude to the gods, answered 'by following the custom[15] of the city.' And no doubt it is the custom everywhere to please the gods as best one can through rites. So how might one honor the gods in a more beautiful and more reverent way than to do as they bid?

"Yet one must not do less than one can. For someone who does less is then clearly not honoring the gods. So one must take heart and hope for the best things, as long as one does not fall short of one's abilities in honoring the gods. For one could not sensibly[16] expect more from anyone than what one expects from those who are able to give the greatest help. Nor can one sensibly have such expectations except by pleasing these beings. And how could one please them except by obeying them to the greatest extent?"

By saying this sort of thing and through his own actions, he caused his companions both to become more reverent and to have more good sense.

Notes

1 The term here is *mēchanikos*, from which is derived the English "mechanical" and "machine." One who is *mēchanikos* is clever at producing stratagems and inventions. In human affairs, we might call such a one "tricky"; in Greek, too, the term is often applied to one whose clever plans may be secret or morally suspect. One who invents a machine or device would also be called *mēchanikos*. The Greeks did not as a rule associate the ability to make such discoveries with the most important kind of knowledge or wisdom.

2 The term translated here as "good sense" is *sōphrosunē*. This term has a wide range of meanings, most of which are associated with a kind of self-knowledge. One important sense is "temperance" or "moderation," the virtue that allows one to not pursue to excess the pleasures of the body. The other is the virtue that enables one to know one's place in regard to one's superiors. It is a sort of humility and lack of arrogance. Here the term is being used primarily in this second sense.

3 Xenophon is probably referring to Plato's *Euthyphro*. He may have other Socratic dialogues in mind, as well.

4 In these several paragraphs, which deal with celestial lights, there are many terms deriving from the root *phainein*, "to appear," "shine," or "be evident." These include the terms for "light," "shine," "mark," and "show." A main theme of this dialogue is that although the gods themselves are not evident, the results of their work are.

5 Socrates is here departing from traditional Greek mythology, according to which the gods wish to ensure their privileged status, and begrudge mortals any aids to their wretched lives. Thus, Greek mythology tells of how Prometheus was punished for giving people fire.

6 On how people acquired fire, see the preceding note.

7 The term *phuein* ("to grow") is related to *phuton* ("plant") and to *phusis*, the philosophic term for "nature."

8 Socrates claimed to have a special *daimon* (a divine intermediary between humans and gods) that never told him what to do, but warned him against doing what he ought not.

9 The sense is that the supreme god is ultimately responsible both for the arrangement of things in the universe and for its very cohesion. We shall see this teaching elaborately developed in Stoic physics.

10 The verb *kosmein* means "to order" or "to arrange." Hence, the term *kosmos* has the sense not only of the totality of things, but of an ordered totality of things.

11 "To put things in order" is my rendering of *oikonomein*, literally, to lay down a law for the household. Our term "economics" is derived from *oikonomikē*, "the art dealing with the law of the household." In traditional Greek gender roles, the wife would establish the rules concerning the things within the household; this involved control of expenditures. Xenophon wrote the lengthy *Oeconomicus* in which Socrates discusses what is fitting for both a man and a woman in the care of an estate.

12 Helios is the sun personified.

13 The term for "prevail" is *krattein*, "to rule over." Socrates is positing a political hierarchy. The one god rules over the many. The many gods rule over their servants, such as lightning. Lightning rules over whatever it strikes. Within this paragraph Socrates asserts that,

within us, the soul rules over the rest of us. We have already seen Socrates draw attention to humans' rule over animals.

14   Apollo had his oracle in Delphi.

15   The term for "custom" is *nomos*. It can refer to any sort of convention, including both written and unwritten law. Part of Xenophon's goal is to show that Socrates was unjustly accused, that he did *not* have contempt for the *nomoi* of Athens.

16   The term employed here is closely related to *sōphrosunē*, on which see n. 2.

CHAPTER TWO

Plato

P<small>LATO'S</small> *Timaeus* is a synthesis and culmination of all previous Greek philosophical thought concerning the natural world. In it Plato presents an account of the universe as a single, living organism. This had an enormous influence on thinkers such as the neoplatonists (including Porphyry), St. Augustine, and John Ray, as well as a less direct influence on other holists such as the Stoics and Spinoza.

The context is a discussion whose main participants are Socrates, Critias (a prominent member of the Athenian aristocracy), and Timaeus (an Italian said to be very learned in philosophy). Socrates begins by presenting a sketch of his ideas for the best society; this follows the main lines of the ideal society discussed in the *Republic,* with notable silence concerning the rule of the lovers of wisdom, or philosophers. He expresses the wish to see in action the society he has described. Critias relates a tale he heard in his childhood, which purportedly originates in Egypt. The ancient Athenians had a society much like that which Socrates described; Critias proposes to tell how they turned back the aggression of the corrupt island of Atlantis. Before he does so, Timaeus situates his tale in a physical and metaphysical account of the whole universe.

Timaeus' account rests on the metaphysical distinction between being and coming-to-be that is argued for in other dialogues (most notably, the *Republic*). Anything that can be sensed is subject to change, and hence cannot be an object of knowledge. Instead, it is an object of mere belief. Such a thing is said to come-to-be. Any true object of knowledge remains what it is, despite any changes in time or perspective. As such it is a "being," sometimes called a "Form." The limited intelligibility that something that comes-to-be does possess proceeds from its status as an image of a "being."

Timaeus argues that the universe as a whole is such an image. Because it is perceptible, it belongs to the realm of coming-to-be. Because it is beautiful and perfect, it has intelligence. The only things that have intelligence have souls. For Plato, a soul is not only the seat of intelligence; it is also the principle responsible for life. Consequently, the universe is a single image of a living thing. Because it contains all particular living things, of every kind, it is an image of the form of living things in general, which comprehends the forms of all particular kinds of living things. Timaeus warns us that his account of the making of this image, by a divine craftsman or "demiurge," cannot be exact or perfectly accurate, as, after all, it concerns a sensible thing, about which true knowledge is impossible.

Through the words of Timaeus, Plato shows himself sensitive to the beauty and integrity of the universe as a whole. Human beings are understood as parts of a much larger, complete, self-regulating organism.

The *Critias* is an unfinished sequel to the *Timaeus*. While Timaeus tells of the very beginnings of the cosmos as a whole, Critias relates a tale, purportedly handed down from Egyptian lore, concerning the first generations of the Greek people. At the center of this tale there was to be an account of how the forces of Atlantis were repulsed by the early Athenians (whose society is said to have followed the model of the best society, as described by Socrates in Plato's *Republic*). For unknown reasons, the dialogue breaks off soon after Critias' account of the island and the people of Atlantis, an account that is the source of much later myth and speculation.

The second selection comes from Critias' account of the land occupied by the early Athenians. The identity of the Attic people is rooted in the land, from which they are said to have sprung. This land was once very fertile, but Critias indicates that much of this remarkable soil has washed away from erosion. In part this erosion is due to periodic floods, which are said to have devastated Greek civilization. But, as evidence of the soil's former health and ability to retain water, Critias points out that, not long before, during a period following the last flood, the mountains around Athens were covered in forest. Plato indirectly indicates that deforestation was a contributory cause of the erosion of the soil.

The ecological lessons of Critias' tale can be integrated with the metaphysics expressed in the passage from the *Timaeus*. Because the land belongs to the world of coming-to-be, it is inevitably subject to decay and imperfection. Yet the *Timaeus* makes clear that the world as a whole is as healthy and perfect a living thing as is possible. It would follow that problems such as those which Critias is indicating are partial and temporary.

PLATO
Timaeus 27D-31A
TR. OWEN GOLDIN

Timaeus: Now in my opinion, one must first make these distinctions: what is that which always is, and involves coming-to-be, and what is that which is always coming-to-be, but never is? Now that which can be grasped by intellect, with the aid of reason,[1] is always uniform, but that which can be an object of belief by means of opinion, with the aid of irrational perception, comes to be and perishes. Again, everything which comes to be necessarily comes to be on account of some cause. For nothing is able to achieve coming-to-be, when it is absent from a cause. Now everything is necessarily beautiful if it is brought to completion when its demiurge[2] always looks toward what is in a uniform state and completes the making of its form, along with its power, by making use of an exemplar of this kind. On the other hand, a thing is not beautiful if its demiurge looks to what has come to be, and makes use of an exemplar which has been born. Now concerning the total heaven, or the cos-mos[3]—should it best take another name, let that be our name for it; at all events our first investigation concerning it must be about what we assume must in every case be investigated at the outset: whether it always existed, having no beginning of its com-ing-to-be, or whether it came to be, having a certain beginning from which it began.

It came to be, for it can be seen and touched and it has body, and all such things are perceptible. As we have seen, perceptible things, which are grasped by belief along with perception, come to be and are born.[4] Further, we say that anything that comes to be must come to be on account of some cause. Now it is quite a task to discover the one who is the maker and father of the universe, and it is impossible for the one who has discovered this to give an account of this to everybody. But we must renew our investigation, considering this: what was the exemplar to which the builder was looking when he was doing his work? Was he looking toward that which holds in respect to the same things and in the same manner, or toward that which has come to be? If this cosmos is indeed beautiful, and if the Demiurge is good, it is clear that he looked toward the eternal. But if the truth is what is improper for anyone to say, he looked toward what has come to be. So it is clear to everyone that he looked toward the eternal. For of all of the things that have come to be, it is the most beautiful, and he is the best of causes. Since it has come into being in this way, it was fashioned by looking toward that which is grasped by reason and intelligence and what holds in respect to the same things.

If these things are granted, it follows by total necessity that this cosmos is an image of something. In all matters it is of the greatest importance to start at the natural starting point. Now, since the accounts that people give are akin to the very things that they explain, the following distinction must be made concerning images and their exemplars. One must say that there are stable and unchangeable accounts[5] for that which is stable, secure, and evident, and that, as far as it is possible and proper for accounts to be irrefutable and immovable, they must not in this respect fall short.

On the other hand, the accounts of what has been made in the likeness of that [original] and is [itself] an image has a likelihood proportionate to these things. For being is to coming-to-be just as the truth is to belief. So, Socrates, there is much to say about many things, and if it should turn out that we are unable to give accounts of the gods and of the coming-to-be of the universe which are entirely and in all respects consistent and precise, you ought not be amazed. But we must be pleased if we come up with images that are inferior to none, remembering that I, who speak, and you, who judge, have a nature that is only human, so that it is proper for us to accept a likely[6] story[7] about these things, and to look for nothing beyond this. *Socrates:* Excellent, Timaeus! This must be accepted, in the way that you ask. We were amazed as we accepted your prelude, so next recite for us the main piece.[8]

Timaeus: Now we ought to tell the cause that is the reason why coming-to-be, that is, this universe, was constructed by the one who constructed it. He was good, and there is no envy concerning anything that ever arises in one who is good. Since he was beyond envy, he wanted everything to become like himself as much as possible. The most correct thing to do is to accept from intelligent men that this above all is an extremely important principle of coming-to-be and of order. For the god wanted all things to be good and for nothing to be bad, as far is this was possible. All that was visible was not at rest—rather it was moving in a confused and disorderly way. He took this up, and from disorder he brought it into order, since he thought that the former is in every way superior to the latter. For it neither was nor is proper for the very best to perform any action that is not the most beautiful of all. By his reasonings, he discovered that, in the case of things that by nature are visible, when one whole piece of work is compared to another, nothing without intellect will ever be more beautiful than something which has intellect, and that it is impossible for intellect to belong to anything that has no soul. This reasoning led him to install intellect within soul, and soul within body, as he was building the universe.[9] In such a way the work he was finishing would be by nature the most beautiful of all and the best. Certainly, then, one must follow the likely account and say that in truth, through the forethought of the god, this cosmos came to be as a living thing, possessing soul and intellect.

Given that this is so, we must tell what comes next. As the likeness of which animal did the one who constructed it construct it? Surely we should think any sort of part unworthy of this. For nothing that is like something imperfect[10] could ever become beautiful. But we should hold that, more than any other animal, it resembles that animal of which the others, taken individually and in respect to their classes, are parts. For within itself it embraces and possesses all of the intelligible animals, just as within itself this cosmos embraces and possesses us and all of the other visible animals that he constructed. For since the god wished it to resemble the most intelligent animals, that which is in all respects complete, he constructed it as a single visible living thing, which had within itself all the animals that are by their nature its kin.

PLATO
Critias 109B-111E
TR. OWEN GOLDIN

Critias: There was a time when the gods divided up the whole earth, on the basis of its [topographic] regions, not on the basis of the outcomes of their battles.[11] For it would not be right to say that the gods do not know what is proper to each of them, nor to say that even though they know what is proper to them they nonetheless fight to possess what belongs to others, instead. When, by Justice, they obtained their own lands by lot, they colonized them, and once these lands were peopled, they nourished us, their possessions and creatures, as though we were their flocks in pasture. That is not to say that they directed us by forcing bodies with bodily force, in the manner of shepherds who strike their sheep when they drive them out to pasture. Rather, with their hands on the soul, they steered us from the stern, from where a living thing is most easily directed, using persuasion as a kind of rudder to guide us in accordance with their plan—and in this way piloted the whole of mortal being.

And so, these things were put in order by having different regions allotted to different gods. But since Hephaistos and Athena have the same nature, she being his sister by having the same father, and as they were active together in the love of wisdom[12] and the arts,[13] they were jointly allotted this land, since its nature is suitable for and conducive to virtue[14] and intelligence. They made good men in this land, who were born from that very ground, and they instilled the order of the community into their minds. While the names of these men have been preserved, the memory of their deeds has disappeared due to the destruction of their descendants and the great amount of time that has passed. For, as was already said, the people that always survive such things are left behind as a group of illiterate mountain-dwellers.[15] These had heard only the names of the rulers in the land, and just a bit about their deeds. They gladly passed down to their descendants the names of the rulers. But they didn't know about the excellent characters and the customs of those who came before, except for some obscure reports they had heard. Further, for many generations they and their children lacked life's necessities. This is why they had their minds set on what they lacked, and their talk was about these things, not paying attention to things that occurred in the distant past. For myth-telling and research into ancient history enter communities only with the coming of leisure, once people have been provided with life's necessities, but not before.

This is how the names of the ancients have been preserved without their deeds. The fact that Solon said that the priests, in telling the history of the war, mentioned the names of Kekrops, Erechtheus, Erichthonius, Erysichthon, and most of the other names that are recalled of those who came before Theseus, including those of the women, is evidence of what I say. Further, the form and image of the goddess, whose statues show her to be armed according to the custom of that time—the practices of war then being common to both women and men,[16] confirm that in the case of all of those animals whose males and females herd together, the whole species, both male and female, has in common the ability to act in accordance with the excellence proper to each kind.

Back then, the warlike class of citizens (who were selected by godlike men back at the beginning) lived apart from the other classes of citizens who lived in that land, namely, those who made things by hand[17] and those who harvested food from the earth. The warriors had everything that was required for nutrition and education.

None of them had any private property, but they looked on everything they had as the common possession of everyone. From the other citizens they asked for nothing more than the food that was needed, and they engaged in all of the activities that were described yesterday, when we were speaking about the guardians whose existence we have assumed.[18]

Further, what was said about the land makes sense and is true. First, Athens at that time was bounded by the Isthmus and, toward the mainland, extending to the peaks of Kithairon and Parnes, and while on the right, the border descended the mountains to Oropia, on the left it was at the Asope, up to the point where it meets the sea.

That soil was pre-eminently excellent, and it is this that allowed the land at that time to feed a great army free from working the soil. The following is significant evidence of this excellence. What remains of the soil is a match for the soil of any land, in bearing large amounts of all sorts of crops, and in being good pasture-land for all animals. But at that time, the land not only gave us fine things, but gave us lots of them.

Now how can we be sure of this, and what is there that is left from the earth in those days, that allows us to speak correctly?

All of it lies like a promontory, extending a long way from the mainland toward the sea. As you know, around this coast there is a steep drop-off into the depths of the sea.

Now since many huge cataclysmic floods have occurred in the last nine thousand years (for these events were that long ago) the earth that erodes during these times and events leaves no deposit worth mentioning, as it does in other places, and it is always carried away, slipping away into the depths. So, just as in the case of small islands, the remaining lands (compared to those back then) are the bones of a body ravaged by disease, with all of the soft fat earth having wasted away, leaving behind only the earth's emaciated body. But then, when the land was still pristine, what are now mountains were high hills, and the plains now called "Rocky" were full of rich earth, and in the mountains there was a good deal of timber, of which there are clear indications even now. Some of the mountains can sustain only bees these days, but it was not long ago that they were wooded, and even now the roofs of some of our largest buildings have rafters cut from these areas, and these rafters are still sound. There were also many tall cultivated trees, and the land offered a vast amount of pasture for animals. What is more, the land enjoyed the yearly rain from Zeus, not, as now, lost when it flows off of the bare earth and heads into the sea. Rather, much of it was retained, since the earth absorbed it, storing it up in the clay, releasing water from the high country into the hollows, and supplying all regions with generous amounts of springs and flowing rivers. That what we are now saying about the land is true is indicated by the holy sanctuaries, which are situated where this water used to spring up.

These were the natural characteristics of the land outside Athens, and it was put in order[19] in a way that benefits true farmers, who practice only farming, who are of good stock and are lovers of beauty, and who have the benefit of the finest earth, unstinting amounts of water, and, in addition to the land, temperate seasons.

Notes

1 "Reason" translates the Greek *logos*, about which see also the Aristotle selection, n. 13.

2 A demiurge is a craftsman, one who makes things with his or her hands.

3 The term *ho kosmos*, here rendered "the cosmos," has the sense of an orderly, well-arranged whole. The term rendered below as "the universe," *to pan*, literally means "the all" or "everything," and refers simply to the totality of things, without the connotation of order or arrangement.

4 There seems to be a fallacy here: just because each individual perceptible thing comes to be does not mean that the totality of perceptible things comes to be. From antiquity to the present day, readers of Plato do not agree whether Plato in fact holds that the universe was created in time. Some point to this fallacy as a clue that Plato means for us to attend to the story not in order to learn how the universe was in fact created in time, but in order to distinguish different metaphysical aspects of the world.

5 The term rendered as "account" is the same as that rendered as "reason": *logos*.

6 The term for "likely" is very closely related to the term for "image": *eikōn*. Timaeus seems to be saying that the account he is about to give is at best probable; it is an image of the true account, which is beyond our powers to give.

7 The Greek term for story is *muthos*. Religious teachings were often conveyed in *muthoi*, "myths."

8 There seems to be a play on words here. The term for "main piece" is *nomos*, which can also mean "law." In Plato's *Republic*, Socrates argues that the telling of myths should be regulated by the enlightened lawgiver.

9 Soul, for Plato, is both that which makes something live, and that which is responsible for intellectual thought. Timaeus argues that, in the physical world, the best things can think, and anything that can think is alive. Accordingly, the best physical things are alive. Because the cosmos as a whole is beautiful and good, it must be alive.

10 The Greek term translated here as "imperfect" also has the sense of "incomplete."

11 According to Greek mythology, Athena and Poseidon fought over control of the land of Attica. In Plato's *Republic*, Socrates had argued that such behavior is unworthy of the gods, and that, in the best society, such religious stories would not be told. Critias himself is presenting a story that conforms to Socrates' standards.

12 "Love of wisdom" is the literal sense of *philosophia,* the term for "philosophy."

13 "The arts" includes what we call the fine arts, as well as those crafts and abilities (such as medicine or shoemaking) that require a certain kind of knowledge and skill.

14 The Greek term that is here and elsewhere translated as "virtue" refers to those qualities that make someone an outstanding instance of a human being. They include, but are not

limited to, moral virtues such as justice and self-control; they also include such qualities as having a keen mind and a strong body.

15 In the *Timaeus*, Critias relates that floods have periodically wiped out the people who have lived in the lowlands, as well as the memory of their culture and achievements.

16 This is another echo of the *Republic*. In that dialogue, Socrates argues for the view (radical for its time) that in the best community men and women would share the responsibilities of political leadership and military defense.

17 The term is "demiurge." Cf. the selection from the *Timaeus*, and n. 2.

18 Critias' description of the class of warriors corresponds to Socrates' account of the warrior class of the best community, in the *Republic*.

19 The Greek term for "put in order" is closely related to the term *kosmos*, on which see n. 3, above.

CHAPTER 3

Aristotle

P<small>LATO'S</small> most important student was Aristotle (384–322 BC), whose groundbreaking work in a number of branches of philosophy and science formed an important basis for almost all subsequent Western thought. A doctor's son who was well acquainted with what the medical theories of that time had to say about the nature of life, Aristotle followed up on Plato's preliminary research into living beings. According to one story, Aristotle's student, Alexander the Great, had numerous specimens sent back to his teacher. The result of Aristotle's study was a large collection of notes concerning the various types of living beings, and a profound philosophical theory concerning the nature of life that was intended to be the basis of biological explanations of these numerous observations. Most scholars today agree that the writings of Aristotle that have been preserved give us notebooks that primarily present the theory and a mass of particular biological facts in need of detailed explanation. What we present here are some of Aristotle's general remarks concerning nature and life. The selected passages provide the reader with Aristotle's arguments for his positions. Interested readers are urged to take a look at his biological writings per se.

Aristotle's thoughts on the nature of life and living beings had an enormous influence on Western thought. Many of the issues of environmental philosophy and the philosophy of biology discussed today were also discussed by Aristotle. His views may be echoed or rejected, implicitly or explicitly, but they continue to serve as a focal reference point.

Aristotle argued that there is a basic distinction to be made between what is "natural" and what is not. Natural things come into being, and do what they do, all by themselves. The principle that allows them to do this is called the "nature" of a thing. This nature is in most cases a metaphysical principle called the "form" of the thing. Such a form only exists when it somehow gets inside some stuff, the "matter," which in and of itself is without that form, but is the sort of stuff that can take on that form. When this form is in matter that is appropriate to it, there exists a basic natural thing, called a natural substance. Aristotle differs from Plato in claiming that things that can be perceived, such as living organisms, can also be known and understood. To know what a natural substance really is, is to know which activities it can engage in, on account of its nature.

Aristotle pays special attention to those natural beings that are said to be "alive." With the exception of divinities, for something to be alive is for it to be a natural substance that can engage in certain activities characteristic of life; at the very least, a living being must be able to eat, grow, and reproduce. Living beings can be placed in hierarchies on the basis of the other activities in which they can engage. Aristotle places human beings at the top of the hierarchy of life, because he takes them to be the only natural substances that can think.

Aristotle's biology was thoroughly teleological. There is purpose to the organization of living beings; they are organized as they are because that benefits them the most. Aristotle argues against any conception of the natural world as a conglomeration of chance microscopic events. The organization of nature does not come about from the providence of the gods or any other conscious agent, as it does for Xenophon's Socrates. Rather, Aristotle takes a natural form to be what orients a natural substance to its own benefit without having reached the threshold of awareness concerning what it is doing. We shall see that, during the "modern" reaction to Aristotelian thought, this conception of purposiveness without consciousness is subject to ridicule. But it was not until Darwin that an alternative explanation was offered of how living beings are organized to their own benefit, without appeal to a providential god.

In his metaphysical and biological writings, Aristotle argues that each living being is to be understood as a good in itself, doing what it does primarily for the sake of its *own* flourishing and that of other members of the same species. This means that nature has basic value, independent of whatever value human beings find in natural things. There is, however, an anomalous passage that continues the sort of teleology we saw in the writing of Xenophon: all other living beings are ultimately for the sake of our use. This anthropocentric passage immediately precedes Aristotle's assertion that only a bit of wealth is required for living well, a central insight for any environmental ethics.

Aristotle's thought has bearing on contemporary issues in environmental philosophy in numerous other areas. A few of these can be pointed out.

Environmental philosophers who advocate duties to the natural world, as such, are concerned with the distinction between what is natural and what is not, or whether such a distinction is even tenable. Something like the Aristotelian position is often advocated. Further, many environmental philosophers argue that the granting of inherent value to natural things requires a metaphysics that views them as wholes, not in principle analyzable as a complex of microscopic entities. Aristotle argued forcefully for such a "nonreductive" account of living beings in advocating his form/matter analysis.

The question of the metaphysical basis of life is another starting point of environmental philosophy. Much discussion in environmental ethics concerns whether humans have more moral standing than other living beings, or whether animals have more moral standing than plants. The traditional answer is that there is indeed a hierarchy of living beings, with humans at the top. The theoretical defense of this position usually has an Aristotelian cast. Arguments against the position often rest on challenges to Aristotelian biology, in the light of evolutionary theory.

The notion of inherent worth often appealed to in environmental philosophy has its basis in the Aristotelian idea that the flourishing of a living being is a good in and of itself, regardless of how it stands in relation to other living beings. Those who argue that ecological communities as such also have inherent worth need to ground this in a metaphysics that, unlike that of Aristotle, locates worth in wholes more encompassing than individual substances. Sometimes the view is put forward that the Earth itself is a single living organism; as such, it would function like an Aristotelian substance.

In *Physics* 2.1 Aristotle explains what he means by "nature" and presents his distinction between what is natural and what is not. In *Physics* 2.8 Aristotle argues against any physical theory that dispenses with teleological explanations and explains everything on the basis of aimless material interactions. *On the Soul* 2 presents Aristotle's most basic account of life and living things, explaining that we call the nature, or form, of living things the "soul," and that the soul is to be understood on the basis of the sorts of activities it makes possible. The selection from the *Politics* is the only selection in which Aristotle suggests that other living beings have their primary good, not in their own flourishing, but in their usefulness to human beings.

ARISTOTLE
Physics
TR. OWEN GOLDIN

2.1[1]

Some beings are by nature, while others have other causes. Those beings that are by nature include animals (as well as their parts), plants, and the simple bodies,[2] i.e., earth, fire, air, and water (for we say that these beings and those like them are by nature). All of these seem different from those that are not composed by nature. For each of these has a principle of change and rest within itself. In some cases the changes concerned are in respect to place, in some cases in respect to growth and diminution, and in some cases in respect to qualitative alteration.[3] But a bed or a cloak, or any other such kind of thing, insofar as each happens to be called by such a name, and insofar as it comes about by art, has no innate[4] impulse to change, though insofar as it happens to be made of stone or earth or some mixture of these, it does have such an impulse, and it has it to that extent, since nature is a certain principle and cause of change and rest in that to which it primarily belongs in itself and not incidentally.[5]

By "not incidentally" I mean this. Someone who is a doctor might himself come to be the cause of his own health. But nonetheless he does not have the medical art on account of the same aspect of him by which he is healed, but it is a coincidence that the same person is a doctor and is healed. This is why being a doctor and being healed are sometimes found apart.

Each of the other things that are made is in the same situation. None of them has the principle of its being made in itself, but some have the principle of their being made in other, external things, for example a house and each of the other things that people make by hand, and some have such a principle in themselves but not in respect to being themselves—these are those that become causes for themselves incidentally.

So nature is what we have said. Everything which has such a principle has a nature. All of these are substances. For each is a subject, and a nature is always in a subject.[6] The things that are by nature are those things, and also the attributes that belong to those things in virtue of themselves. For example, it is by nature that fire goes up. This upward motion is not a nature, nor does it have a nature, but it occurs by nature and naturally.

So we have said what nature is, as well as what is by nature and occurs naturally.

It would be absurd to try to prove that nature exists. For it is obvious that there are many things such as we have described. Only someone who is unable to distinguish what is immediately knowable and what is not would try to prove obvious points by appealing to obscure points. (But it is not unclear that someone could be in that situation. For someone blind from birth might make inferences concerning colors.) For such people discourse necessarily deals with words alone, and there is no intellectual insight.

To some people it seems that the nature, that is, the essence of the beings that are by nature, is the primary constituent of each, which in itself is not ordered.[7] For example, the nature of a bed would be the wood, and the nature of a statue would be the bronze. To prove this, Antiphon says the following. Suppose someone were to plant a bed, and the rotting stuff were to have the power to send up a shoot. It would not be a bed that would come to be, but wood. This means that being a bed belongs to the thing incidentally, and the disposition and art are by convention,[8] while being wood is the essence which persists continuously even while these changes happen to it.

But if each of these stuffs stand in this same relation to some other stuff—for example, if bronze and gold stand in this relation to water, and bones and wood stand in this relation to earth, and similarly in regard to any other stuff whatever—that other stuff would be their nature and essence. This is why some people say that the nature of beings is fire, and others earth, others air, others water, and others all of these. Whichever of them someone takes to be of this kind, whether one or more than one, this (or these) they affirm to be the whole essence, while all of the others are things that happen to these, or their states and dispositions. Whatever they say is the essence they take to be eternal (for it is not possible for it to change into something else), but they say that the other things come to be and pass away endlessly.[9]

This is one way to talk about nature: to say that it is the primary underlying matter of each thing that has a principle of change and motion in itself. Another way is to say that it is the structure, that is to say, the form[10] in accordance with its account.[11] For we talk about nature and what is by nature and the natural just as we speak of art and what is by art and what is artificial. In the latter case, we would not say that something is by art, if it is only potentially a bed, not yet having the form of a bed, and we do not say that there is art involved. The case is parallel for things that are constituted by nature. What is potentially[12] blood or bone does not yet have its nature, prior to its assuming the form in accordance with its account, according to which we, in giving a definition, say what blood or bone is. Nor is such a thing by nature. So another way of talking about nature is to say that it is the structure, that is, the form of those things that have in themselves a principle of change. This is not separable except in our speech (*logos*).[13] (What comes from these two kinds of nature, for example a human being, is not itself a nature, but is by nature.)

The second kind of nature is "nature" in a more proper sense than is matter. For each thing is said to be what it is when it is what it is in actuality, more than when it is what it is potentially. Another point is that a human being comes to be from a human being, but a bed does not come to be from a bed. This is why people do not say that the structure is the nature, but rather the wood, on the grounds that if the wood were to send up shoots, there would not come to be a bed, but wood. But if we do grant that this wood is nature, that is even more reason to say that the structure is nature. For a human being comes to be from a human being.

Another point is that nature, said in the sense of coming to be, is a process directed toward nature. The case is not the same as that of practicing medicine, which is a process directed not toward the medical art, but toward health. Practicing medicine has its source, not its goal, in the medical art. This is not the way in which nature is related to nature. What grows[14] insofar as it grows has a source and a destination. What is it which is growing? It is not its source, but its destination. This is why the structure is nature.[15]

There are two senses to each of the terms "structure" and "nature." For in a sense the privation is a form. But whether or not there is privation and some contrary in the case of generation in the strict sense is something we must investigate later.[16]

2.8

... Here is a problem: why can't it be the case that Nature makes things, not for the sake of something, nor because it is better that it do so, but in the manner that Zeus lets the rain fall?[17] For it does not rain in order that the grain grow, but it rains of necessity (for that which is drawn up must cool off, and that which is chilled, having turned into water, must go down, and once this has occurred, the grain happens to grow). Likewise, if the grain rots on the threshing floor, it did not rain so that the grain would rot, but this is simply how things happened.[18] So why can't this be the case in the natural world, in respect to bodily parts? For example, it is necessary that the front teeth come up sharp, well suited for biting off pieces, and the molars come up flat, good for chewing the food. Why can't one say that such growth is not for the sake of this beneficial result, but that this is simply how things fall together? The case would be similar for all of the other bodily parts that seem to be as they are for the sake of something. Then, whenever all of the parts coincided, just as if this had occurred for the sake of something, these suitable combinations of parts were by chance preserved. Unsuitable combinations were destroyed, as Empedocles tells us occurred in the case of cattle with men's heads.[19]

It would be this or some other such argument that would lead one into puzzlement. But this cannot be how things are. For these things, as well as all things that are by nature, come about in all cases, or for the most part, but none of the things that are due to luck or chance do so.[20] For the fact that it often rains in winter does not seem to be due to luck or chance, as would rain in the dog days of summer. Nor would a heat wave during the dog days seem to be due to chance or luck as it would if this were to occur in the winter. Then if these things[21] are apparently either random events or for the sake of something, and if they are not random and do not occur by chance, they are for the sake of something. Yet all of these sorts of things really are by nature, as is granted even by those who argue in the above manner. Therefore, in the natural world there are events that occur, and things that exist, for the sake of something.

Another point is this. In the case of those things for which there is a goal, the order of priority and posteriority by which things are done is determined with a view to this goal. The course of natural processes is like that of human deeds, and, as long as nothing interferes, humans do things according to the course of natural processes. Now human deeds are for the sake of something. Therefore natural processes are also for the sake of something. For example, suppose that a house were one of the things that come about by nature. Its coming to exist would then take the same course as it does now, by art. And if the things that are by nature were to come about not only by nature, but also by art, the processes by which they come into existence would take the same course as they do by nature. For each step in such a process is for the sake of another. Speaking generally, in some cases art sometimes attains those goals which nature cannot produce, and in other cases it imitates nature. Then if the things that come about through an art are for the sake of something, clearly this is also so for the things that are by nature. For in the realms of art and nature, the later stages are similarly related to the earlier stages.

This is especially evident in the case of those other animals that make things, though not by art, and following neither inquiry nor deliberation. This is why some people are puzzled about whether the work of spiders, ants, and other such animals is due to intellect or something else. Going a little farther in the same direction, it seems that even in the case of plants things happen that are advantageous in regard to the goal; for example, leaves grow so that they can shelter the fruit. So if by nature the swallow makes its nest and the spider its web for the sake of something, and plants grow leaves for the sake of the fruit, and roots grow down, not up, for the sake of getting food, it is evident that such a cause holds for what occurs and exists in the natural world. And since there are two sorts of nature, matter and form, and the latter serves as goal, the other aspects of the thing are for the sake of the goal, and this is the cause, that for the sake of which there are the others. ...

It is strange that people refuse to believe that an occurrence has a purpose when they do not see that the cause of motion has deliberated. Yet even art does not deliberate. Also, if the art of shipbuilding were in the wood, it would make the ship in a manner similar to the workings of nature. So if there is purposiveness in art, it exists in nature, as well. This is especially clear, when someone practices the art of medicine on oneself. For nature is like this.

So it is clear that nature is a cause, and the manner in which it serves as cause is also clear: it is for the sake of something.

ARISTOTLE
On the Soul
TR. OWEN GOLDIN

2.1

Let the above be our account of what our predecessors have said about the soul. Let us go back as though we were making a new beginning, and try to determine what the soul is and what is the most general account that can be given of it.[22]

We say that substance is a certain single kind of being,[23] and of this, one kind is material, which is not in itself a particular thing, and another kind is the structure, that is, the form, in respect of which something is said to be a particular thing, and a third kind comes from the other two.[24] Matter is potentiality, form is actuality—and "actuality" here has two senses: one, in the sense in which knowledge is an actuality, the other, in the sense in which contemplation is an actuality.[25]

Bodies, and among these, natural bodies seem to be substances most of all. For these are the principles of the others.[26] Some natural bodies have life, and some do not. By "life" we mean the ability to nourish oneself, and to grow and waste away. It follows that every natural body partaking in life is a substance, that is, a composite substance.

But the body is not the soul, since the living substance is such-and-such a kind of *body* (for it is a body having life). For a body is not something that is in a subject. Rather, it plays the role of subject and matter. So, the soul must be a substance in the sense of being the form of a natural body having life potentially.

A substance is an actuality. The soul is an actuality of this kind of body.[27] But "actuality" has two senses: one, in the sense in which knowledge is an actuality; the other, in the sense in which contemplation is an actuality. It is clear, then, that it is actuality in the sense in which knowledge is an actuality. For both sleep and wakefulness occur when there is soul, and being awake is analogous to contemplation, and sleep is analogous to having soul but not being awake. Knowledge comes about prior to the contemplation that comes from it.

This is why the soul is the first actuality of a natural body that has life potentially. This sort of body is the sort that has organs. The parts of plants, too, are organs, albeit extremely simple ones. For example, the leaf is a covering of a pod, and the pod is a covering of fruit. The roots are analogous to a mouth, for both take in food.

Then if we must say what is common to all soul, it would be "the first actuality of a natural body having organs."

This is why one must not ask whether the soul and the body are one, just as one must not ask whether the wax and the impression are one. Nor, speaking generally, must one ask whether the matter and that of which it is the matter are one. For "one" and "being" have many senses, but "unity" and "being" in the strictest sense are "actual unity" and "actual being."

We have said in general terms what soul is. For it is the essence, in respect to its account. This is the essence of such-and-such a body. It is as though a certain tool, say an ax, were to be a natural body; the being of the ax would be its essence, and this would be its soul. If this were to be separated from the ax, it would no longer be an ax (although we could *call* it an ax), but as it stands it *is* an ax[28]—for it was not of this sort of body that the essence, i.e., the account, is the soul, but of a certain kind of natural body, having within it a principle of change and rest.

We must consider what we have said in regard to the parts of the body. If the eye were an animal, its soul would be its ability to see. For this is the essence of the eye, in respect to its account. For the eye is the matter for the ability to see, and when this is taken away, it is no longer an eye (though we could *call* it an eye, as we do the eye of a statue and one depicted in a drawing).

What we have said about the part, we must apply to the whole living body. For the part is related to the part as is the whole ability to perceive to the whole perceptive body, insofar as it is such a thing.[29]

It is not that which has lost its soul which has the potential being which is life, but that which has the soul. The seed and the fruit are this sort of body in potentiality.

Like the cutting and the seeing, the waking state is an actuality, while the ability to see and the potentiality of the organ is the soul. The body is that which is, in potentiality. But just as the pupil and sight are an eye, here the soul and the body are a living being.

So it is evident that the soul is not separable from the body—or at least some parts of the soul are not separable, if the soul is by nature divisible. For in the case of some of the parts the actuality is of the parts themselves. However, nothing prevents some parts of soul from being separable, on account of the fact that they are not actualities of any bodies.[30]

Another point is that it is unclear whether the soul is the actuality of the body as the pilot is the actuality of a ship.

Let this outline provide our definition and sketch of the soul.

2.2

... Let us begin our inquiry. We say that what has a soul is distinguished from what does not have a soul by the presence of life. But "life" has many senses, and we say that something lives even if there is life in only one of its senses, for example, intellect, perception, motion and rest (in respect to place), as well as the change involved in nutrition, that is, both wasting away and growth. This is why even all plants are thought to live. For they seem to have within them this sort of faculty and principle, on account of which they take part in growth and wasting away in opposite directions. Consider all beings that are continually nourished, and stay alive until the end, for as long as they are able to take in nourishment. It is not the case that their growth is upwards, but not downwards, but there is the same sort of growth in both directions, or in all directions. It is possible for this faculty to exist apart from the others, but, for mortals, the others cannot exist apart from this.[31] This is clearly how things are for plants, for they have no other faculty of soul.

So it is on account of this principle that life belongs to living things, but it is perception, first and foremost, that makes something an animal. ...

Concerning whether each of these is soul or a part of soul, and if it is a part, whether it is separable only in speech or it is also spatially separable: in some of these cases it is not hard to know this, but in others the issue is problematic.

For just as in the case of plants, when some parts are cut from each other, the parts appear to live (since in each plant there is a soul that is one in actuality, though this soul is potentially many) so, in the case of insects that are cut, we see this same thing happen for other varieties of soul. For each of the parts has the ability to perceive and to move about. And if it can perceive, it has imagination[32] and appetite. For wherever there is perception, there is pleasure and pain, and where these exist, there must also be desire.

So far, nothing has been clarified concerning intellect and the faculty of thought. But this seems to be the case: it is another variety of soul, and this alone can exist separate from the rest, just as the eternal can exist separate from the perishable. But these considerations show that the other parts of the soul are not separable, as some say they are. But it is clear that they are different in how we talk about them. For to be able to perceive is different from being able to have a belief, if perceiving is different from believing. The case is the same for each of the other abilities that we have mentioned.

Another point is that some animals have all of these, some have some of these, and others have only one. This accounts for the distinctions to be made among animals. The reason for this must be considered later. For some animals have all of these, some have some, and some have one, that is the most necessary: touch. ...

[A]s we have said, "substance" has three senses: one being "form," another "matter," and another "what is made of these two," and of these, matter is potentiality and form is actuality. Since it is that which is made up of these two that has a soul, the body is not the actuality of the soul, but the soul is the actuality of some body.[33]

This is why it is a fine thing to hold that while the soul is not found without a body, it is not itself a body. For while it is not a body, it belongs to a body, and is in a body of a certain kind. This is in contrast to the view of previous thinkers who fitted the soul to a body without making further distinctions concerning in which body and what sort of body a particular soul belongs, even though it is apparent that a given soul does not belong to any chance body.[34] Our position on this matter makes sense. For the actuality of each X naturally comes to be in what is already X, and in the appropriate matter.

So it is clear from these considerations that soul is an actuality and essence (*logos*) of that which has the potentiality for a being of a certain kind.

2.3

As we have said, some living things possess all of the aforementioned faculties of the soul, while some possess some of them, and others possess only one. We have named the following faculties: those of nutrition, perception, appetite, moving in respect to place, and thought. Only the faculty of nutrition belongs to plants, while this faculty and that of perception belongs to other living beings. And where there is the faculty of perception, there is that of appetite, too. For appetite consists in desire and fervor[35] and wish.

Yet all animals have one of the senses—touch. Whatever has the faculty of sensation is able to experience pleasure and pain, and what is pleasant and painful. Those able to experience these things have the faculty of desire too, for desire is an appetite for what is pleasant. ...

Those living beings that have the faculty of touch also have the faculty of desire.

The situation concerning imagination is unclear, and must be considered later. In addition to these faculties some living things possess that of motion in respect to place, and still others possess the faculties of thought and intellect, for example human beings and any other living being which is similar or on a higher plane.[36]

It follows that in each case our inquiry into what the soul is must concern the soul of each living thing (that is, the soul of a plant, the soul of a human, or the soul of a beast). We must also inquire why they are arranged hierarchically.[37] For while there is no sensitive faculty apart from the nutritive faculty, in the case of plants the nutritive faculty is found apart from the sensitive faculty. Again, while none of the other senses is found apart from the sense of touch, touch is found apart from the other senses. For there are many animals that can neither see nor hear nor smell.[38] Even among those that can perceive, some have the faculty of moving around and some do not. At the highest level and finally, a very few animals also have the faculty of reasoning and thinking. For those perishable animals[39] that have the faculty of reasoning have all of the rest, but it is not the case that anything that has any of the other faculties has the faculty of reasoning as well. Rather, some of them do not have the faculty of imagination, while others live by this faculty alone.[40] The theoretical intellect is another story.

So it is clear that the most appropriate account (*logos*) of soul is the account of *each* of these faculties.

✛══✛

ARISTOTLE
Politics 1.8
TR. OWEN GOLDIN

There are many kinds of food, and this is why for both animals and humans there are many ways of living. For life depends on food, so that, among animals, differences in what is eaten have been responsible for differences in how life is led. Some wild beasts live in herds and some live apart from any group, each kind living in the manner that best allows it to get its food, since some are carnivores, some herbivores, and some are omnivores.[41] So Nature has given them different ways of life, to allow them to have an easier time getting the food. Since not all animals by nature take pleasure in the same things—rather, different animals enjoy different things—even within the classes of carnivores or herbivores there are distinct ways of living.

This holds true in the case of human beings, too. Their ways of living differ greatly. Nomads lead the most idle life. For without any trouble these people get food from the animals they herd, while they are leading a leisurely life, but since their flocks must move through the pastures, they themselves are compelled to follow, as though they were farmers whose farm were itself an animal. Some people live off of wild animals, different people living off of different wild animals. For example, some live from piracy,[42] and some from fishing, namely, all of those who live near lakes, marshes, rivers, and in certain kinds of coastal areas. Some live off of birds, and others off of wild beasts. But the largest group of people live off of the land and off of the fruits of cultivated plants. These are in effect all of the ways of life that there are, of those whose business arises independently, that is to say, of those who do not acquire their food through trade or commerce. These are the lives of nomads, farmers, pirates, fishermen, and hunters. Some people live in a pleasant manner by combining these ways of life, by granting to the more deficient way of life whatever it happens to lack in regard to self-sufficiency. For example, some live the lives of nomads and pirates at the same time, or live as both farmers and hunters, and there are similar combinations for the other ways of life. For these people lead their lives as their need compels them.[43]

A certain kind of property seems to be given to all beings by Nature itself. Such property exists right away, when first born, and likewise exists for those who have matured. For, right from the start, from the time of birth, some animals supply their offspring with enough food to last until it is able to provide for itself. Examples are those that produce grubs, and those that lay eggs. Also all the viviparous[44] animals possess food for their offspring within themselves, until their young reaches a certain age. We call food of this nature "milk."

For the same reasons, it clearly follows that we must believe this[45] about what has been already generated: plants are for the sake of animals, and the other animals are for the benefit of humans. This is so for tame animals, because of the use to which they are put, and because they are our food. Most, if not all, wild animals are for the sake of food and other benefits, so that clothing and other tools might come to be from them.

Then, if Nature does nothing imperfect or in vain, it must have made all of these things[46] for the sake of humans. And this is why, in a sense, the art of war, by virtue of its nature, will be an art of acquiring things. For the art of hunting is part of this,[47] an art[48] that must be employed against both wild animals, and against all of those human beings that by nature are to be ruled, but are unwilling, since by nature this is a just war.

Now one kind of acquisitive art is by its nature a part of the art of running a household.[49] The reason for this is that there are certain goods that are required for life, and are the sort of thing that can be stored and are of service to civic or household communities. These must either already exist, or they must be supplied by this art. These are the things that make up true wealth. For the amount of such things that one needs, in order to be self-sufficient in regard to the good life, is not unlimited, as it is according to Solon, who wrote "for men, no bounds to wealth have been established." But such bounds exist, as they do in the case of the other arts. For there is no art that uses an instrument infinite in multitude or magnitude, and wealth is a plurality of instruments for the use of those managing the household or the city.[50]

It is therefore clear that there is by nature a certain art of acquisition for the management of both households and cities, and why this is so.

Notes

1 This chapter has to do with "nature," understood not as a deity (e.g., Pan or Mother Nature) or as simply the totality of things in the world that humans have not made, but as a principle that can help explain why things are the way they are. In English, the word "nature" may still be employed with this meaning. For example, if someone asks why dogs are loyal, we might respond "that's their nature."

2 The "simple bodies" of which Aristotle speaks are "elements." These, like the elements of today's chemistry, are basic kinds of stuff. Aristotle identified the elements as earth, air, fire, water, and ether. Earth is the heaviest and most solid element; it is drawn to the center of the earth, which, for almost all of the Greeks, occupies the center of the cosmos. Water is also drawn to the center of the universe, but it occupies a place above that of earth. Air, too, is drawn to the center of the universe, but it occupies a place above that of water. Fire is drawn up, away from the center of the universe. These are the four "sublunary" elements, the ones found beneath the moon. If left by themselves, they would constitute four separate spherical layers, but as Aristotle sees it, they keep getting shaken up and moved around by the celestial bodies, which are made of a special kind of shining stuff called ether, not found down here on earth. For Aristotle, the motion proper to ether is circular motion; that's why we see the sun, moon, and stars go around the earth.

3 Qualitative alteration is change of quality. A quality for Aristotle is a non-quantitative feature of a thing that can be sensed: its color, temperature, etc.

4 Like our term "innate" the Greek term here (*emphuton*) is made up of the roots meaning "in" and "nature."

5 "In itself" (or "in virtue of itself" or "per se") and "incidentally" (or "accidentally" or "by virtue of an accident") are technical terms whose sense is very complex. The basic idea is this: Aristotle holds that things have essences—making them the sort of thing they really are. Each of us, for example, has the essence of humanity. To have an attribute "in virtue of ourselves" or per se is to have the attribute insofar as we are the sort of thing with our essence. For example, you are capable of learning language in virtue of yourself. This is because your being human is the feature that is responsible for your being able to learn a language. For something to have an attribute incidentally is to have that attribute not insofar as it is the sort of thing with its essence. The two things just happen to have "stepped together" (the literal meaning of Aristotle's word for "accident"). In such a case the attribute is said to be "incidental" or "an accident." For example, the fact that you are learning something about Aristotle is incidental to you; your being human is not what is responsible for this. (If it were, every human being would learn something about Aristotle.) In English, the fact that a certain subject happens to have a certain incidental attribute can be called a "coincidence."

6 "Substance" and "subject" (or "underlying subject," "substrate," or "substratum") are also very important terms in Aristotelian metaphysics. "Substance" refers to the most basic kind of being—a true "thing." Aristotle stresses that a substance isn't an attribute of something else, but is that "something else" in which attributes inhere. For example, the color of this paper isn't a thing. It is the paper, of which the color is an attribute, that is a real thing in the world.

Subjectus in Latin means "that which is thrown under"; the Greek *hupokeimenon*, which is translated by "subject," means "what is underlying." This root meaning should be kept in mind when trying to understand the Aristotelian notion of "subject." The subject or substrate of something is that in which the "something" inheres. For example, a subject of color is a surface. The surface in turn inheres in a body, but the body is not the "first" or "primary" substrate of the color; the surface is.

7 "The primary constituent ... which is not ordered" is, as Aristotle's examples and the passages that follow make clear, the matter that makes up a thing. Matter is the stuff that can become a certain sort of thing, but need not be that thing. Material things come into being when matter accepts a certain form. The basic idea in this passage is that one can think of a thing, for example, a bed, not as being an ultimate subject, but as being a certain kind of stuff, such as wood, whose shape and function is a feature of that stuff. From that point of view, the nature of the bed would be wood.

8 The Greek term for "convention" is *nomos*, which can also be rendered "law" or "custom." For several generations, Greek intellectuals wondered which features of human life were by *phusis* (nature) and which were by *nomos* (convention). Ethical relativists suggested that many basic standards of decency and justice were by convention (*nomos*) alone, not grounded in human nature. These standards of human interaction were adopted by human agreement, to serve certain ends; they did not have to be adopted. Likewise here, the suggestion is that there is nothing in reality to compel one to regard a certain object as a bed. It is called a bed only out of human agreement, because this too serves certain ends.

9 Aristotle is here wondering: If we are going to be consistent in saying that the material substrate of a thing is its nature, and the elements are the basic substrates for all other stuffs, won't we have to say that the elements themselves are the only real natures? Aristotle points to the historical example of some of the presocratics, who tried to explain all phenomena in terms of one or more of the basic elements.

10 "Form" is another important term in Aristotelian metaphysics. (The Greek term here, *eidos*, is the same word that Plato used for "Form," with the sense he gave to it. The Greek literally means "look," denoting the way something looks.) Both "form" and "structure" can refer to either physical shape or essence. In the former sense, the form of a bronze sphere is its sphericity. In the latter sense, the form of a human being is humanity.

11 The Greek term translated here by "account" is *logos*, which can have the sense of "law," "word" (as in John 1.1), "reason," "sentence," "statement," or, as here, "definition."

12 Potentiality and actuality are important concepts for Aristotle, who was the first to crystalize them. To say that some lumber is potentially a bed is to say that it could become a bed, but is not a bed yet. Once it is a bed, one can say that it is a bed in actuality.

13 When Aristotle says that form is separable in speech, he means that one can define or reason about the form, without paying attention to the matter in which it happens to inhere. But one never actually finds a natural form existing apart from such matter (as do the forms of animals, in Plato's *Timaeus*). That is why a natural form is separable only in *logos*.

14 There is an etymological connection between the verb "to grow" and the noun "nature."

15 Many of the ancient Greeks hold a teleological view of nature, that is, the view that things in nature have purposes. For example, a teleologist might hold that because the purpose of the acorn is to grow into a tree, the acorn itself has a tendency to become a tree.

16 In a sense we can answer a "What is it?" question by identifying what it is not. But Aristotle's considered position is that such an answer does not really identify what it is, that is, its form or nature.

17 Aristotle here notes that the scientific explanations of some sorts of events do not require any appeal to teleology. We can explain rainfall by noting that it is necessitated by certain conditions of air, water, and temperature, without any appeal to any benefit that is gained from this rainfall. He asks why we cannot say that all natural processes are like this.

18 The word for "happen" here is the same as that for "to be an accident." The passage can also be translated "(… once this has occurred, the growth of the grain is an accident.) Likewise, if the grain rots on the threshing floor, it did not rain so that the grain would rot, but this is an accident."

19 Empedocles advocates an evolutionary theory of the origin of the various kinds of living things. General processes of combination and separation lead to various conglomerations, such as loose, isolated organs and various monstrosities, which are unable to survive and propagate.

20 If two or more things just happen to be found together, that is, if their connection is accidental, there is no causal bond between the two. In such a case, we say that this is by luck or chance. For example, if, when purchasing a lottery ticket, you choose a certain number, because it is the birthday of a loved one, and you win, this is on account of luck or chance, because there is no causal bond between the birthday of the loved one and the selection of that ticket. We know that there is no causal connection, because most of the time, these things (in this case, the birthday and the ticket number selected) are not found together. Aristotle believes that if they are always, or usually found together, we could infer some causal connection.

21 "These things" apparently refers to natural organisms, and their parts.

22 Literally, "the most common account." Aristotle is after the account of soul that holds of all kinds of souls. "Account" translates *logos* (see n. 13, above); here it may have the sense of "definition."

23 This is a reference to Aristotle's teaching of the "categories." Here it suffices to say that not all beings are substances, that is, basic things. For example, a color or a place is not a substance, or basic thing, for these are features of basic things, and as such are dependent on them.

24 This third kind of substance is the matter/form composite.

25 Aristotle's term for "knowledge" refers to what we might call "scientific understanding," the ability to explain things. You can have this ability even if you are not exercising it. For example, you can be a geometer at a certain time even if you are then planting seeds, because you *could* at that time give a geometrical explanation if you wanted to. "Contemplation" is Aristotle's word for the active exercise of scientific knowledge. So we have two kinds of actuality: an actualized ability—what Aristotle calls a first actuality—and the exercise of an actualized ability—what he calls a second actuality.

26 Aristotle's point is that all events are in some sense natural; all motions have their ultimate source in the natures of things. This is why natures are the principles of other things. For example, the motion of an automobile has its source in the natural motion of my feet and hands in operating the vehicle; natural processes of combustion and the like

are also involved. Only if we consider the motion of the car *as* being of a car must we say that the motion is not natural, for a car as such has no nature.

27   "This kind of body" clearly refers to "a natural body having life potentially."

28   Aristotle's point is that although a broken ax isn't really an ax at all (for it is essential to an ax that it be able to cut) we could still speak loosely and, pointing to the broken ax, say, "Look at that broken ax over there!"

29   As the eye (a part of the body) is to sight (one of the first actualities that constitute our life), so is the body to the soul.

30   Aristotle will argue that intellectual activity is not the actuality of any body. It follows that the human intellect does not exist as enmattered, as do other aspects of the human soul. The implications of this are far-reaching but not at all clear.

31   Aristotle takes a god to be an eternal, intelligent, immaterial being.

32   For Aristotle, "imagination" is the place of mental images and memories.

33   An animal's body is matter, for it (as a corpse) is what is left when the animal loses its form as a living being. This body is the sort of thing that can perform life functions; that is to say, it is understood as the bearer of the potentiality for these things. The soul is that which actualizes this potentiality. That is why Aristotle says that soul is actuality.

34   The Pythagoreans and Plato believed that after death the souls of human beings are re-born in the bodies of various animals.

35   For Aristotle, appetite is the encompassing faculty, under which are classed desire and fervor. ("Fervor" translates *thumos*, the principle of anger and self-preservation.)

36   This is an oblique reference to Aristotle's highest god, and the other celestial souls and intellects in which he believes.

37   Though Aristotle does take those living beings that are marked by more faculties of soul to have greater value, the term here translated "hierarchically" does not itself point to a ranking in terms of value; literally, it means "in sequence."

38   Examples are worms, sponges, and shellfish.

39   The gods and the celestial intellects are imperishable living beings that can think, but engage in none of the other life activities.

40   That is to say, some animals make their way around in the world by means of imagination, unaided by reason.

41   The Greek text can be interpreted to the effect that herbivores live in groups and carnivores live alone. On this interpretation, Aristotle would be pointing to a purpose behind this correlation. Presumably herbivores would live in groups for protection, and carnivores would hunt more efficiently if they did so independently. But the Greek need not be interpreted as pointing to such a correlation.

42   We cannot help but be puzzled by Aristotle's employing piracy as a natural form of hunting, especially since it is presented as an example of living off of *wild* animals. Though popular Greek thought did sometimes glorify the life of plunder and conquest, one would think that a great ethicist such as Aristotle would not hesitate to condemn the life of thievery in all its forms. But Aristotle's writings on justice do not clearly condemn theft outside the parameters of a particular human community.

43 Aristotle recognizes that humans must live their lives in accordance with the specific characteristics of the land, which gives them sustenance. We would, however, expect Aristotle to take location to be primary. A culture in a certain geographical location is constrained in its choice of food, and the ways of human life must be determined by the nature of the food available. Instead, Aristotle extends his biological analysis to human beings. Choice of food is primary; it is this that determines where human beings live.

44 Like our term "viviparous," the Greek term Aristotle uses has the root sense of "giving birth to what is alive." Aristotle does not deny that a grub or an egg is in some sense alive; there is present a soul that is responsible for self-development. But on Aristotle's view, a grub or an egg does not yet have all of the capacities for life-functions that are possessed by the adult animals. Perhaps this is why they are not taken to be fully alive; the soul is somehow present only in a partial way.

45 The reference seems to be to the notion that food is a kind of natural property. As such, any form of eating constitutes a kind of appropriation that is grounded in the nature of things. There are problems with this inference, if it is indeed Aristotle's. For Aristotle uses the natural basis of food to argue for a teleological hierarchy among living beings; yet animals lower on the hierarchy eat those higher up, as when people are bitten by mosquitoes. Also, it would seem to provide an ethical foundation for cannibalism.

46 "These things" can refer to animals, or only wild animals, or both animals and plants.

47 Although it is not certain, Aristotle is probably saying that the art of hunting is an art of acquiring things.

48 Although this is not certain, the reference is probably to the art of war. Accordingly, we can see Aristotle as saying that the world has been teleologically organized so that more developed beings by rights have claim over less developed beings, so that the more developed beings can achieve their natural goal. Thus highly developed human cultures by rights have dominion over both less developed animals and less developed cultures. In each case, the art of hunting is to be employed so that a highly developed culture can get what it needs. When this hunting has human beings as its object, we call this hunting "war."

Aristotle is here comparing the hierarchy of species with the hierarchy found within all human beings. Aristotle openly asserts that the rule of some people over others has a natural basis. In the most extreme case, those who are ruled are "natural slaves." Although Aristotle nowhere gives the hierarchy he advocates a racial or ethnic basis, his political thought is bound to be highly controversial in our democratic age. A proper evaluation of Aristotle's thought would necessarily have to rest on a close reading of his arguments, which is beyond the scope of the present volume.

49 The Greek term for "the art of running a household" is *oikonomikē*, on which see n. 11 of the passage from Xenophon included in this volume. Aristotle takes the knowledge of how to supply the household with what it needs as being of the same kind as the knowledge of how to supply the whole society with what it needs.

50 Wealth is a tool required for the good life, a means to an end. Aristotle indicates that in all spheres of life, an end is to be achieved given a good enough instrument; an indefinite increase in the number of instruments, or in their size, would not result in an indefinite increase in the good one is trying to achieve. Likewise, Aristotle asserts that a certain amount of material wealth is necessary for the good life, but an increase above this amount will not lead to a better life.

CHAPTER FOUR

Cicero

THE HISTORY OF ancient philosophy does not end with Plato and Aristotle. For centuries, the body of thought of the presocratics, as well as of Plato and Aristotle, was developed and adapted by thinkers who followed. New schools of thought appeared, too. This period, up until the beginnings of Christian and Islamic philosophy, is usually referred to as the Hellenistic period.

Although most of the key texts of Hellenistic philosophy have been lost, enough of them remain to show evidence of a vibrant and highly influential period. Far from being trapped within the language and dogma of their own schools, Hellenistic philosophers were constantly confronting and addressing radically contrasting ways of conceptualizing the world. Thus, much Hellenistic philosophy has been preserved in the form of accounts by writers who were not themselves exponents of the philosophical ideas they were presenting.

Two schools of Hellenistic thought are especially important for our topic: Epicureanism and Stoicism. Although both are based on an insistently materialistic metaphysics, they are greatly opposed in many other respects. Epicureanism regards the world as resulting from random bodily processes, taking all morality to be based on conventions devised by people for their survival. Stoicism (in the version of Chrysippus, 280–207 BC, which for centuries was the standard form of these teachings) views the cosmos as a single, teleologically oriented organism, permeated throughout by a material stuff, *pneuma*, which is a divine intelligent ordering principle. This principle is rational in nature; indeed it is sometimes called the *logos*, "reason." The goal of the cosmos is to live in accordance with this *logos*. Because, of all the parts of the cosmos, only human beings are rational (only humans are directly animated by the special, pure form of the *pneuma* that is rational), all nonhuman organisms in the cosmos are there for the sake of human beings. We thus see that the Stoics present a philosophical argument for the same anthropocentric hierarchy that was presented (if not argued for) by Xenophon and Aristotle. In Stoic thought we also see the idea of the cosmos as a single, self-regulating, living thing. This is a precedent for the Gaia hypothesis, the notion that the earth is a super-organism that perpetuates its own life by regulating the global environment. (Originally propounded by Dr. James Lovelock in order to explain certain facts concerning atmospheric chemistry, the Gaia hypothesis is now entertained within many scientific disciplines and is sometimes employed as a principle of environmental ethics.)

Although best known for his role in Roman political history, Cicero (106–43 BC) played an equally important role in the history of philosophy. He was extremely interested in Greek philosophy, and produced numerous works presenting Greek philosophical ideas in Latin; these provided the foundation for the vocabulary of philosophical Latin, developed subsequently. Although his own thought was eclectic, borrowing from each of the major schools, Cicero took care to present each school's ideas independently and accurately. For this reason his work is an important source of Hellenistic philosophy. Further, his work was well known to later generations, and it is primarily through Cicero's writings that much of Greek philosophy was transmitted to such thinkers as St. Thomas Aquinas and Kant.

Much of ancient philosophy was concerned with developing arguments and speculations regarding the divine and its relation to the physical universe. In the unfinished *On the Nature of the Gods*, Cicero presents a dialogue on this theme. The participants are an Epicurean, a Stoic, and a Skeptic (a member of a school that argued that definitive knowledge on such matters is impossible). Balbus the Stoic presents his views in the following selection.

CICERO
On the Nature of the Gods Book 2
TR. BRAD INWOOD AND L. P. GERSON

Next I must show that everything is subordinate to nature and is ruled by it in the finest possible manner. But first, I must give a brief explanation of what nature is, to facilitate the understanding of what I want to show. For some think that nature is a type of non-rational force which induces necessary motions in bodies;[1] others[2] that it is a force endowed with reason and orderliness, proceeding methodically, as it were, and showing what the cause of each thing brings about and what follows upon it, [a force] whose cleverness could not be emulated by any craft, skill or craftsman. [They say] that the power of a seed is such that, despite its minute size, if it meets with a receptive and favourable nature,[3] and gets hold of the sort of matter which can nourish it and foster its growth, the seed can produce each sort of thing, according to its kind—some things which are nourished only via their roots, others which can set themselves in motion and perceive and desire and produce others like themselves.[4] And there are also those who use the term "nature" to refer to everything, like Epicurus, who makes the following division: the nature of all things which exist is bodies and void and their attributes. But since we say that the cosmos is constituted and governed by nature, we do not mean that it is like some lump of mud, piece of stone, or anything else with only a natural power of cohesion, but rather that it is like a tree or animal. For nothing is random in them; rather, it is evident that they possess a certain orderliness and craftsmanlike quality.

But if nature's craft is responsible for the life and vigour of plants which are held together by being rooted in the earth, certainly the earth itself is held together by the same force, since when the earth is impregnated by seeds she gives birth to and brings forth all things, embraces their roots, nourishes them, fosters their growth, and is herself nourished in turn by external and superior natural elements.[5] And the air and the aither and all superior entities are nourished by vapours produced from the earth. So, if the earth is held together by nature and owes its vigour to nature, then the same rational force is present in the rest of the cosmos. For the roots [of plants] are bound to the earth, while animals are sustained by inhalation of air and the air itself helps us to do our seeing, helps us to do our hearing and speaking; for none of these functions can be carried out without air. Indeed, it even helps us to move, since wherever we go or we move to, it seems to give way and yield to us.

And the motion of things to the central, i.e., lowest, region of the cosmos, and the motion of other things from the middle to the upper regions, and the circular orbit of others around this mid point all combine to make the nature of the cosmos a single and continuous whole.[6] And since there are four kinds of bodies, nature is rendered continuous by their mutual interchange. For water comes from earth, air from water and aither[7] from air; then in reverse air comes from aither, then water and from water comes earth, the lowest element. Thus the union of the parts of the cosmos is held together[8] because the elements from which everything is composed move up and down and back and forth. And this union must either be everlasting, exhibiting the very order which we now see, or at the very least very stable, enduring for a long, nearly boundless expanse of time. And either way it follows that the cosmos is governed[9] by nature.

Consider the sailing of a fleet of ships, the formation of an army, or (to return to examples drawn from the works of nature) the reproduction of vines or trees, or furthermore the shape and organization of the limbs of an animal: which of these points to as great a degree of cleverness as the cosmos itself does? Either, therefore, there is nothing ruled by a nature capable of perception or one must admit that the cosmos is so ruled. Moreover, how can that which contains[10] all natures and the seeds which produce them fail to be itself governed by nature? So, if someone were to say that the teeth and body hair exist by nature but that the man to whom they belong was not constituted by nature, he would simply be failing to understand that those things which produce something from themselves have natures more perfect than the things produced from themselves. But the cosmos is the sower and planter and (if I may so put it) the parent and nurse and nourisher of all things governed by nature; the cosmos nourishes and holds together[11] everything as though those things were its limbs and parts of itself. But if the parts of the cosmos are governed by nature, it is necessary that the cosmos itself be governed by nature.[12] And the governance of the cosmos contains nothing which is subject to criticism; the best possible result which could be produced from those natures which existed was indeed produced. Let someone, then, show that something better could have been produced! But no one will ever show this. And if someone wants to improve on something [in the cosmos], either he will make it worse or he will be longing for something which simply could not have happened.

But if all parts of the cosmos are so constituted that they could neither have been more useful nor more beautiful, let us see whether they are the products of chance[13] or of such a character that they could never even have held together if not for the control exerted by a perceptive and divine providence. If, therefore, the products of nature are better than those of the crafts and if the crafts do nothing without the use of reason, then nature too cannot be held to be devoid of reason.[14] When you look at a statue or a painting, you know that craftsmanship was applied; and when you see from afar the course steered by a ship, you do not doubt that it is moved by rational craftsmanship; when you gaze on a sundial or waterclock, you understand that the time is told as a result of craft and not as a result of chance. So what sense does it make to think that the cosmos, which contains these very crafts and their craftsmen and all else besides, is devoid of deliberative ability and reason?

... So Aristotle puts it splendidly:[15] "If," he says, "there were people who lived under the earth in fine and splendid houses adorned with statues and paintings and outfitted with all those things which those who are considered happy have in great abundance, but who had never come out onto the surface of the earth, though they had heard by rumour and hearsay that some divine force and godly power existed; and then one day the earth opened its maw and they could emerge from those hidden places and come out into the regions which we inhabit, and they then became aware of the huge clouds and the force of the winds and saw the sun in all its great size and beauty, and also became aware of its creative power (for it created the day by spreading its light throughout the entire heaven); and then when night darkened the earth they could see the whole heaven adorned and ornamented with stars, and the changes in the illumination of the moon as it waxed and waned, and the risings and settings of all those heavenly bodies moving in courses immutably fixed for all of eternity—when they saw all of this, certainly they would think both that there are gods[16] and that these things are their handiwork."

... All of man's senses are far better than those of the lower animals.[17] First, in those crafts in which the eyes make the crucial distinctions, painting, sculpture and engraving, and also in distinguishing bodily motion and gestures, [in all of these] the [human] eye makes many distinctions more subtly; for the eyes judge the beauty and order and and, I may say, the propriety of colours and figures; and there are other, even more important distinctions which it makes, since it recognizes the virtues and the vices, and an angry or friendly person, a happy or sad one, a brave or cowardly one, a bold or timid one. The ears too possess a remarkably craftsmanlike sense of judgement, by which we can distinguish, in vocal music and in wind or string instruments, timbre, pitch and key, and a great many vocal qualities as well: a melodious or "dark" voice, a smooth or rough one, a flexible or inflexible one. These distinctions are made only by the human ear. Smell, taste and touch also possess [to some extent] great powers of judgement. ...

Moreover, he who does not see the divine effort which was put into the perfection of man's mind, intelligence, reason, deliberative ability and prudence, seems to me to lack these same qualities. And in discussing this topic, I wish, Cotta,[18] that I had your eloquence. How [wonderfully] you could describe, first of all, human understanding; and then our ability to link conclusions with premises and grasp the result, i.e., the ability by which we judge what follows from what and prove it in the form of a syllogism, and define in a compact description each kind of thing. And from this we can grasp the power and characteristics of knowledge, a thing whose excellence even the gods cannot surpass. How extraordinary, indeed, are those powers which you Academics[19] try to undermine and even to destroy: the ability to perceive and grasp external objects with our senses and mind. It is by comparing and contrasting these with each other that we can produce the crafts, some of which are necessary for the practicalities of life and some for the sake of pleasure.

Indeed, the mistress of all, as you call it, is the power of eloquence—how wonderful and divine it is! First, it enables us to learn what we do not know and to teach others what we do know; next, we use it to exhort and persuade, to comfort the unfortunate and to distract the timid from their fears, to calm those who are passionate and dampen their desires and anger; it is the bond which unites us in law, legislation and civil society; it is eloquence which has raised us from a state of uncouth savagery.

What then? Does human reason not penetrate even to the heavens? For we are the only animals who know the risings, settings, and courses of the heavenly bodies; it is the human race which has defined the day, the month, and the year, has learned about solar and lunar eclipses and predicted their dates of occurrence and degree for all time to come. By contemplating these things our mind attains to knowledge of the gods, and that is the origin of piety, which is closely linked with justice and the other virtues, which are in turn the source of a life which is happy and similar, even equivalent, to that of the gods—yielding to the heavenly beings only in respect to immortality, which is quite irrelevant to the good life. After explaining this, I think that I have shown clearly enough by how much human nature is superior to the [other] animals. And from that one ought to see that chance could never have created the form and arrangement of our limbs or the power of our mind and intelligence.

It remains for me to come to my conclusion at last by showing that everything in this cosmos which is of use to men was in fact made and provided for their sake. First of all, the cosmos itself was made for the sake of gods and men, and the things in it were provided and discovered for the use of men. For the cosmos is like a common home for gods and men, or a city which both [gods and men] inhabit. For only creatures who use reason live by law and justice.[20] So just as one must hold that

Athens and Sparta were founded for the sake of the Athenians and Spartans and everything in these cities is properly said to belong to those peoples, in the same way one must hold that everything in the entire cosmos belongs to gods and men. Moreover, although the orbits of the sun and moon and the other stars help the cosmos hold together, they also serve as a [wonderful] spectacle for men. For no sight is less likely to become boring, none is more beautiful and none more outstanding with respect to rationality and cleverness; for by measuring out their courses we learn when the various seasons change and reach their peaks. And if men alone know these things, one must judge that they were created for the sake of men.

The earth is rich with grain and other kinds of vegetables and pours them forth with the greatest generosity; do you think that it was made for the sake of beasts or of men? What should I say about vines and olive trees? Their most rich and fertile fruits are of no use at all to beasts. Beasts have no knowledge of sowing, cultivating, of reaping and bringing in the harvest at the proper time, nor of putting it up and storing it; only men can use and care for these things. Just as we should say that lyres and flutes are made for the sake of those who can use them, so one must admit that the things I have been talking about are provided only for the sake of those who use them; and if some animals steal or snatch some of it from them, we shall still not say that those things were made for their sake. For men do not store grain for the sake of mice or ants, but rather for the sake of their wives, children, and households. So animals use such things by stealth, as I said, but their masters do so openly and freely. So one must concede that this generous supply of goods was provided for the sake of men, unless the great richness and variety of fruits, and their pleasant taste, odour, and appearance, leave any doubt about whether nature presented them to men alone.

So far is it from being true that these things were provided for the sake of the beasts, that we can see that even the beasts themselves were created for man's sake. What are sheep for except to provide wool which can be worked and woven into clothes for men? And without man's cultivation and care they could not have been nourished or maintained, nor produced anything of use to others. What can be the meaning of the faithful guard service of dogs, their loving admiration of their masters, their hatred of outsiders, and their remarkable skill in tracking and speed in the hunt? Only that they were created to serve man's needs. ...

... It would take too long to recount the useful services provided by mules and asses, which were certainly provided for man's use. What is there in pigs, except food? Chrysippus says that the pig was given a soul in place of salt, to keep the meat from spoiling.[21] Because it is well-suited for feeding humans, no other type of animal is more prolific of offspring.

... You can scan the land and all the seas with your mind, as though with your eyes, and you will immediately see huge expanses of land which bear fruit [for man], and densely forested mountains, pasture land for cattle, and also sea-lanes for ships to sail in with remarkable speed. It is not just on the earth's surface either; but even in the deepest, darkest bowels of the earth there lies hidden a great store of useful materials which were made for man and are only discovered by man.

There is another point too, which both of you will perhaps seize on for criticism, you, Cotta, because Carneades loved to attack the Stoics, Velleius because Epicurus ridiculed nothing so much as the prediction of future events; but I think that it proves better than anything else that divine providence takes thought for human affairs. For divination certainly does exist, since it shows up in many different places and at many different times, in both private and public affairs.[22]

Notes

1 This may be a reference to Aristotle. As we have seen, Aristotle takes the nature of a thing to be an internal principle responsible for the motions and changes undergone by that thing. Although its activity is teleologically directed, its workings are not themselves rational (unless the thing is itself rational, for in that case, the nature is the same as the rational soul). The Stoics differ from Aristotle in taking teleological action to be evidence of rational planning. Since a nonhuman terrestrial organism is not itself rational, the natural activity of such an organism must be due to some rational agent, outside of the organism as such. For the Stoics, this is God, the *logos*, and the *pneuma* interpenetrating all things.

2 The reference is to the Stoics themselves.

3 The terms translated as "receptive" and "favourable" could also be given a purely spatial sense. The first, cognate with the English word "conceive," could mean "taking in." The second can mean "embrace" or "get hold of." Cicero is referring to the taking of a seed by the womb, or by appropriate earth.

4 The distinction, of course, is between plants and animals.

5 In Aristotelian biology, the earth merely provides the matter and background conditions that make it possible for the nature in a plant seed to initiate the growth and development of that plant. As such, there is no need to consider the earth a single, living being. Cicero has the Stoic Balbus argue that this is an incomplete conception of the workings of the earth. Just as animal seed requires not only suitable matter and background conditions, but the active guidance of the mother's nature, so plants require an analogous maternal activity from the earth. As such, the earth must itself be invested with the sort of nature that justifies our considering it a single natural being.

6 Balbus presents an argument for considering the whole cosmos a single natural organism. We have seen him argue that the earth must be a natural organism, on the grounds that it actively nurtures plants. But air, too, plays an active role in animating us, allowing us to live as we do. (The Stoics give air an active role in animating and nurturing organisms.) Hence the air that surrounds the earth also has an active nature. Stoic geology and meteorology explain how this nature is dependent on the agency of the earth. So the earth and air together can be considered interrelated parts of a larger, integrated natural system. Such moves can presumably be made until the cosmos as a whole is understood as a single natural organism.

7   "Aither" here takes the place of fire, which is present in Aristotle's classification of the terrestrial elements as earth, air, fire, and water. The Stoics believed that the fire we see on earth is an impure variety of the aither seen among the stars.

8   The term translated "held together" (*continēre*, the source for the English "contain") is very closely related to the term translated as "continuous" just above. The mutual transformation of the elements not only allows the cosmos to cohere so that it does not fall apart; this same process is what makes the cosmos a single, continuous whole.

9   Balbus has shown that the nature of the universe as a single whole is key to understanding the workings of any individual thing within this whole. The use of the political term "govern" here would be unjustified unless this single nature is rational, exercising forethought in its operations and caring for the welfare of the things it controls. This is what Balbus is about to show.

10   The verb is *continēre*; see note 8 above.

11   See note 8 above.

12   Balbus has argued that the cosmos is a single natural organism. That is not quite the same as saying that it is a single *living* being, a claim made of the Earth in our times by the Gaia hypothesis. The Stoics sometimes take "life" to be said of anything able to move and change by itself, as does a plant (but not, on their view, a clod of earth). In this sense, Balbus has already shown the cosmos to be alive. Occasionally the Stoics reserve the word "life" for what is able to perceive and have awareness, as do animals. Balbus has not yet indicated that the cosmos as a whole has any awareness of what is going on within it. This must wait until he has argued that the rational element in the cosmos governs and controls everything that occurs within it.

13   This is the view of the Epicureans.

14   Aristotle had argued that the workings of crafts and skills imitate the nonrational teleological workings of nature. This would make no sense for the Stoics. Balbus claims that it is reason that allows the crafts to achieve their goals so effectively. Nothing other than reason could allow natural processes to likewise achieve their goals.

15   Cicero provides a translation of a passage from Aristotle's lost dialogue *On Philosophy*.

16   The Stoics supposed there to be a single god ruling over the cosmos as a whole, whom they identified with Zeus (or Jupiter). The stars were also taken to be gods. The plurality of gods in classical mythology was considered by the Stoics to be a metaphor for these divine principles and their workings.

17   Sections of the text in which Balbus relates in detail examples of the gods' providential care have been omitted. The present passage, part of this larger discussion, is important insofar as it presents the Stoic view of the crucial distinction between human beings and nonhuman animals. Humans are not distinguished by their having some immaterial principle; for the Stoics, nothing is immaterial. Rather, human beings are exceptional in the excellence of their share in the material processes of sensation and knowledge.

18   Cotta is a member of the Academic skeptical school.

19   Velleius, the third party to the discussion, is the Epicurean participant in the dialogue.

20   As adherence to law and standards of justice requires rationality, and human beings and the gods are the only rational beings in the cosmos, only human beings and gods can

adhere to standards of law and justice. But membership in a community requires adherence to standards of law and justice. Hence the cosmos can be considered a single community whose members include only human beings and gods. As we shall see in chapter 5, Porphyry takes pains to refute this argument.

21 For the Stoics, soul is *pneuma* undergoing a certain motion, by which a body is unified as a single living organism. This prevents the body from decomposing, as would meat from a dead animal, unless preserved by salt. Chrysippus says that this preservation is for our benefit, so that our meat will not rot. On this, see also Porphyry, *On Abstaining from Animals* 3.20, in the present volume.

22 Stoics argued for the validity of astrology and the reading of omens. They saw nothing irrational in this. Rather, for them it was evidence of the fact that the cosmos is a seamless whole, with changes in one part correlated with changes in a seemingly unrelated part. The fact that human beings can improve their lives by paying attention to such changes is fuller evidence that the cosmos has been designed by a rational agent for their benefit.

CHAPTER FIVE

Porphyry

W<small>E HAVE SEEN</small> that for Plato, Aristotle, and the Stoics, rationality is the most important feature of human beings, insofar as what is rational is marked by a divine orderliness and beauty. But it was far from settled just what rationality is, or which animals possess it. In the *Timaeus*, as we have seen, the entire world is a single animal, controlled by a single, intelligent soul. Each individual human being, in some unclear manner, has a share of this single World Soul. Further (in passages not excerpted for the present volume), Plato takes all other living beings to have a share of this same soul, for, at bottom, there is only one soul. Plants are said to have sentience, but not reason. Timaeus further teaches that animals other than human beings do have reason, but it is impaired by the soul's undue attachment to the body; animals are the reincarnations of human beings who have failed to achieve wisdom.

Plato does not explore the ethical implications of the view that human beings and other animals share the same sort of soul. This is most likely because, for Plato, virtue is at bottom a matter of perfecting the individual soul. A virtuous person will not harm others, primarily because wisdom, the chief desire of such a person, is not to be thereby gained.

Nevertheless, the issue of whether living beings other than people are worthy of moral consideration did become a major issue in later Greek philosophy. Like so much of Hellenistic philosophy, most of this debate has not been preserved. But its main lines can be reconstructed, largely on the basis of Porphyry, *On Abstaining from Animals*. Porphyry (232/3–305?) was the student of Plotinus, whose systematization of the metaphysical thought of Plato has earned him the reputation as the greatest neoplatonic philosopher. Although he is nowhere near Plotinus' equal as a thinker, Porphyry's erudite and philosophically acute writings preserve important evidence of this debate.

One of Porphyry's main arguments for vegetarianism is that a simpler diet serves to purify the soul from being chained to bodily desires that block the path to wisdom. But he also argues that there are real ethical obligations to other kinds of living beings.

He begins by reviewing the arguments that had been presented against such obligations. The followers of Epicurus take all ethical obligation to be a matter of joint expediency. By entering into certain compacts, people form communities. By upholding the community's standards of behavior, the pleasure of each individual human life is to be maximized. As other animals are not able to form contracts with people, there is nothing to be gained in maintaining strict standards of behavior in regard to them. Porphyry never directly addresses their arguments, but he makes clear that he rejects their presuppositions. The good life is not simply one of maximizing pleasure. It involves acting rationally, and purifying the soul.

The Stoics likewise reject the Epicurean account of justice. For the Stoics, to act rightly is to act in accordance with the *logos* that governs the whole cosmos. This involves recognizing that there are certain bonds to others whereby their interest becomes identified with our own. A fully rational being will recognize that we have such a bond, not only to members of our family, or to fellow citizens, but to all rational beings. But because human beings are the only rational animals, there is no reason to take a direct interest in the welfare of animals other than human beings.

Porphyry, at least provisionally, accepts the theoretical basis of Stoic ethics. But he rejects the Stoic view (expressed by Cicero in the present volume) that animals ultimately exist for the sake of human beings. He also argues that the Stoics err in denying rationality to other animals. Animals other than human beings communicate by producing true *logoi*; it follows that they have reason (*logos*). Further, many of the things that animals do can be explained only by attributing to them some rational thought.

In rejecting the view that animals are on the earth for our benefit, and in calling into question the existence of a clear and fundamental distinction between animal and human abilities, Porphyry anticipates many contemporary challenges to the granting of an ethically privileged status to human beings.

PORPHYRY
On Abstaining[1] from Animals
TR. OWEN GOLDIN

Book 1

1. Firmus, from some of our visitors I learned that you have found fault with your vegetarian diet and have gone back to eating meat. At first I did not believe them, since I considered how much self-control[2] you have and how much care we had taken in going over what ancient, god-fearing men have revealed about these things. But, soon after I first heard the news from these people, the news was confirmed by information I received from others. I decided not to scold you, even though you neither "avoid evil, by finding a better life," as the old proverb has it, nor "atone for your old life, and turn toward the better," as Empedocles recommends.[3] For it seemed to me that scolding would be crude, and removed from the sort of persuasion that comes from reasoning things out. Rather, I thought it worthy both of our friendship and of those who order their lives according to truth, to bring to light a rational refutation of your errors (in regard to both the place from which you have begun and the level to which you have fallen).

2. For when I am by myself and think about the reason for this change, I do not say that you changed your mind in the interests of health or strength, which is what most people (that is, the uneducated rabble) would say. This is because, as you yourself agreed when you were among us, the contrary is true: a vegetarian way of life contributes to both health and the powers of endurance that are required for philosophy. In saying these things you spoke the truth; this can be learned from experience. So it appears that you went back to your old unlawful ways either because you were deceived, or because you think that how you choose to live your life makes no difference in regard to intelligence; or perhaps there is some other cause of which I am unaware, involving a fear which is more threatening to you than the impiety of transgression. I would not say that it is from weakness of will or through succumbing to the cravings of a gourmand that you look down on our ancestral laws concerning the philosophy you once zealously pursued. Nor would I say that your nature is inferior to that which belongs to the uneducated people of certain regions, who, when they accept laws different from those under which they had been living, allow themselves to be mutilated,[4] and are so serious about abstaining from eating certain animals (with which they had been previously gorging themselves) that they would sooner eat human flesh.

3. But when some of my visitors recounted the very arguments that you were using against those who abstain, I had cause to not only raise objections, but to show real anger, since you persisted both in deceiving yourselves[5] and in trying to overturn a teaching that is both ancient and loved by the gods, when you were convinced by insipid and stale sophistic arguments. This is why it seemed appropriate that I not only explain how things stand from our point of view, but that in addition I lay out and disprove the arguments of our opponents. These are superior to yours, since they are more numerous, have more force, and show more resourcefulness. I will thus show that truth cannot be defeated by apparently serious arguments, let alone by stupid and superficial sophisms. Perhaps you do not know that more than a few people have made a case against abstaining from animals. Even among philosophers, there have been Peripatetics, Stoics, and Epicureans who devoted much time to arguing against the philosophy of Pythagoras and Empedocles, which you once took up with zeal. Also, many intellectuals, including a certain Neapolitan named Clodius, have written books opposing those who abstain from meat. Of these I will cite those investigations that have the most general relevance for this teaching, leaving aside the arguments that they resorted to in addressing Empedocles in particular.

4. Now those who argue against vegetarianism begin by saying that if we extend the term "just" not only to rational beings, but also to irrational beings, justice will be overturned and the unshakable will be shaken. This is what happens if one not only takes gods and human beings to be related, but deals with irrational wild animals, which are in no way related to us, as though they were our kin.[6] We would not

make use of them in our work, nor use them as food, since we would not take them to be unrelated to us, nor would we exclude them from the respect we give to those within our community, the way we exclude those who are not citizens. For someone who is as considerate of these animals as they are of humans, and does not hurt them, attributes to justice what it cannot bear; its power is destroyed and the notion of what is appropriate is ruined by what is alien to us. So one of two things happens to us.[7] Either we do not spare them, and are obliged to commit injustice, or we do not make use of them, and life becomes impossible and without the means to carry on. In some sense, renouncing the use of wild animals forces us to live like wild animals.

5. I leave aside the countless multitudes of Nomads and Troglodytes,[8] who know of no food but meat. But what sort of work on land or at sea is left to us, who think that we live in peace and with love for our fellow human beings? What productive art, what orderly way of life is left if our relation to animals is, like that toward our kin, one of doing no harm, and we are careful to treat them well? There is no work that can be mentioned. We have no cure or medicine for this problem, which would have us dispense with either life or justice, unless we maintain the old law and rule, which, according to Hesiod, was followed by Zeus when he distinguished natural kinds and put each in its own group:

> "Fish, wild beasts, and wingéd birds,
> He gave these leave to eat each other,
> Since for them there's neither right nor wrong
> But right and wrong he gave to humans . . ."[9]

in their conduct toward one another.

6. It is not possible for us to be unjust to those beings who cannot act in an unjust manner toward us.[10] So anyone who disregards this argument has left no road, either broad or narrow, by which justice is able to come in.[11] We have already said why this is so. Our nature is not self-sufficient, but is in need of many things. So if one were to deny it the benefit of animals, it would be annihilated, trapped in a life without any means of dealing with problems, with no resources and possessing nothing that it needs. According to them, the first generations did not lead prosperous lives. For their superstitious beliefs did not stop at animals. Rather, superstition forced people to behave in a certain way even toward plants. For why does one who slaughters a cow or sheep commit an injustice any greater than one who chops down a pine or oak, if, as the doctrine of rebirth has it, a soul emerges within these, as well? These are the most important Stoic and Peripatetic arguments.

7. The Epicureans tell their story as though it were a long genealogy. They say that once the ancient lawgivers paid attention to the communal life of human beings and their mutual interaction, they called the eating of humans "unholy" and ascribed to it a special dishonor. Perhaps among human beings there exists a certain natural

appropriation toward other human beings, which comes about from their similarity in bodily shape and in soul, and perhaps this contributes to the fact that no one destroys an animal that is similar in kind as readily as one might another animal whose destruction is permitted. Nonetheless, according to them, the most important reason why this is held in disgrace and is called "unholy" is the fact that the lawgivers held that it is disadvantageous for the entire organization of life. So things started out in this way, and from that time on, those who understood the advantage behind distinguishing things in this way needed no other consideration to cause them to hold back from such an action. But those who could not have sufficient awareness of how this was to their advantage readily hold back from killing one another on account of their fear of the severity of the penalty. Even today, it seems, there are both kinds of attitudes. For those who see the advantage of the arrangement that has been decreed willingly adhere to it. But those who are not receptive adhere to the arrangement because the laws frighten them with their threats, which were issued for the sake of those who could not reason through the usefulness of the arrangement. Most people accepted these threats. ...

10. But those who first distinguished what people are required to do and not do quite properly did not prohibit the destruction of animals other than human beings. For in the case of these animals, acting in the opposite way results in what is to our advantage. For it is not possible for people to survive unless they try to protect themselves from these animals by banding together into societies. Some of the brightest people who lived at that time kept in mind that they held back from killing others because of how useful that is in keeping themselves safe from harm, and they reminded the rest of the consequences of living in a community with one another, that when they hold back from their kin they protect the community, which made a contribution toward each individual's own survival. There were two reasons why it was useful for them to live together, apart from others, and to do harm to no one who had gathered in the same area. First, this is how they expelled animals of other kinds. Second, in this way they were able to deal with people who might come up to them in order to do harm. So this is why for a period of time they held back from their kin, insofar as they all had entered into the same community for the necessities of life, and furnished something required for attaining each of the above two goals. But as more time passed, human interaction led to a great increase in population. As nonhuman animals were driven out of the areas in which people lived, the threat of predatory attacks was reduced. In these circumstances, there were some people who went beyond the point of having only an irrational memory, and calculated the advantages that come from forming societies for mutual support.

11. This is why they tried to more securely constrain those who were poised to destroy each other and were coming up with less adequate means of defending themselves, having forgotten the past. When they tried to do this, they issued the legisla-

tion that persists to this day among the various cities and nations. The multitude willingly went along with this, since they were aware of the advantages of people coming together. For the indiscriminate killing of all that is harmful, along with the careful maintenance of the means for doing this, contribute to living without fear. This is why they took the reasonable step of prohibiting the killing of some of the things we mentioned, while the killing of others was not prevented. No one can respond by saying that the law has permitted us to destroy some animals, which neither put human nature in danger nor harm our lives in any way. For it could be said that no animal which the law permits us to kill is harmless in this way, since we would find it harmful to allow there to be an overabundance of any animal. But when we make sure that they remain in their present numbers, they furnish some of what we need in life. For sheep and cattle and all such animals help us with the necessities of daily life, as long as their numbers stay within bounds, but if they were to freely multiply and their numbers were to greatly exceed a set limit, our natural lives would suffer harm. This can happen when they employ their force, since Nature has been so lavish in this, or merely when they eat up all of the food which the earth yields to us. This is the why the destruction of such animals is not prohibited, in order that there are enough of them left for us to use to our advantage, and not so many that we cannot easily master them. For the situation in regard to cattle, horses, sheep, and, in general, the animals that are called "tame," differs from that of lions, wolves, and the animals, small as well as large, that are said to be fierce. For one cannot say of the latter kind of animal that the hard necessities of life would be softened if there remained a certain number of them. This is why we destroy the one kind of animal without mercy, but we do away with only the surplus of the other kind.

12. We must believe that those who originally regulated these things by law made distinctions concerning which living things were to be eaten, for reasons very much like those we have described, and that something was determined to be unsuitable to serve as food, based on whether or not it would be of some advantage. So we must regard as really foolish anyone who says that everything that has been legislated concerning beauty and justice is a matter of personal belief. For that is not how things are; rather, the situation is the same as it is for other kinds of advantage, such as health and thousands of others. There are many ways to be mistaken, both in the concerns of the community as well as in individual matters. For some people do not keep in mind those conventions that would be applicable to all people. Rather some people neglect them because they take them to be a matter of indifference, while others make the opposite mistake. This is to mistakenly take conventions that are without universal advantage to in fact be advantageous everywhere. This is why they cling to laws that are inapplicable, even if in other cases they have discovered some that are good for them in particular and others that help the community. For most nations, decrees concerning the slaughter of living things and their use as food are of this kind, since

they are determined by the peculiar characteristics of the land. In such a case we need not comply with them, since we do not live in the same place. So if they were able to have made a compact with the other animals, as one does with people, to neither kill them nor have them killed by us without good reason, it would have been a fine thing for justice to apply even up to this point. For this compact would have been established with security in mind. But since there is no way to contrive things to allow those animals that do not accept reason[12] to share in law, one cannot employ such means to one's advantage in achieving security against other kinds of living things, any more than one can against lifeless things. Only through being allowed to kill them, as we now are, can we have the security that can be achieved.

The Epicureans say these things, and other things similar to them. ...

27. First of all, it must be known that what I have to say will not be addressed to all human lives. I will not say these things to people who pursue menial crafts, or to athletes, soldiers, sailors, orators, or those who go into business. Instead, I will speak to the person who thinks through the issue of what he or she is, whence he or she comes and to what things he or she must be devoted, as well as obligations concerning food and other duties that are very different from what has been established for people who live other kinds of life.[13] ...

53. If everyone were as intelligent as possible, there would be no need for the art of hunting birds or its practitioners; nor would there be need of fishermen or swineherds. When animals are left to themselves, and there is no one in charge to take care of them, they are quickly destroyed and consumed by other animals that attack and devour most of them, just as occurs in the case of thousands of animals which human beings do not eat. ...

Book 3

1. Firmus Castricius, in the first two books we have proven that eating living things makes no contribution to self-control and the simple life, nor toward reverence, which are virtues[14] that are especially conducive to the contemplative life. Rather, eating such things works against this goal. Since justice toward the gods is at its finest in reverence toward the gods, and abstinence brings about its goal to the greatest possible degree, there is no need to fear that we somehow do away with justice in regard to people, as long as we are faithful in our obligations toward the gods. Indeed, consider what Socrates said when speaking to those who contended that pleasure is the goal: that, even if every pig and goat should agree, we would not be persuaded that our happiness lies in pleasure, as long as intellect is the ruler of the universe. And this is what we say: even if every wolf and vulture should think highly of eating meat, we would not concede that they are speaking with justice, as long as there is nothing harmful in human nature, and as long as one ought to hold back from harming others in order to get pleasure for oneself.

Let us proceed to our account concerning justice. Since our opponents contend that we have an obligation to extend justice only to those who are like us, and for this reason they exclude irrational animals, come then, let us ask them to consider a view which is true, and was also held by the Pythagoreans, and declare that every soul is rational, insofar as it has a share of sensation and memory. For once this has been proven, it is reasonable for us to extend the notion of justice to every animal,[15] even according to their way of thinking. But let us quickly summarize what was said by the ancients.

2. Now according to the Stoics there are two kinds of *logos*, that which is internal and that which is uttered. *Logos* can also be divided another way, into that which is correct and that which is in error. So we ought to determine which sort of *logos* they deny to animals. Do they deny to animals only correct *logos*, as opposed to *logos* in general? Or do they utterly deny all *logos*, both the inner *logos* and that which proceeds outwards? Apparently they predicate of animals a total privation of *logos*, not merely a privation of correct reason. For otherwise, animals would not be irrational;[16] they would still be rational, just as, in their view, almost all human beings are. For according to them there have been only one or two sages, in whom alone there has been correct *logos*, but other human beings have all been fools.[17] Even if some have made progress, while others have a profusion of foolishness, nevertheless they all share the same status in regard to whether they are rational or not. Self-love leads them to immediately declare that all other animals are irrational, meaning by "irrationality" a total privation of *logos*. But, to tell the truth, not only is *logos* in general to be seen in all animals, in many cases there is the basis for achieving perfection.

3. So, since there are two kinds of *logos*, one which consists in the utterance, and one in having the disposition,[18] let us begin with the *logos* that is uttered and ordered in speech. Let us say that the *logos* that is uttered is a sound made by means of the tongue that signifies what is going on internally, that is, the affections of the soul, for this is the most common definition of it, which involves only the concept of *logos*, not a commitment to the thought of any particular sect. What aspect of this is not present in all of the animals that vocalize? Why doesn't a certain animal think about the things that it experiences even before it says what it is going to say? By "thought" I mean that which is silently sounded within the soul. So as long as something is said by means of language, however it is said, whether in Greek or in some foreign language, whether in dog-talk or in cow-talk, the animals that speak have a share of real *logos*. The difference is that while human beings vocalize in accordance with human conventions, animals do so in accordance with laws[19] that each has obtained from the gods and Nature. ...

7. We must also show that there exists the internal *logos*, that which is within them. As Aristotle somewhere states,[20] their *logos* does not seem to be essentially different from ours, but the difference is seen to be a matter of more or less. This is how many people understand the transition from the gods to us, too. They believe

that there is no essential difference here; rather, the difference lies in the precision or imprecision of the *logos*. Almost everyone agrees that the similarity of animals to us extends as far as having a share in sensation and the general organization of the sense organs and the flesh. For they have not only the affections[21] that occur in accordance with nature, and the changes that these affections bring about, but they also have the diseases that are seen to occur in them contrary to nature. No sane person, who sees that even in the case of human beings there are great differences in their character on account of their race and nationality, and who agrees that they are nonetheless all rational, would say that animals cannot have a rational disposition because their body is of a different character. ...

9. We must therefore show that they have rational souls and are not devoid of intelligence. First, each animal knows which parts of it are weak and which are strong, and it protects the parts that are vulnerable, while it makes use of the other ones, as the panther uses its teeth, the lion its claws as well as its teeth, the cock its spur, and the scorpion its stinger. Egyptian serpents use the venom that they spit out to blind the eyes of those who approach, which is why they are called "venom-spitters." Different animals make use of different parts, each one ensuring its own survival. Again, all of those animals that are strong live at a distance from human beings, but animals that belong to an inferior kind live in the midst of human beings, keeping their distance from the animals that are stronger than they are. Some do so from farther off, such as sparrows and swallows who live on the roofs of houses, and some, like dogs, are right at people's sides. Animals migrate with the seasons and they know everything that is to their advantage. One can see such reasoning even among fish and birds. A great number of such facts have been collected by the ancients in their writings on animal intelligence. Aristotle, who devoted much of his time to these matters, described how all animals devise a home for themselves with a view to living and ensuring their own survival.

10. But anyone who ascribes these abilities to animals does not realize that this is to say that they are by nature rational, or, alternatively, that logos does not arise in us by nature, and that there can be no movement toward its perfection, in accordance with our nature. The rationality of a god, at any rate, has not come about from any teaching, for there has never been a time when a god has been irrational. Rather, its existence has always been accompanied by its rationality, and nothing interfered with its rationality. This is because it did not acquire its *logos* from having been taught. Still, while the other animals, like humans, have been taught much of what they know by nature, they acquire some of what they know from having learned it. For they teach some of these things to one another, while, as we have said, other things are taught by people. (For they have the faculty of memory, which is crucial for the acquisition of reasoning and intelligence.) There are vices and instances of envy among them, too, even if there is not the profusion of these that one finds among human

beings. This is because evil is less serious for animals than it is for human beings. For example, a man who is building a house is incapable of laying the foundation unless he is sober. A shipbuilder is incapable of having the keel put in place, if he is ill. Nor can a farmer plant grapes unless he is paying attention to what he is doing; yet almost everyone is able to beget children, even while drunk. But things are different for animals. For them, the act of procreation is intended to lead to offspring, and, in the case of most animals, the male does not try to mount the female once she is impregnated, nor does she permit such a thing. (On the other hand, everyone knows how arrogant and lecherous people are in these matters.) The males of some animals are aware of the pains their partners feel in begetting their young, and often, as in the case of cocks, they feel these pains alongside the females. In some cases, for example, doves, the males help incubate the eggs. They also think ahead concerning where they will beget their young. Further, after childbirth each animal washes itself and its offspring. Anyone who observes animals carefully can see that they all go about their business in an orderly way, and that they wag their tails or act in a servile manner when meeting the one who feeds them. It can also be seen that they know their master, and point out anyone who is up to no good. ...

11. Doesn't everyone know that social animals watch over one another to make sure they maintain standards of justice toward each other? For this is done by each individual ant, bee, and similar animal. And who doesn't know about the self-control the ring-doves show, in their faithfulness toward their partners? They kill any of their number that they catch being unfaithful. Who has not heard of the justice that storks show to their parents?[22] For each animal has a certain virtue of its own, to which it is naturally disposed. (Granted, they do these things by nature, and these virtues are permanent, but this does not mean that they are not rational.) It is incumbent on the one who holds that virtuous deeds do not accompany a rational aptitude to refute the point that we have just made. Because of our inability to enter into their reasoning, we do not understand how it is that they do these things. But that is no reason for us to declare them irrational. For it is not possible to enter into the mind of the god, either. But when we accepted the assertions of those who declared it intellectual and rational, it was on the basis of what the sun does.[23]

12. One could well wonder at those who do not extend the notion of justice all the way to those animals that are found within our community, though they take justice to be constituted by reasoning, and call the animals that live outside of our community "fierce" and "unjust." For, like human lives, the lives of the animals within our community depend on that community. For example, birds, dogs, and many quadrupeds (for example, goats, horses, cattle, asses, and mules) perish when they are isolated from being in a community with human beings. The Demiurge[24] Nature caused them to need people, and caused people to need them, and it provided them with an innate sense of justice toward us, while also providing us with an innate sense

of justice toward them. It is no surprise if some of them respond to us with ferocity. For Aristotle spoke the truth when he said that, if all beings had been provided with copious amounts of food, they would not have been fierce toward each other, or to us. For their enmities and alliances are for the sake of food (though only for the small amount they need) as well as territory. But if people had been put in the dire straits in which animals find themselves, how far would they have gone beyond the ferocity of those they now consider fierce? Both war and famine have shown the lengths to which people would go, since during those times people do not shrink from eating each other. Even without conditions of war and famine, people eat those with whom they live, the tame animals.

13. But someone might say that, even if they are rational, they do not stand in any relation to us. These are the people who denied any relation toward them on the grounds that they are without *logos*, and consequently were among those who ascribe the community they have with them to their usefulness, not to their *logos*. But our project was to show whether they are rational, not whether we and they have entered into any compacts, since not all human beings have entered into a compact with us, and no one would say that someone with whom we have no compact is without *logos*. Yet many animals are the slaves of humans, and, as someone rightly said, even if people have been presumptuous enough to make them their slaves, these animals have made use of their wisdom and justice to turn their masters into their attendants and helpers. At any rate, their vices are obvious, and these, more than anything else, show how rational they are. For the males show jealousy and envy over the females, and the females do the same over the males. But there is one vice that they do not have, and that is malevolence toward those with good will toward them. Instead, the animals always have nothing but good will in return. They have so much confidence in those showing good will toward them that they follow wherever one of them should lead, even to the point of death or obvious danger. For even if someone who owns animals should give them food for his or her sake, not theirs, they have good will toward that owner. But people rebel against no one as they do against the one who feeds them, and for no one else do they harbor such hopes of death.

14. To see how animals reason about the things that they do, consider that it is not unusual for them to know that someone has set out some bait in order to trick them, and they approach it only on account of incontinence or hunger. Some of them have gone up to the bait, though not right away, while others remain before it, hesitating, trying to find a way to take the food without falling into the trap. Often their reasoning has been more powerful than their feelings, and they have left it behind. Sometimes when this happens they become infuriated and urinate on the traps that humans have laid. Some animals know that they will be taken but they indulge themselves and eat, as they allow themselves to die. In this they behave no worse than did the companions of Odysseus.[25] ...

18. These considerations and others (which we will soon recall when we review the views of ancient thinkers) show that animals are rational, and that they are not wholly deprived of *logos*, even though, for most of them, it is imperfect.[26] But if, as our adversaries admit, justice pertains to rational beings, why aren't we required to act in a just way toward them? For we do not extend the obligations of justice all the way to plants, since in their case there seems to be much that has nothing to do with *logos*. Yet even here, we are wont to make use of the fruit, without cutting down the trunk together with the fruit. We collect grains and beans once they have dried out and died, and are falling to the ground. On the other hand, no one would deal with the flesh of dead animals in this way (except for fish, and we employ violence to get them, too). It follows that in these matters we are very unjust.

First, as Plutarch too says,[27] just because our nature needs many things, of which it makes use, it does not follow that we should act unjustly in every way toward everything. For he grants permission to inflict a certain amount of harm, for the sake of necessities, if to take something from plants without killing them counts as harm. But to destroy and kill other things gratuitously, for the sake of pleasure, is the utmost of cruelty and injustice. Abstaining from these is detrimental neither to our life nor to our living well. For had our lives happened to depend on the slaughter of animals and the consumption of their flesh, just as we require air, water, plants, and fruit in order to live, our nature would have been necessarily interwoven with such injustice. On the other hand, this sort of food is never even touched by many of the gods' priests and many barbarian[28] rulers, as they try to stay pure, nor by countless varieties of animals, yet they live and attain their natural end. So wouldn't it be strange if someone were to tell us that since we have to wage war, we cannot have peaceful relations with those with whom this is possible, but are confronted with the choice of either staying alive, dealing justly with none, or losing our lives, dealing justly with all? The situation is similar to the way in which we deal with people. If someone who seizes the goods of others or lays waste to a land or city does so for the sake of his own survival, or that of his children or country, the injustice is excused by the agent's having been compelled to act in this way, while someone who does these things while reveling in wealth, luxury, or pleasure, and assuring that one's desires (not needs) are satisfied appears antisocial, incontinent, and wicked. In the same way, the god is understanding and allows people to injure plants, to consume fire and deplete springs of water, to shear and milk our livestock, and to tame and yoke our cattle, for their own maintenance and survival. But to lead them to death and to butcher them, tainted with murder, not for the sake of food, to assure that we acquire what we lack, but to supply ourselves with the utmost in pleasure and gluttony, is to do something exceedingly lawless and terrible. It is enough that we employ animals that do not themselves need to work hard, subduing and putting under the yoke "steeds, asses, and the seed of bulls," as Aeschylus says, "taking our toils, serving as slaves."[29]

19. But if someone is against turning cattle into a meal, extinguishing and destroying their spirit and life in order to put sauces and garnishes on our table with which to stuff ourselves, how could anyone say that this person withholds from life anything that one needs to survive or anything that is admirable in respect to virtue? But not discriminating between animals and plants does violence to things. For animals have a nature by which they perceive, experience pain and fear, and can undergo injury. This is why they have a nature enabling them to be victims of injustice. But plants are able to perceive nothing, and hence nothing is alien to them, and there is no evil, injury, or injustice that we can do against them. For sensation is the principle of all appropriation and recognition of what is alien. But the followers of Zeno[30] posit appropriation as the principle of justice. We see many people who live by sensation alone, and have neither intellect nor *logos*, and many who outdo the most fearsome of wild animals in their savagery, fervor, and feistiness, who kill their own children and parents, who are tyrants and the lackeys of kings. How is it not irrational to think that we have standards of justice toward them, but not toward the ox that we use for ploughing, the dog with whom we live, the animals that nourish us with their milk, and the creatures whose hair adorns us? Wouldn't this opinion be extremely paradoxical?

20. But, by Zeus, Chrysippus[31] made a credible case when he said that the gods made us for the sake of ourselves and each other, and that animals were made for our sake. Horses were made to aid us in battle, and dogs were made to aid us in the hunt. On the other hand, panthers, bears, and lions were made so that we could have practice in courage. But most delightful of all of these things that are for our sake is the pig.[32] For it was born for nothing except being sacrificed, and the god mixed some soul into the flesh as a kind of salt,[33] devising for us quite a tasty meal. So that we might have copious amounts of gravies and side dishes, he supplied us with all kinds of oysters, purple fish, sea nettles, and a great assortment of winged animals. These things did not have some transcendent source; rather, the god turned a large part of himself to this world.[34] His kindheartedness was greater than that of the nurses of children; he filled the terrestrial region with pleasures and amusements. But anyone who thinks that these arguments have a bit of credence, and are the sort of thing that is worthy of being said of the god, ought to see what he has to say about the argument which is given by Carneades:[35] each thing that has come to be by nature is benefitted[36] when it achieves the end that is the aim of its nature and that for which it was born. But here "benefit" has to be taken in its less specialized sense, which is what they call "usefulness." But by nature the pig is born to be slaughtered and devoured. When this happens, it achieves that at which its nature aims, and it is benefitted. But if the god has devised animals for human use, what use will we make of mice, mosquitoes, bats, beetles, scorpions, and vipers? Some of these things are ugly to look upon and foul to the touch, with an intolerably bad smell, and make a

terrible, horrible sound. Others simply come right out and destroy those they en-counter. Why hasn't the Demiurge taught us how it is useful for Nature to have brought forth whales, saw-fish, and other great sea creatures,

> And roaring Amphitrite feeds
> the thousands and thousands of these[37]

as Homer tells us? But if they reply that not all animals are made for our sake (that is, because of us), doesn't this greatly confuse things? Hasn't this muddied the distinction between the different kinds of animals? Moreover, our attacks on animals (animals that are not meant for us, but, like us, have come into being on account of their own na-ture) and our maltreatment of them, show that we are not keeping clear of injustice. I don't even mention the fact that those who define animals on the basis of their useful-ness toward us cannot help but concede that they themselves have been born for the sake of the most dangerous animals, such as crocodiles, whales, and snakes. This is be-cause there is absolutely no benefit that we derive from them. They, on the other hand, attack and destroy any human being they meet, and make use of them as food. This is no more cruel than doing what we do. The difference is that their needs and hunger lead them to this injustice, but when we slaughter animals it is usually out of arrogance and luxury, often while amusing ourselves during a hunt or at the theater.[38]

These things strengthen the part of us that is murderous, like a wild animal, and they make us immune to pity. The part of us that is tame was weakened mostly by those who dared to act in this way. The Pythagoreans made kindness toward wild animals a sort of practice for loving other people and for compassion. So how can one deny that justice is strengthened by these people, more than it is by others, who declare that these actions destroy the familiar sort of justice? For it is astonishing how familiarity leads people to make moral progress, by means of certain feelings which have little by little found a home within us. ...

23. ... It should come as no surprise that there is such a difference between hu-man beings and animals, in regard to learning and acuity of mind, and in what has to do with justice and community. For many of them surpass all people in size and speed, and in power of vision and acuity of hearing. But this does not mean that people are deaf or blind or without any strength. Rather, we do run, even if we do so more slowly than deer, and we do see, even if our vision is not as keen as that of hawks. Also, Na-ture has not deprived us of strength and size, though in such things we are nothing compared to an elephant or a camel. Likewise, we ought not to say that wild animals cannot think or be intelligent or have *logos*, even if their intelligence is slower than ours and they do not think as well as we do. Rather, their *logos* is weak and muddy, like an eye with a disorder, which does not see well.

24. ... These are the sorts of things that are said by Plutarch, in many of his books, in response to the Stoics and Peripatetics.

25. But Theophrastus[39] has made use of an argument like the following. We say that those who were begotten by the same ones (I mean, the same father and mother) are by nature kin[40] to one another. And for this reason we think that those who are descended from the same distant ancestors are kin to one another, as are fellow citizens, since they have in common their land and mutual relations. For we do not judge such people to be kin to each other on the grounds of being descended from the same people, unless the very founders of the clan are their first forebears. For just as we think that a Greek is kin and family to a Greek, and a barbarian to a barbarian, so we say that every human being is kin and family to every other. We say this for one of two reasons. First, all people have the same forebears. Second, all people have in common their food, culture, and membership in the same kind. Thus we also posit a single family of all humankind along with all animals. For by nature their bodies have the same principles. By this I am not referring to the fact that they have the same primary elements, for plants also come from these. More important, humans and animals have the same principles because there is no natural basis for making distinctions among them. I have in mind the fact that they are subject to desire and anger, and, further, the ways in which they reason, and most of all, the ways in which they all perceive things. But, just as is the case in respect to their bodies, some of their souls are more highly developed, and some are less developed. This is shown by the kinship of their passions.

If what has been said is true—namely, that the factors mentioned above are responsible for the emergence of their patterns of conduct—every sort of animal is intelligent, but they differ in how they have been brought up, and in how the primary constituents have been mixed. It would follow that in every respect we would form one family with the other kinds of animals. For, as Euripides tells us, all of them eat in the same way, sharing the same breath, and within all of them there are blood-red streams, and these things show that heaven and earth are the common ancestors of all.

26. Since they are family to us, if it should appear that Pythagoras[41] was right and they have a share of the same soul, it would be just to consider impious someone who does not hold back from doing injustice to our kin. Just because some of them are fierce does not mean that they are not our kin. Among human beings, one finds more (not fewer) instances of those who do evil to their neighbors, and are impelled to hurt anyone they encounter, as though carried by the wind of their own nature and wickedness. This is why we get rid of these fierce animals, but that does not take away the relationship we have with the animals that are tame. So even if some animals are fierce, and we must get rid of them, as we do with people of that kind, it is wrong to distance ourselves from the relationship that we have with the rest of the animals, those that are more tame. Yet we don't eat people who are unjust; likewise, we are to eat neither kind of animal. But as things stand we act in an exceedingly unjust manner, getting rid of tame animals as well as those that are fierce and unjust;

we eat tame animals. For our injustice is twofold. First, we destroy them, even though they are gentle. Second, we feast ourselves on them, and they die for no reason other than to be turned into food. ...

All of those who thought that justice makes its entry on account of appropriation in regard to human beings are apparently also unaware of the distinctive characteristic of justice. For this would make it a kind of love for human beings, but justice consists in abstaining from and doing no harm to anything whatever that itself does no harm. The just person is to be understood in this way—as having justice, which consists in doing no harm, extend to all living things; justice is not to be understood in the other way. For the same reason its essence is found in having the rational part of the soul rule over the irrational part, and in having the irrational part follow.[42] The reason for this is that when the one rules and the other follows, it is altogether necessary for a person to do no harm to anything at all. For when the passions have been kept in check, desires and angers have withered away, and when the rational part of the soul has the rule that is appropriate for it, what is inferior immediately becomes like what is superior. That which is superior in the universe as a whole is, as we have seen, wholly blameless. By virtue of its power, it maintains all things; it brings about the good for all things; it has no further need of anything. Yet justice leads us to harm no one, while it is the mortal part of us that makes us depend on necessities. But we can get what we need without harming plants, when we take the things that fall from them. We do no harm to fruits, if we make use of fruits that have already died. Nor do we do any harm to sheep when we crop their wool (on the contrary, they are benefitted by this), and we care for them when we share their milk. This is why the just person may seem to neglect himself or herself concerning the things of the body. Yet no harm is done to the self. For inner goodness grows through the disciplining of the body and through continence. Thus one becomes like the god.

Notes

1   The Greek term for "abstain," *apechein*, literally means "to hold back." In English, it is appropriate to talk of abstaining from certain foods and drinks; this refers to keeping oneself away from consuming these things. On the other hand, it is awkward English to speak of abstaining from other sorts of behavior, such as murder. For this reason, *apechein* has been rendered as "abstain" or "hold back," depending on context; likewise for *apoche* ("abstinence," holding back).

2   The term here translated as "self-control" is *sōphrosunē*, the term translated as "good sense" in Xenophon, *Memorabilia* 4.3, above. On this term see n. 2 of the Xenophon reading.

3   Empedocles was a presocratic philosopher who presented a materialistic account of life and consciousness, advocated vegetarianism, and taught that souls are reborn in successive bodies of different kinds of living things. Scholars do not agree on whether Porphyry is quoting here a genuine fragment from his lost writings.

4   Some Gallic converts to the cult of Cybele voluntary had themselves castrated.

5 This plural is our only indication that Firmus was a member of a group, the members of which had renounced their vegetarianism.

6 This is the first occurrence in this work of the term *oikeios*. This term and its cognates have a great importance in this work. Like "economics" (see n. 11 to Xenophon, *Memorabilia* 4.3, included in this volume), the term derives from *oikia*, home. At its root, *oikeios* is that with which one is at home; it is one's own. The Stoics took the notion of what is *oikeios* to be fundamental to their ethics. There is an ethical obligation to act in accordance with the divine law, which is expressed in the teleological structure of the human person. All organisms are teleologically designed to care for that which is *oikeios* to them. This includes one's family, one's immediate community, and, ultimately, all rational beings. As is made clear both by Porphyry and the selection from Cicero excerpted in this volume, this community does not include nonhuman animals. These animals are taken to be *allotrios* (alien). This is why for the Stoics the notion of justice extends only to other rational beings, which includes human beings and the gods.

The process by which one comes to recognize the things that are *oikeios* to one is *oikeiōsis*. In some sense this is a process of taking things initially external to oneself to be among the things that are one's own. For this reason, and for lack of any clear English equivalent, the term is usually translated as "appropriation." It should be kept in mind, however, that unlike "appropriation," the Greek term does not carry with it connotations of forcibly seizing what initially belongs to another.

The terms *oikeios*, *oikeiōsis*, and *allotrios* accordingly present a significant problem to the translator. The point of Porphyry's argument that other animals are related to us in a fundamental way would perhaps be lost if we were to uniformly render *oikeios* as "appropriate." Further, he sometimes uses the term to merely refer to those to whom one is biologically related, which is part, but not all, of the Stoic sense of the term. We have translated *oikeios* as both "kin" (or "akin") and "appropriate." *Oikeiōsis* is translated as "appropriation," and *allotrios* as "alien."

7 With this sentence there begins an extract that is taken almost verbatim from Plutarch's *On the Cleverness of Animals*, 964a–c. Porphyry has no compunction about inserting long extracts from other writers, sometimes with no signal that this is what he is doing.

8 These are names of tribes living near the Red Sea.

9 Hesiod, *Works and Days*, 277–79.

10 Porphyry, following Plutarch, supports the argument against vegetarianism by means of the Stoic principle that there are obligations of justice only toward other rational beings. This would exclude young children from the moral community; one would have obligations toward young children only insofar as one has obligations toward their parents or others who have an interest in the children's welfare. It may be surprising to see that Porphyry does not criticize the Stoics' position on these grounds. Instead, he attempts to show that many animals do in fact possess rationality. One can partially account for this by noting that infanticide was an accepted practice within ancient Greek and Roman culture. For example, it is advocated in the account of a perfectly just society related by Socrates in Plato's *Republic*.

11 The extract from Plutarch ends here.

12 The term for reason is *logos*; it can also mean "language." Much of Book 3 is spent discussing whether animals other than people have *logos* or not.

13 Porphyry makes clear that he is not establishing an ethical code applicable for all human beings. Rather, he is indicating that for a certain elite, who are capable of the best life, this best life is made possible only though paying meticulous attention to how their conduct, especially in regard to matters of food, impacts on other rational beings, and to how such conduct serves to purify or sully the soul.

14 On "virtue" see n. 14 to Plato's *Timaeus*.

15 The term for "animal" can also have the sense of "living being." But the arguments that Porphyry presents bear almost exclusively on animals, not plants.

16 The term for "irrational" is *alogos*, "without *logos*."

17 Notoriously, the Stoics argued that, at most, only a handful of people have achieved moral perfection, and were therefore happy. All others were unhappy, even if they had made relatively more progress in living a life in accordance with the divine *logos*.

18 In Stoic thought, a disposition (*diathesis*) is a permanent attribute of a thing.

19 The same term is translated "convention" and "law."

20 Aristotle, *History of Animals*, 4.9 536b17ff.

21 An affection is either something that is experienced, or something that happens to the body.

22 The Greeks believed that younger storks fed their parents, when the latter were too old to take care of themselves.

23 Plato and his followers took the celestial bodies to be divine. Porphyry is pointing to the fact that one is able to infer that the sun is endowed with a rational soul on the basis of the perfect regularity of its motions.

24 This is a reference to the creation story of Plato's *Timaeus*.

25 In Homer's *Odyssey*, Odysseus' men are overcome by hunger on the Island of Thrinakia and, although prohibited to do so, they eat the oxen of the Sun (Book 12, 260–419). At the Sun's request, Zeus destroys Odysseus' ship once it sets sail, and the entire crew is lost.

26 The Greek term translated here as "imperfect" can also mean "incomplete."

27 Here begins a long extract from a lost work of Plutarch.

28 As used here, a barbarian is a non-Greek.

29 This is from one of the lost plays of Aeschylus.

30 Zeno (335?–263? BC) was the founder of the Stoic school.

31 On Chrysippus, see the introduction to the selections from Cicero.

32 There is a play on words here. The pig is delightful to eat; also, according to Porphyry, the notion that pigs are only for our sake is delightfully absurd.

33 On this, see n. 21 of Cicero, *On the Nature of the Gods*, in this volume.

34 As a Platonist, Porphyry holds that the cause of the existence of certain animals in the world is the Demiurge, who is modeling the world on the Forms. For the Stoics, however, the divinity that is responsible for the order in the world is a thin body called *pneuma*, which permeates all of the physical world.

35 Carneades (214?–129? BC) was the founder of Academic skepticism. His aim was to show that philosophical arguments can convey no certainty; an opposing argument is always available. For this reason, Carneades argued that we should be reconciled to accepting the view that is the most probable.

36 In other contexts in this selection the term for "benefit" has been translated as "help." As Porphyry is about to point out, the term has two senses. In one sense, a thing is "benefitted" when it fulfills its teleology, as humans do when they acquire moral perfection. In another sense, a thing is "helped" when something is useful to it. If an animal like a pig really were for the sake of human enjoyment, it would be fulfilling its teleology when it is eaten. Porphyry asks, can one thereby say that being eaten is helpful or of some use to the pig?

37 *Odyssey* 12.97.

38 The extract from the lost work of Plutarch ends here. There then begins another extract from Plutarch: *On the Cleverness of Animals* 959E–963F, which continues until section 24.

39 Theophrastus was a student of Aristotle, and succeeded him as head of Aristotle's school, the Lykeum. He was a noted botanist.

40 On this term, see note 6, above.

41 Pythagoras, who lived in the sixth century BC, was a spiritual leader and philosopher who apparently advocated vegetarianism for his followers, and preceded Plato in arguing that the human soul can be successively reborn in the bodies of different kinds of living things.

42 In Book 4 of the *Republic*, as well as in the *Timaeus*, Plato had argued that the soul has three parts: one rational part and two irrational parts, the seat of desire and the seat of feelings of anger, shame, and possessiveness. It is by virtue of the latter two parts that the soul as a whole cares for the body. In a just, or properly ordered soul, the rational part governs the irrational parts (and thereby governs the body).

Faith and Nature

CHAPTER 6

Genesis

THE ANCIENT philosophers set for themselves the project of arriving at explanations of the most important features of the world on the basis of reason alone. The religious views of their societies had no special immunity from philosophical criticism, although some philosophers discreetly disguised their criticisms, and others saw poetic expositions of truth in religious myth.

Sacred texts play a much different role in medieval philosophy. In the Jewish, Christian, and Islamic medieval philosophical traditions, sacred texts are at least explicitly taken to be direct revelations of divine wisdom. The problem lies in interpreting them, and arriving at as comprehensive a rational understanding of them as is possible. The thought of the ancient pagan philosophers was put into service toward this end.

It is for this reason that several pages of the Hebrew Scriptures are included in this volume. Medieval philosophical authors (and many philosophers living after the medieval period) accept the stories of Creation, Adam and Eve, Noah's Ark, and the Psalms of David as containing important wisdom. The initial chapters from Genesis depict a world all of whose components are good in God's eyes. Human beings have a special status, which is altered because of the unique human capacity for moral error. Moral error, again, is responsible for a massive change in the world: the great Flood. In this story, Noah and his family have a special role as caretakers for the other animals.

These texts allow themselves to be interpreted in many different fashions, each interpretation leading to a very different understanding of the nature of human beings, their place in the cosmos as a whole, and their relation to the nonhuman world. Although space does not permit discussion of the various interpretations and their philosophical implications, we can indicate the following questions as fundamental to a philosophy of nature or an environmental philosophy that finds guidance in Biblical writings:

1. In what sense does God declare the various aspects of the created world to be "good"? Does this entail ascribing inherent value to the nonhuman world?
2. In the most fundamental state (i.e., in the Garden of Eden), in what sense are human beings set apart from all other living things? Why is it significant that Adam gave names to all the animals?
3. What are the metaphysical implications of the eating of the Tree of the Knowledge of Good and Evil? In what sense does this act rupture the bond between human beings and all other living things? In what new sense are Adam and Eve now a fundamentally different kind of thing than all other living beings?

4. In what manner is the nonhuman world altered by human wickedness?
5. Why is Noah called upon to aid God in making sure that the various species perpetuate themselves? Does this have implications for the ethical obligation that human beings today have in regard to other living things?

Genesis

TR. BY A BOARD OF EDITORS; MAX L. MARGOLIS, EDITOR-IN-CHIEF.

Chapter 1

1 In the beginning God created the heaven and the earth. 2 Now the earth was unformed and void, and darkness was upon the face of the deep; and the spirit of God hovered over the face of the waters. 3 And God said: "Let there be light." And there was light. 4 And God saw the light, that it was good; and God divided the light from the darkness. 5 And God called the light Day, and the darkness He called Night. And there was evening and there was morning, one day.

6 And God said: "Let there be a firmament in the midst of the waters, and let it divide the waters from the waters." 7 And God made the firmament, and divided the waters which were under the firmament from the waters which were above the firmament; and it was so. 8 And God called the firmament Heaven. And there was evening and there was morning, a second day.

9 And God said: "Let the waters under the heaven be gathered together unto one place, and let the dry land appear." And it was so. 10 And God called the dry land Earth, and the gathering together of the waters called He Seas; and God saw that it was good. 11 And God said: "Let the earth put forth grass, herb yielding seed, and fruit-tree bearing fruit after its kind, wherein is the seed thereof, upon the earth." And it was so. 12 And the earth brought forth grass, herb yielding seed after its kind, and tree bearing fruit, wherein is the seed thereof, after its kind; and God saw that it was good. 13 And there was evening and there was morning, a third day.

14 And God said: "Let there be lights in the firmament of the heaven to divide the day from the night; and let them be for signs, and for seasons, and for days and years; 15 and let them be for lights in the firmament of the heaven to give light upon the earth." And it was so. 16 And God made the two great lights: the greater light to rule the day, and the lesser light to rule the night; and the stars. 17 And God set them in the firmament of the heaven to give light upon the earth, 18 and to rule over the day and over the night, and to divide the light from the darkness; and God saw that it was good. 19 And there was evening and there was morning, a fourth day.

20 And God said: "Let the waters swarm with swarms of living creatures, and let fowl fly above the earth in the open firmament of heaven." 21 And God created the great sea-monsters, and every living creature that creepeth, wherewith the waters swarmed, after its kind, and every winged fowl after its kind; and God saw that it was

good. 22 And God blessed them, saying: "Be fruitful, and multiply, and fill the waters in the seas, and let fowl multiply in the earth." 23 And there was evening and there was morning, a fifth day.

24 And God said: "Let the earth bring forth the living creature after its kind, cattle, and creeping thing, and beast of the earth after its kind." And it was so. 25 And God made the beast of the earth after its kind, and the cattle after their kind, and every thing that creepeth upon the ground after its kind; and God saw that it was good. 26 And God said: "Let us make man in our image, after our likeness; and let them have dominion over the fish of the sea, and over the fowl of the air, and over the cattle, and over all the earth, and over every creeping thing that creepeth upon the earth." 27 And God created man in His own image, in the image of God created He him; male and female created He them. 28 And God blessed them; and God said unto them: "Be fruitful, and multiply, and replenish the earth, and subdue it; and have dominion over the fish of the sea, and over the fowl of the air, and over every living thing that creepeth upon the earth." 29 And God said: "Behold, I have given you every herb yielding seed, which is upon the face of all the earth, and every tree, in which is the fruit of a tree yielding seed—to you it shall be for food; 30 and to every beast of the earth, and to every fowl of the air, and to every thing that creepeth upon the earth, wherein there is a living soul, [I have given] every green herb for food." And it was so. 31 And God saw every thing that He had made, and, behold, it was very good. And there was evening and there was morning, the sixth day.

Chapter 2

1 And the heaven and the earth were finished, and all the host of them. 2 And on the seventh day God finished His work which He had made; and He rested on the seventh day from all His work which He had made. 3 And God blessed the seventh day, and hallowed it; because that in it He rested from all His work which God in creating had made.

4 These are the generations of the heaven and of the earth when they were created, in the day that the LORD God made earth and heaven.

5 No shrub of the field was yet in the earth, and no herb of the field had yet sprung up; for the LORD God had not caused it to rain upon the earth, and there was not a man to till the ground; 6 but there went up a mist from the earth, and watered the whole face of the ground. 7 Then the LORD God formed man of the dust of the ground, and breathed into his nostrils the breath of life; and man became a living soul. 8 And the LORD God planted a garden eastward, in Eden; and there He put the man whom He had formed. 9 And out of the ground made the LORD God to grow every tree that is pleasant to the sight, and good for food; the tree of life also in the midst of the garden, and the tree of the knowledge of good and evil. 10 And a river went out of Eden to water the garden; and from thence it was parted, and became four heads. 11 The name of the first is Pishon; that is it which compasseth the whole land of Havilah, where there is gold;

12 and the gold of that land is good; there is bdellium and the onyx stone. 13 And the name of the second river is Gihon; the same is it that compasseth the whole land of Cush. 14 And the name of the third river is Tigris; that is it which goeth toward the east of Asshur. And the fourth river is the Euphrates. 15 And the LORD God took the man, and put him into the garden of Eden to dress it and to keep it. 16 And the LORD God commanded the man, saying: "Of every tree of the garden thou mayest freely eat; 17 but of the tree of the knowledge of good and evil, thou shalt not eat of it; for in the day that thou eatest thereof thou shalt surely die."

18 And the LORD God said: "It is not good that the man should be alone; I will make him a help meet for him." 19 And out of the ground the LORD God formed every beast of the field, and every fowl of the air; and brought them unto the man to see what he would call them; and whatsoever the man would call every living creature, that was to be the name thereof. 20 And the man gave names to all cattle, and to the fowl of the air, and to every beast of the field; but for Adam there was not found a help meet for him. 21 And the LORD God caused a deep sleep to fall upon the man, and he slept; and He took one of his ribs, and closed up the place with flesh instead thereof. 22 And the rib, which the LORD God had taken from the man, made He a woman, and brought her unto the man. 23 And the man said: "This is now bone of my bones, and flesh of my flesh; she shall be called Woman, because she was taken out of Man." 24 Therefore shall a man leave his father and his mother, and shall cleave unto his wife, and they shall be one flesh. 25 And they were both naked, the man and his wife, and were not ashamed.

Chapter 3

1 Now the serpent was more subtle than any beast of the field which the LORD God had made. And he said unto the woman: "Yea, hath God said: Ye shall not eat of any tree of the garden?" 2 And the woman said unto the serpent: "Of the fruit of the trees of the garden we may eat; 3 but of the fruit of the tree which is in the midst of the garden, God hath said: Ye shall not eat of it, neither shall ye touch it, lest ye die." 4 And the serpent said unto the woman: "Ye shall not surely die; 5 for God doth know that in the day ye eat thereof, then your eyes shall be opened, and ye shall be as God, knowing good and evil." 6 And when the woman saw that the tree was good for food, and that it was a delight to the eyes, and that the tree was to be desired to make one wise, she took of the fruit thereof, and did eat; and she gave also unto her husband with her, and he did eat. 7 And the eyes of them both were opened, and they knew that they were naked; and they sewed fig-leaves together, and made themselves girdles. 8 And they heard the voice of the LORD God walking in the garden toward the cool of the day; and the man and his wife hid themselves from the presence of the LORD God amongst the trees of the garden. 9 And the LORD God called unto the man, and said unto him: "Where art thou?" 10 And he said: "I heard Thy voice in the garden, and I was afraid, because I was naked;

and I hid myself." 11 And He said: "Who told thee that thou wast naked? Hast thou eaten of the tree, whereof I commanded thee that thou shouldest not eat?" 12 And the man said: "The woman whom Thou gavest to be with me, she gave me of the tree and I did eat." 13 And the LORD God said unto the woman: "What is this thou hast done?" And the woman said: "The serpent beguiled me, and I did eat." 14 And the LORD God said unto the serpent: "Because thou hast done this, cursed art thou from among all cattle, and from among all beasts of the field; upon thy belly shalt thou go, and dust shalt thou eat all the days of thy life. 15 And I will put enmity between thee and the woman, and between thy seed and her seed; they shall bruise thy head, and thou shalt bruise their heel."

16 Unto the woman He said: "I will greatly multiply thy pain and thy travail; in pain thou shalt bring forth children; and thy desire shall be to thy husband, and he shall rule over thee."

17 And unto Adam He said: "Because thou hast hearkened unto the voice of thy wife, and hast eaten of the tree, of which I commanded thee, saying: Thou shalt not eat of it; cursed is the ground for thy sake; in toil shalt thou eat of it all the days of thy life. 18 Thorns also and thistles shall it bring forth to thee; and thou shalt eat the herb of the field. 19 In the sweat of thy face shalt thou eat bread, till thou return unto the ground; for out of it wast thou taken; for dust thou art, and unto dust shalt thou return." 20 And the man called his wife's name Eve; because she was the mother of all living. 21 And the LORD God made for Adam and for his wife garments of skins, and clothed them.

22 And the LORD God said: "Behold, the man is become as one of us, to know good and evil; and now, lest he put forth his hand, and take also of the tree of life, and eat, and live for ever." 23 Therefore the LORD God sent him forth from the garden of Eden, to till the ground from whence he was taken. 24 So He drove out the man; and He placed at the east of the garden of Eden the cherubim, and the flaming sword which turned every way, to keep the way to the tree of life. ...

Chapter 6

... 11 And the earth was corrupt before God, and the earth was filled with violence. 12 And God saw the earth, and, behold, it was corrupt; for all flesh had corrupted their way upon the earth.

13 And God said unto Noah: "The end of all Flesh is come before Me; for the earth is filled with violence through them; and, behold, I will destroy them with the earth. 14 Make thee an ark of gopher wood; with rooms shalt thou make the ark, and shalt pitch it within and without with pitch. 15 And this is how thou shalt make it: the length of the ark three hundred cubits, the breadth of it fifty cubits, and the height of it thirty cubits. 16 A light shalt thou make to the ark, and to a cubit shalt thou finish it upward; and the door of the ark shalt thou set in the side thereof; with lower, second, and third stories shalt thou make it. 17 And I, behold, I do bring the

flood of waters upon the earth, to destroy all flesh, wherein is the breath of life, from under heaven; everything that is in the earth shall perish. 18 But I will establish My covenant with thee; and thou shalt come into the ark, thou, and thy sons, and thy wife, and thy sons' wives with thee. 19 And of every living thing of all flesh, two of every sort shalt thou bring into the ark, to keep them alive with thee; they shall be male and female. 20 Of the fowl after their kind, and of the cattle after their kind, of every creeping thing of the ground after its kind, two of every sort shall come unto thee, to keep them alive. 21 And take thou unto thee of all food that is eaten, and gather it to thee; and it shall be for food for thee, and for them." 22 Thus did Noah; according to all that God commanded him, so did he.

Chapter 7

1 And the LORD said unto Noah: "Come thou and all thy house into the ark; for thee have I seen righteous before Me in this generation. 2 Of every clean beast thou shalt take to thee seven and seven, each with his mate; and of the beasts that are not clean two [and two], each with his mate; 3 Of the fowl also of the air, seven and seven, male and female; to keep seed alive upon the face of the earth. 4 For yet seven days and I will cause it to rain upon the earth forty days and forty nights; and every living substance that I have made will I blot out from off the face of the earth." 5 And Noah did according unto all that the LORD commanded him.

6 And Noah was six hundred years old when the flood of waters was upon the earth. 7 And Noah went in, and his sons, and his wife, and his sons' wives with him, into the ark, because of the waters of the flood. 8 Of clean beasts, and of beasts that are not clean, and of fowls, and of every thing that creepeth upon the ground, 9 there went in two and two unto Noah into the ark, male and female, as God commanded Noah. 10 And it came to pass after the seven days, that the waters of the flood were upon the earth. 11 In the six hundredth year of Noah's life, in the second month, on the seventeenth day of the month, on the same day were all the fountains of the great deep broken up, and the windows of heaven were opened. 12 And the rain was upon the earth forty days and forty nights.

13 In the selfsame day entered Noah, and Shem, and Ham, and Japheth, the sons of Noah, and Noah's wife, and the three wives of his sons with them, into the ark; 14 they, and every beast after its kind, and all the cattle after their kind, and every creeping thing that creepeth upon the earth after its kind, and every fowl after its kind, every bird of every sort. 15 And they went in unto Noah into the ark, two and two of all flesh wherein is the breath of life. 16 And they that went in, went in male and female of all flesh, as God commanded him; and the LORD shut him in. 17 And the flood was forty days upon the earth; and the waters increased, and bore up the ark, and it was lifted up above the earth. 18 And the waters prevailed, and increased greatly upon the earth; and the ark went upon the face of the waters. 19 And the waters prevailed exceedingly upon the earth; and all the high mountains that

were under the whole heaven were covered. 20 Fifteen cubits upward did the waters prevail; and the mountains were covered. 21 And all flesh perished that moved upon the earth, both fowl, and cattle, and beast, and every swarming thing that swarmeth upon the earth, and every man; 22 all in whose nostrils was the breath of the spirit of life, whatsoever was in the dry land, died. 23 And He blotted out every living substance which was upon the face of the ground, both man, and cattle, and creeping thing, and fowl of the heaven; and they were blotted out from the earth; and Noah only was left, and they that were with him in the ark. 24 And the waters prevailed upon the earth a hundred and fifty days.

Chapter 8

1 And God remembered Noah, and every living thing, and all the cattle that were with him in the ark; and God made a wind to pass over the earth, and the waters assuaged; 2 the fountains also of the deep and the windows of heaven were stopped, and the rain from heaven was restrained. 3 And the waters returned from off the earth continually; and after the end of a hundred and fifty days the waters decreased. 4 And the ark rested in the seventh month, on the seventeenth day of the month, upon the mountains of Ararat. 5 And the waters decreased continually until the tenth month; in the tenth month, on the first day of the month, were the tops of the mountains seen.

6 And it came to pass at the end of forty days, that Noah opened the window of the ark which he had made. 7 And he sent forth a raven, and it went forth to and fro, until the waters were dried up from off the earth. 8 And he sent forth a dove from him, to see if the waters were abated from off the face of the ground. 9 But the dove found no rest for the sole of her foot, and she returned unto him to the ark, for the waters were on the face of the whole earth; and he put forth his hand, and took her, and brought her in unto him into the ark. 10 And he stayed yet other seven days; and again he sent forth the dove out of the ark. 11 And the dove came in to him at eventide; and lo in her mouth an olive-leaf freshly plucked; so Noah knew that the waters were abated from off the earth. 12 And he stayed yet other seven days; and sent forth the dove; and she returned not again unto him any more.

13 And it came to pass in the six hundred and first year, in the first month, the first day of the month, the waters were dried up from off the earth; and Noah removed the covering of the ark, and looked, and behold, the face of the ground was dried. 14 And in the second month, on the seven and twentieth day of the month, was the earth dry.

15 And God spoke unto Noah, saying: 16 "Go forth from the ark, thou, and thy wife, and thy sons, and thy sons' wives with thee. 17 Bring forth with thee every living thing that is with thee of all flesh, both fowl, and cattle, and every creeping thing that creepeth upon the earth; that they may swarm in the earth, and be fruitful, and multiply upon the earth." 18 And Noah went forth, and his sons, and his wife,

and his sons' wives with him; 19 every beast, every creeping thing, and every fowl, whatsoever moveth upon the earth, after their families, went forth out of the ark.

20 And Noah built an altar unto the LORD; and took of every clean beast, and of every clean fowl, and offered burnt-offerings on the altar. 21 And the LORD smelled the sweet savour; and the LORD said in His heart: "I will not again curse the ground any more for man's sake; for the imagination of man's heart is evil from his youth; neither will I again smite any more every thing living, as I have done. 22 While the earth remaineth, seedtime and harvest, and cold and heat, and summer and winter, and day and night shall not cease."

Chapter 9

1 And God blessed Noah and his sons, and said unto them: "Be fruitful, and multiply, and replenish the earth. 2 And the fear of you and the dread of you shall be upon every beast of the earth, and upon every fowl of the air, and upon all wherewith the ground teemeth, and upon all the fishes of the sea: into your hand are they delivered. 3 Every moving thing that liveth shall be for food for you; as the green herb have I given you all. 4 Only flesh with the life thereof, which is the blood thereof, shall ye not eat. 5 And surely your blood of your lives will I require; at the hand of every beast will I require it; and at the hand of man, even at the hand of every man's brother, will I require the life of man. 6 Whoso sheddeth man's blood, by man shall his blood be shed; for in the image of God made He man. 7 And you, be ye fruitful, and multiply; swarm in the earth, and multiply therein."

8 And God spoke unto Noah, and to his sons with him, saying: 9 "As for Me, behold, I establish My covenant with you, and with your seed after you; 10 and with every living creature that is with you, the fowl, the cattle, and every beast of the earth with you; of all that go out of the ark, even every beast of the earth. 11 And I will establish My covenant with you; neither shall all flesh be cut off any more by the waters of the flood; neither shall there any more be a flood to destroy the earth." 12 And God said: "This is the token of the covenant which I make between Me and you and every living creature that is with you, for perpetual generations: 13 I have set My bow in the cloud, and it shall be for a token of a covenant between Me and the earth. 14 And it shall come to pass, when I bring clouds over the earth, and the bow is seen in the cloud, 15 that I will remember My covenant, which is between Me and you and every living creature of all flesh; and the waters shall no more become a flood to destroy all flesh. 16 And the bow shall be in the cloud; and I will look upon it, that I may remember the everlasting covenant between God and every living creature of all flesh that is upon the earth." 17 And God said unto Noah: "This is the token of the covenant which I have established between Me and all flesh that is upon the earth." ...

CHAPTER 7

St. Augustine

As THE CHRISTIAN religion swept over much of Europe, the Near East, and Northern Africa, many leading Christian intellectuals turned to the pagan philosophers for the resources to solve certain metaphysical problems standing in the way of their accepting the tenets of the Church. Among these was St. Augustine (354–430), Bishop of Hippo, whose version of neoplatonic thought, integrated with Christian teachings, dominated Latin philosophy for almost a millennium.

Augustine accepted the Platonic dualistic conception of soul and body, with soul an independent being dominant over body, and bodily beings inferior to the intelligible, eternal beings that can be grasped only with the mind. He is often said to have an attitude of contempt for bodily, earthly things, but, as the following sermon makes clear, this is not the whole story. Augustine recognized the beauty and order of the physical world, and, like many Christian thinkers who followed him, saw the goodness of the physical world as bearing witness to the Biblical God. By appealing to the Platonic teaching that the world is an animal, with its body given order and goodness by the World Soul, he mitigates the harsh dualism of pagan neoplatonic philosophers by indicating that the human soul, too, taken alone, is fundamentally incomplete without a body. In this way Augustine grants to the body a dignity of its own, and allows his congregation to accept that it is good for souls, at the time of resurrection, to once again live in bodies of their own.

As Augustine ushered in Christian philosophy, he set a number of important precedents for philosophical thought concerning Nature. He taught that the natural world is genuinely beautiful, and for this reason it points to God as its source. A study of the workings of the natural world can lead to knowledge of spiritual truths. The human body, too, is part of the physical world; it shares in the order and beauty of the world, even if it does occupy a rank lower than that of soul. Although Augustine did not explicitly endorse the view that the world is a single sentient organism, he showed respect for the Platonic teaching of the World Soul, and used it to argue against neoplatonic contempt for bodily things.

ST. AUGUSTINE
Sermon 241,
On the Resurrection of Bodies, against the Pagans[1]
TR. DAVID CHURCH

1. The resurrection of the dead is an article of faith that distinguishes Christians. Christ our head gave proof of the resurrection in his own person, thus providing a

model for our faith, so that we, the members of his body, might hope that what had first taken place in our head would be accomplished in us as well. Yesterday I told you that the most eminent of those wise men whom the pagans call "philosophers" had scrutinized nature and had come to know its artificer from his works. They had not heard the prophets nor received the law of God, but God was somehow speaking to them silently through the works of his world, and the beauty of that world was inviting them to seek the artificer of things; and they could not bring themselves to believe that heaven and earth could exist without a creator. St. Paul the Apostle has this to say about these men: "For the wrath of God is revealed from heaven against all ungodliness."[2] What is meant by "against all ungodliness"? The wrath of God is revealed from heaven not only against the Jews, who received the law of God and sinned against its giver, but also against all the ungodliness of the pagans. And lest someone should ask: "Why is God angry at the pagans, when they have not received the Law?", He adds the following: "And against the wickedness of men who by their wickedness suppress the truth." Now answer this question: What truth did they suppress? For they had not received the Law, nor had they heard the Prophets. Listen to Paul's explanation: "For," he says, "what can be known about God is plain to them." How is it plain to them? Listen further: "Because God has shown it to them." If you still ask how he showed this to those to whom he had not given his Law, listen once more to the Apostle: "Ever since the creation of the world, his invisible nature has been clearly perceived in the things that have been made." "Ever since the creation of the world": that is, from the time when God created the world; "his invisible nature": that is, the invisible nature of God; "has been clearly perceived in the things that have been made": that is, that invisible nature is perceived by being understood through these created things. "His eternal power and deity": I'm quoting these additional words of the Apostle, with which you are to understand "are clearly perceived." "So they are without excuse." Why without excuse? "Because, although they knew God, they did not honor him as God or give thanks to him." Note that he does not say, "They did not know God," but "although they knew God."

2. What was the source of their knowledge of God? They knew him from the things that he created. Question the beauty of the earth, the beauty of the sea, the beauty of the air, spread out and dispersed everywhere. Question the beauty of the heavens and the orderly arrangement of the constellations. Question the sun, lighting up the day with its radiance, and the moon, mitigating with its splendor the darkness of the night that follows. Question the living things swimming in the sea, walking on land, and flying through the air—though their souls are hidden and their bodies in plain sight, their invisible souls have dominion over their visible bodies, which must be directed. Question all these creatures, and they reply: "Look at us! We are beautiful!" Their beauty is their witness to their creator. Who made these beautiful yet changeable things, if not one who is both beautiful and unchangeable?

Finally, in order to know and comprehend God, the creator of the whole world, the pagan philosophers questioned, in man himself, these two parts, his body and his soul; they questioned, that is, what they themselves were carrying about. They saw their body, they could not see their soul, but they did not see their body except through the agency of their soul; for the eye which enabled them to see was within the body, and peered out through its windows.[3] ... Hence the philosophers questioned these two parts of man, his body, which can be seen, and his soul, which cannot be seen, and they found that what cannot be seen is better than what is seen: that the hidden soul is better, the visible flesh worse.[4] They looked at these two parts, examining and discussing both of them, and they found that both parts are subject to change. The body changes because of the stages it passes through during its life, because of the degeneration occurring within it, because of the food it eats, because it recuperates, then declines, because it lives and dies. Then those philosophers went beyond the body to consider the soul, which they certainly understood to be superior to the body, and which, even though it was invisible, they held in great esteem. And they found that it too is changeable; now willing, now unwilling; now knowing, now ignorant; now remembering, now forgetting; now frightened, now daring; now progressing towards wisdom, now lapsing into foolishness. Seeing that it too is changeable, they finally went beyond the soul itself; for they were seeking something unchangeable.[5]

3. Thus the pagan philosophers came to a knowledge of God from the things which he made. "But they did not honor him as God or give thanks to him," the Apostle himself says, "but they became futile in their thinking and their senseless minds were darkened; claiming to be wise, they became fools." By claiming as their own the knowledge they had received, they lost the good sense they had once possessed. Declaring themselves to be somehow great, they became foolish. And to what extreme did they go in their folly? "They changed," he says, "the glory of the immortal God for images resembling mortal man" (he is speaking about idols). And the pagans were not content to make their idols in the form of man, thus attributing to the artificer the likeness of one of his works. This was not enough for them; they went much further: they made idols in the form "of birds and beasts and serpents."[6] ...

4. The pagan philosophers, then, as I reminded you yesterday, sought the truth about what comes after this life. They sought this truth as men, but when would they find it, since they were men? They did not have God's teaching, nor had they heard the Prophets; they could not find the truth about life after death, they could only guess at it. Yesterday I told you about their conjectures: evil souls, they say, leave the body, and because they are impure, they immediately begin another cycle of life on earth but in different bodies; the souls of the wise and the just also leave the body, and because they have lived well, they fly to heaven. ...

6. ... Away with such nonsense![7] Let us either ridicule this doctrine because it is false, or deplore it because it is held in high repute. For, my brothers, these are the

gross ravings of famous teachers; how much better it is to put our faith in the sublime mysteries transmitted to us by our great saints! Those philosophers say that souls who have been purified, cleansed, and become wise return to earth out of love of bodies: that these souls, although purified, enter again into bodies because they love them. Is this the love of a purified soul? Isn't it rather a great defilement?

7. "But every body must be shunned." These are the words of Porphyry, a famous man among the later generation of philosophers. He lived in the Christian era, and was a bitter foe of the Christian faith.[8] But although he was ashamed of his insane accusations when censured for some of them by the Christians, he nevertheless said in his writings, "Every body must be shunned." He says, "Every body," as if every body were a miserable prison for the soul. And certainly, if every body of whatever kind is to be shunned, you cannot praise the body to Porphyry, nor tell him how our faith does so under the influence of God's teaching. For although the body we now have is the source of the punishment for sin that we suffer, and "a corruptible body weighs down the soul" (Wisdom 9.15), nevertheless this body has its own beauty: the arrangement of its parts, the differentiation of its senses, its upright posture, and the rest of its qualities, which amaze those who think about the body in the right way. And despite its present condition, this body will become completely incorruptible and immortal, completely nimble and adept in its movements.

But Porphyry says: "You have no reason for praising the body to me; if a soul wishes to be happy it must shun every body, no matter what kind of body it may be." This is what the philosophers assert, but they are wrong, they rave. Since I don't want to argue this point at length, I offer this instant proof: The thing that is exalted must have something subject to it,[9] for these two, what is exalted and what is subject, are intimately connected: God, for instance, is superior to all things, and all things are subject to him. Thus the soul too, if it holds a place of honor before God, must have something subject to it. But rather than prolong this discussion, I appeal to what I have read in your own books. You call our world an "animal"; by this you mean that the heavens, the earth, and the seas, together with all the huge bodies existing in them and the vast expanse of the elements, constitute collectively a single body, which is a great living thing: that is, has its own soul.[10] Although this animal has no bodily senses, because there is nothing outside it that could be perceived, it does have an intellect and is in contact with God. You also say that its soul is named "Jupiter" or "Hecate," as if it were a universal soul that rules over the world, thus forming with it a single living thing, a kind of animal.—This same world, you say, will exist forever and will never come to an end. If, then, the world is eternal and will endure forever, and if it is an animal whose soul is forever enclosed within it, is it true without qualification that every body must be shunned? What do you mean when you say this? I say that blessed souls will always possess incorruptible bodies. Slay the world, you who say: "Every body must be shunned." You tell me to flee from my flesh; then let your Jupiter take flight from heaven and earth!

8. What of the fact that in the book he wrote about the formation of the world, this same Plato, the teacher of all those philosophers, portrays God as the maker of gods, that is, as producing the celestial deities: all the stars, the sun and the moon? Hence he calls God the "artificer"[11] of the celestial deities, and says that the stars themselves have intellectual souls that know God, as well as the visible bodies that we see. ... Is it, then, true without qualification that every body must be shunned?—It seems to me that I have answered the philosophers in a way that you can understand; I have answered them to the extent that the time of this sermon allows me to speak and your capacity enables you to comprehend. Yet I still have much to tell you about what they say with respect to the resurrection of bodies—they argue, as they think, so cleverly that I shall be incapable of replying to them. But since I once promised you that I would deal, during the paschal season, with the question of the resurrection of the body, go home now and, with God's help, prepare your ears and your hearts for the rest of this instruction tomorrow

Notes

1 This sermon was delivered by Augustine at Hippo during the Easter season, between 400 and 412.

2 Augustine is commenting on St. Paul's Epistle to the Romans, 1.18-23: "For the wrath of God is revealed from heaven against all ungodliness and wickedness of men who by their wickedness suppress the truth. For what can be known about God is plain to them, because God has shown it to them. Ever since the creation of the world his invisible nature, namely, his eternal power and deity, has been clearly perceived in the things that have been made. So they are without excuse; for although they knew God they did not honor him as God or give thanks to him, but they became futile in their thinking and their senseless minds were darkened. Claiming to be wise, they became fools, and exchanged the glory of the immortal God for images resembling mortal man or birds or animals or reptiles" (Revised Standard Version of the King James Bible).

3 That is, the soul perceives the external world through the sense organs of the body.

4 Augustine is unaware of the Aristotelian account of soul. In referring to pagan philosophers, he is primarily referring to Plato and his followers. On Plato's distinction between the soul and the body, see the selection from the *Timaeus*, n. 9, in the present volume.

5 In seeking something unchangeable, the Platonic philosophers discovered the Forms. But thinking about the Forms led them to become aware of the source of all of the Forms, which Plato called the Form of the Good. Neoplatonic philosophers identified this with a single transcendent god.

6 Augustine is surely aware that the use of idols in pagan religion preceded the thought of Plato. Perhaps he has in mind later Platonists, such as Porphyry (mentioned later in the sermon) who endorsed the polytheistic rites of nonphilosophic religion as expressions of philosophic truth.

7   In the omitted section, Augustine presents pagan philosophical accounts of what happens to the souls of the dead, and reveals inconsistencies in these accounts. Plato and other ancient philosophers took there to be a cycle of rebirth, so that souls return to exist once again in bodies; Augustine points out that the cause of this rebirth is unexplained, especially if this is said to occur in the case of those souls that have been purified of bodily desire. Further, the pagan Platonists (like Augustine) equate happiness with knowledge. But if purified souls are aware of their destiny of rebirth, how can they be happy? If they are ignorant, again, it would seem as though they could not be happy.

8   Porphyry wrote a lengthy treatise, *Against Christians*, which provoked refutations by Christian apologists, notably Methodius of Olympus and Eusebius of Caesarea. These refutations, along with Porphyry's treatise, are now lost, but Augustine is apparently referring to them when he says that Porphyry was "censured by the Christians."

In 3.26 of *On Abstaining from Animals*, excerpted above, Porphyry says that the soul must discipline the body; at the conclusion of 3.27, he makes the stronger claim that the soul must free itself from the servitude of the body.

In *The City of God*, Augustine attributes the words quoted here to a work of Porphyry entitled *On the Return of the Soul*, which survives only in fragments, most of them found in the writings of Augustine himself, who quotes a longer version of the formula: "every body must be shunned, so that the soul may remain happy with God" (*De civ. Dei*, X, 29).

9   There is a play on words here. This line can also be translated as the grammatical principle "everything that is predicated must have a subject."

10 This teaching can be found in Plato, *Timaeus* 30B, found in the present volume: "Certainly, then, one must follow the likely account and say that in truth, through the forethought of the god, this cosmos came to be as a living thing, possessing soul and intellect." The Greek term for "living thing" can also mean "animal."

11 The designation of the creator of the world as *opifex* ("artificer") is an attempt to render Plato's *demiourgos* ("craftsman").

CHAPTER 8

Hildegard of Bingen

For almost a millennium, St. Augustine's writings provided the philosophical foundation for nearly all Roman Catholic theological writings. As we have seen, this involves a fundamentally Platonic metaphysics, located in a Christian context. The natural world can be cherished as providing an image for the beauty and goodness of God, but only rational beings have moral standing, since only they have a direct share of rational soul.

Nonetheless, according to this world view, all living things are alive by virtue of soul. It is therefore a short move from traditional Augustinian thought to a view, such as that of St. Francis, that minimizes the differences between human beings and other living things.

Another such view was put forward by Hildegard of Bingen (1098–1179), a leading religious leader, scientist, and composer of her time, who is often considered a precursor of ecofeminism. Hildegard is best known for her vivid accounts of the mystical visions she experienced throughout her life. She was greatly influenced by the language and imagery of the Biblical prophets, as well as the ways in which wisdom is considered a powerful feminine being in certain "wisdom writings," such as the books of Proverbs, the Wisdom of Solomon, and the Wisdom of Sirach (Ecclesiasticus). Her accounts are poetical expressions of a unique philosophical and theological world view. God has a number of manifestations. That which serves to relate God to the created world, and the created world to God, has a distinctly feminine character, and is referred to as "Wisdom" or "Charity." It is this same aspect of the Divine that animates the natural world (and hence plays the role of Soul in neoplatonic thought). Wisdom or Charity allows all things, including people, animals, and plants, to come to fruition and create. Human beings and natural things that thus achieve spiritual, artistic, and physical fecundity are said to do so by virtue of a special spiritual characteristic that Hildegard calls "greenness," a characteristic associated with moisture and warmth. According to this view, God is as much of a nurturer as a ruler.

The following passages depict visions of Caritas, who is also Wisdom—that aspect of God that is the principle of "greenness," love, and intelligence within the world.

HILDEGARD OF BINGEN
The Book of Divine Works
TR. ROBERT CUNNINGHAM

First Vision: On the Origin of Life

Vision One: 1

And I saw within the mystery of God, in the midst of the southern breezes, a won-drously beautiful image. It had a human form, and its countenance was of such beauty and radiance that I could have more easily gazed at the sun than at that face. A broad golden ring circled its head. In this ring above the head there appeared a second countenance, like that of an elderly man, its chin and beard resting on the crown of the first head. On both sides of the figure a wing grew out of the shoulders. The wings rose above the above-mentioned ring and were joined there. At the topmost part of the right wing's curve appeared an eagle's head. Its eyes were like fire, and in them the brilliance of angels streamed forth as in a mirror. On the topmost part of the left wing's curve was a human head, which shone like the gleaming of the stars. Both faces were turned toward the East. From the shoulders of the figure a wing extended to its knees. The figure was wrapped in a garment that shone like the sun. Its hands carried a lamb, which shone like a brilliant day. The figure's feet trod upon a monster of dreadful appearance, poisonous and black, and a serpent which had fastened its teeth onto the monster's right ear. Its body was wound obliquely across the monster's head; its tail extended on the left side as far as the feet.

Vision One: 2

"I, the highest and fiery power, have kindled every spark of life, and I emit nothing that is deadly. I decide on all reality. With my lofty wings I fly above the globe: With wisdom I have rightly put the universe in order. I, the fiery life of divine essence, am aflame beyond the beauty of the meadows, I gleam in the waters, and I burn in the sun, moon, and stars. With every breeze, as with invisible life that contains every-thing, I awaken everything to life. The air lives by turning green and being in bloom. The waters flow as if they were alive. The sun lives in its light, and the moon is enkindled, after its disappearance, once again by the light of the sun so that the moon is again revived. The stars, too, give a clear light with their beaming. I have established pillars that bear the entire globe as well as the power of the winds which, once again, have subordinate wings—so to speak, weaker winds—which through their gentle power resist the mighty winds so that they do not become dangerous. In the same way, too, the body envelops the soul and maintains it so that the soul does not blow away. For just as the breath of the soul strengthens and fortifies the body so that it does not disappear, the more powerful winds, too, revive the surrounding winds so that they can provide their appropriate service.

And thus I remain hidden in every kind of reality as a fiery power. Everything burns because of me in such a way as our breath constantly moves us, like the wind-tossed flame in a fire. All of this lives in its essence, and there is no death in it. For I am life. I am also Reason, which bears within itself the breath of the resounding Word, through which the whole of creation is made. I breathe life into everything so that nothing is mortal in respect to its species. For I am life.[1]

I am life, whole and entire—not struck from stones, not blooming out of twigs, not rooted in a man's power to beget children. Rather all life has its roots in me. Reason is the root, the resounding Word blooms out of it.

Since God is Reason, how could it be that God, who causes all divine actions to come to fruition through human beings, is not active? God created men and women in the divine image and likeness, and marked each of these creatures according to a fixed standard in human beings. From eternity it was in the mind of God to wish to create humanity, God's own handiwork.[2] And when God completed this action, God gave over to act with it just as God had formed the divine handiwork, humanity.

And thus I serve by helping. For all life lights up out of me. I am life that remains ever the same, without beginning and without end. For this life is God, who is always in motion and constantly in action, and yet this life is manifest in a threefold power. For eternity is called the "Father," the Word is called the "Son," and the breath that binds both of them together is called the "Holy Spirit." And God has likewise marked humanity; in human beings there are body, soul, and reason.[3] The fact that I am aglow above the beauty of earthly realms has the following meaning: The Earth is the material out of which God forms human beings. The fact that I am illuminated in the water signifies the soul, which permeates the entire body just as water flows through the entire Earth. The fact that I am afire in the sun and moon signifies reason; for the stars are countless words of reason. And the fact that I awaken the universe with a breath of air as with the invisible life that contains everything, has the following significance: Through air and wind whatever is growing toward maturity is enlivened and supported, and in no way does it diverge from its inner being."

Vision One: 3

And again I heard a voice from heaven saying to me:

"God, who created everything, has formed humanity according to the divine image and likeness, and marked in human beings both the higher and the lower creatures. God loved humanity so much that God designated for it the place from which the fallen angel was ejected, intending for human beings all the splendor and honor which that angel lost along with his bliss. The countenance you are gazing at is an indication of this fact.

"For what you see as a marvelously beautiful figure in God's mystery and in the midst of southern breezes—a figure similar to a human being—signifies the Love[4] of our heavenly Father. It is Love[5]—in the power of the everlasting Godhead, full of exquisite beauty, marvelous in its mysterious gifts. Love appears in a human form because God's Son, when he put on flesh, redeemed our lost humanity in the service of Love. On this account the countenance is of such beauty and splendor that you can more easily gaze at the sun than at it. For the abundance of Love gleams and shines in the sublime lightning flash of its gifts in such a way that it surpasses every insight of human understanding by which otherwise we can know in our soul the most varied things. As a result, none of us can grasp this abundance with our minds. But this fact will be shown here in an allegory so that we can know in faith what we cannot see with our outward eyes."

✛═══✛

HILDEGARD OF BINGEN
The Book of the Rewards of Life
TR. BRUCE W. HOZESKI

Part 3

5. The Words of Envy

This image answered: "I am the shepherd and guardian of excess, and I cast out all greenness from men whenever I want to. I also strike down appropriate tongues. I also bite them, as skillfully as serpents that are as plentiful as the sand of the sea. They cannot resist me since I am called Gehenna. And so I draw many to myself and pollute all things that God does. If I cannot have the things that are bright, I value them as nothing. If those who call me night were to sprinkle water on me, I would quickly dry myself. In addition, I aim my words like hidden arrows and wound the heart of those who call themselves righteous. For my strengths are like the North. All the things that are mine, however, I give with hatred because hatred was born from me and is smaller than me."

6. The Response of Charity

Again from the storm cloud I heard this response given to this image: "O most filthy filth, you are like a snake that attacks itself, for you cannot sustain anything that is stable and honorable. You, however, are the shadow that is against God and that attacks people through unfaithfulness. You rightly call yourself Gehenna since it holds out excess against all just moderation and tears to pieces everything that springs from wisdom. Neither is Gehenna strong against anything bright. I, however, am the air, I who nourish all greenness and bring flowers to mature fruit. For I have been taught by the inspiration of the Spirit of God so that I pour out the clearest of streams. Of course, I bring forth tears from a good sigh as I also bring forth a good aroma from tears through most holy works. I am also the rain that rises from the dew through which the grass rejoices with rich life. You, however, the most wicked and worst poison, devour these things with your punishments, but you cannot trample all these things under your feet. For the more you rage, the more they grow. Whereas you are mortal, these strengths live on and through God's power they appear like flowers on a vine. You, however, are the most abominable and darkest abomination and the hissing sound of the devil. You do not even want to be any other way and with pride in your mind you say: 'I draw more people to me than there are grains of sand by the sea.' But you will fail, for I make the power of good works equal throughout the day and night. I spread my mantle upon the day and night; I do a lot of good works during the day and I anoint the sorrows of the night. Thus no one can accuse me either way. I am the most prized of friends on God's throne; God hides no counsel from me. I have a royal dwelling place and all the things that are from God are mine. Where the Son of God wipes away men's sins with his tunic, there I also bind men's wounds with the sweetest of linen. You, however, blush because what is the better part is not for you."

Notes

1 As in the neoplatonic tradition, the principle of soul, which gives life to both the whole cosmos and the individual human being, is also the principle of wisdom, by which the cosmos, as well as the individual life, is put into a rational order.

2 In the neoplatonic tradition, conveyed to Christianity primarily through the writings of St. Augustine, all created beings are what they are by virtue of the Forms, which eternally exist in the mind of God, even during the period prior to creation.

3 In this vision, God is personified as the principle of both wisdom and life. In the individual human being, on the other hand, reason (the principle of wisdom) and soul (the principle of life), are distinguished as two different things.

4 The Latin is *Caritas*, Charity.

5 Hildegard here makes clear that, ultimately, Charity is both the principle of life and the principle of Wisdom.

CHAPTER 9

St. Francis of Assisi

Lᴉᴋᴇ ᴛʜᴇ Sᴄʀɪᴘᴛᴜʀᴀʟ texts included in this volume, the following writings about St. Francis of Assisi (1181?–1226) are nonphilosophical texts that nevertheless cast a long philosophical shadow. St. Francis was the first major Christian figure to take creatures other than human beings to have moral standing, and to be the sort of being that can be the object of compassion or charity. The life of St. Francis, who has been declared the patron saint of ecology by Pope John Paul II, has often been cited by modern-day environmental philosophers as evidence that Christian teachings can lead to an ethic of concern for all natural things.

The following biographical texts contain three important philosophical aspects. First, St. Francis looks to the beauty and perfection of the natural world as evidence of the greatness of God. Here he is following the Augustinian tradition, which dominated the Christian philosophical thought of his time. Francis differs from St. Augustine, however, in taking the beauty of the natural world as a means by which these things engage in active praise of God. Second, St. Francis takes all natural creatures to be kin to humans, insofar as all are children of God. It is owing to this that he shows charity to them (which, as we shall see, St. Thomas Aquinas take to be impossible). It would follow that a Christian ethic, based on the obligations of charity, would grant moral standing to creatures other than human beings. Third, we see St. Francis taking special interest in certain natural things, insofar as they are images of key attributes of God. This is a distant ancestor of the view, expressed very differently by Kant and Thoreau, that the natural world has value for human life insofar as it allows us access to the divine.

CELANO
The First Life of St. Francis (1229)
TR. PLACID HERMANN, O.F.M.

Chapter 29 *Of the love Francis bore all creatures on account of their Creator; a description of the inner and outer man*[1]

It would take too long and it would be impossible to enumerate and gather together all the things the glorious Francis did and taught while he was living in the flesh. For who could ever give expression to the very great affection he bore for all things that are God's? Who would be able to narrate the sweetness he enjoyed while contemplating in creatures the wisdom of their Creator, his power and his goodness? Indeed, he was very often filled with a wonderful and ineffable joy from this consideration while he looked upon the sun, while he beheld the moon, and while he gazed upon the stars and the firmament. O simple piety and pious simplicity! Toward little worms even he glowed with a very great love, for he had read this saying about the Savior: *I am a worm, not a man.*[2] Therefore he picked them up from the road and placed them in a safe place, lest they be crushed by the feet of the passers-by. What shall I say of the lower creatures, when he would see to it that the bees would be provided with honey in the winter, or the best wine, lest they should die from the cold? He used to praise in public the perfection of their works and the excellence of their skill, for the glory of God, with such encomiums that he would often spend a whole day in praising them and the rest of creatures. For as of old the three youths in the fiery furnace[3] invited all the elements to praise and glorify the Creator of the universe, so also this man, filled with the spirit of God, never ceased to glorify, praise, and bless the Creator and Ruler of all things in all the elements and creatures.[4]

How great a gladness do you think the beauty of the flowers brought to his mind when he saw the shape of their beauty and perceived the odor of their sweetness? He used to turn the eye of consideration immediately to the beauty of that flower that comes "from the root of Jesse"[5] and gives light "in the days of spring"[6] and by its fragrance has raised innumerable thousands from the dead. When he found an abundance of flowers, he preached to them and invited them to praise the Lord as though they were endowed with reason. In the same way he exhorted with the sincerest purity cornfields and vineyards, stones and forests and all the beautiful things of the fields, fountains of water and the green things of the gardens, earth and fire, air and wind, to love God and serve him willingly. Finally, he called all creatures "brother," and in a most extraordinary manner, a manner never experienced by others, he discerned the hidden things of nature with his sensitive heart, as one who had already escaped "into the freedom of the glory of the sons of God."[7] O good Jesus, he is now praising you as admirable in heaven with all the angels, he who on earth preached you as lovable to every creature.

┼══╾═══╾┼

ST. BONAVENTURE
Major Life of St. Francis (1263)
TR. BENEN FAHY, O.F.M.

Chapter 8 *Francis' Loving Compassion and the Love Which Creatures Had for Him*

Compassion, as St. Paul tells us, is all-availing and it filled the heart of St. Francis and penetrated its depths to such an extent that his whole life seemed to be governed by it. It was loving compassion which united him to God in prayer and caused his transformation into Christ by sharing his sufferings. It was this which led him to devote himself humbly to his neighbor and enabled him to return to the state of primeval innocence by restoring man's harmony with the whole of creation.

Loving compassion made him regard everything with affection, but especially the souls which Jesus Christ redeemed with his precious blood. ...

The realization that everything comes from the same source filled Francis with greater affection than ever and he called even the most insignificant creatures his brothers and sisters, because he knew they had the same origin as himself. However, he reserved his most tender compassion for those creatures which are a natural reflection of Christ's gentleness and are used in Sacred Scripture as figures of him. He often rescued lambs, which were being led off to be slaughtered, in memory of the Lamb of God who willed to be put to death to save sinners.

While he was staying at the monastery of San Verecundo in the diocese of Gubbio one time, a lamb was born there during the night. It was attacked immediately by a vicious sow which had no mercy on the innocent creature and killed it with one hungry bite. When he heard about it, the saint was deeply moved as he remembered the immaculate Lamb of God and he mourned for the death of the lamb before them all saying, "Brother lamb, innocent creature, you represented Christ in the eyes of men. A curse on the wicked beast which killed you. May no human being or any animal ever eat of it." There and then the vicious sow fell sick and after suffering for three days it eventually expiated its crime by death. The carcass was thrown into the monastery moat where it lay for a long time and became as hard as a board, so that even the hungriest animal refused to eat it.

If cruelty in an animal led to such a terrible end, what will be the lot of evil men when the time of punishment comes eventually? In this incident the faithful, too, can see the power of Francis' tender love and how abundantly it filled him, so that it was acclaimed in their own way even by the animals.

When he was traveling near Siena, St. Francis came upon a large flock of sheep grazing in a field. He greeted them lovingly, as usual, and immediately they stopped grazing and ran to him, standing there with their heads erect and their eyes fastened on him. They showed their appreciation of him so clearly that the shepherds and the other friars were amazed to see the shearlings and even the rams jumping excitedly about him. ...

... A rabbit which was caught on an island in Lake Trasimene was afraid of everyone else, but entrusted itself to Francis' embrace as if that were its home. When he was crossing Lake Piediluco on his way to Greccio, a fisherman offered him a water-bird. Francis took it gladly and then opened his arms to let it off but it would not go. The saint stood there praying with his eyes raised to heaven, and after a long time he came back to himself and once more encouraged the bird to fly away and praise God. When he had given it his blessing, the bird showed its joy by the movements of its body and then it flew off. On the same lake he was offered a live fish which he addressed as brother, as usual, and put it back in the water beside the boat. The fish played about there in front of him as if it were attracted by his affection, and would not go away until he gave it his permission with a blessing.

Notes

1 The "inner man" is the soul; the "outer man," the body.

2 Psalm 22:7.

3 Daniel 3.

4 The reference is to St. Francis's "Canticle of Brother Sun," which contains the following lines:

> All praise be yours, my Lord, through Brothers Wind and Air,
>> And fair and stormy, all the weather's moods,
>> By which you cherish all that you have made.
> All praise be yours, my Lord, through Sister Water,
>> So useful, lowly, precious and pure.
> All praise be yours, my Lord, through Brother Fire,
>> Through whom you brighten up the night.
>> How beautiful is he, how gay! Full of power and strength.
> All praise be yours, my Lord, through Sister Earth, our mother,
>> Who feeds us in her sovereignty and produces
>> Various fruits with colored flowers and herbs. *(tr. B. Fahy)*

5 Isaiah 11:1.

6 Ecclesiasticus 50:8.

7 Romans 8:21.

CHAPTER 10

St. Thomas Aquinas

As THEY DO for so many areas in the history of Western thought, the writings of St. Thomas Aquinas (1225?–1274) play a key role in the development of views concerning nature and the relation that human beings have to it.

Aquinas belonged to the second generation of Christian scholars who had access to the writings of Aristotle and his commentators in good Latin translations. He was among those who saw in Aristotelian principles a way of making better sense of Scriptural teachings than the Augustinian neoplatonic metaphysics that had been followed for almost a thousand years.

Aquinas's highly original and powerful synthesis of Biblical, Aristotelian, neoplatonic, and Stoic teachings were at first the subject of great controversy, but within fifty years his body of work served as the theoretical framework for much of the Catholic intellectual tradition (a role it retains today). Although Aquinas's views did not go unchallenged until the dawn of "modern" thought in the seventeenth century, the predominant "scholastic" philosophy was largely based on Thomistic (i.e., Aquinas's) principles.

There are two aspects of Aquinas's thought that are especially important for tracing the history of Western attitudes toward nature and natural things.

First, Aquinas locates within a Christian context the Stoic notion of a hierarchy of earthly natural things with human beings at the summit. Although agreeing with Aristotle that each living thing is a substance unto itself, and hence possessing its own internal teleology directed toward its own good, Aquinas adopts the Stoic notion that the whole cosmos can, at the same time, be considered a single organism, whose intrinsic goal is the knowledge and love of God. Like the Stoics, Aquinas takes human beings to be the only beings on earth capable of achieving this goal. Accordingly, he follows the Stoics in seeing everything on Earth as designed by a providential deity for the sake of the benefit of human beings. The Genesis story is interpreted in this light.

Second, Aquinas employs explicit arguments against the notion that people have ethical obligations to living things other than human beings. He does so when he argues against the possibility of showing charity to animals. "Charity" is understood as a special kind of friendship (friendship with God), made possible only through revealed religion. In contrast to friendship in the ordinary sense, which can be shown only to good people with whom we have a special bond, charity ought to be shown toward all human beings, because of the special relationship that each person has to God, the true object of charity. Animals other than human beings lack the faculties that would make it possible for a human being to be a friend on the level of ordinary friendship. Further, they are without the special rela-

tionship to God that would allow them to warrant special consideration as objects
of charity. Aquinas infers from this that there are no ethical obligations to animals
other than human beings but gives two reasons why cruelty to animals is to be
avoided. First, cruel behavior is a sign of disrespect for God, to whom these animals ultimately belong. Second, cruel behavior toward animals would tend to make
one more cruel toward other humans as well, and this is a direct violation of our
nature as social beings.

ST. THOMAS AQUINAS
Summa Contra Gentiles
TR. VERNON J. BOURKE

Book Three

Chapter 78: That Other Creatures Are Ruled by God by Means of Intellectual Creatures

1. Since it is the function of divine providence[1] to maintain order in things, and
since a suitable order is such that there is a proportional descent from the highest
things to the lowest, it must be that divine providence reaches the farthest things by
some sort of proportion.[2] Now, the proportion is like this: as the highest creatures are
under God and are governed by Him, so the lower creatures are under the higher
ones and are ruled by them. But of all creatures the highest are the intellectual ones,
as is evident from what we said earlier. Therefore, the rational plan of divine providence demands that the other creatures be ruled by rational creatures.

2. Again, whatever type of creature carries out the order of divine providence, it
is able to do so because it participates in something of the power of the first providential being; just as an instrument does not move unless, through being moved, it
participates somewhat in the power of the principle agent. So, the beings that participate more fully in the power of the divine providence are executive agents of divine
providence in regard to those that participate less. But intellectual creatures participate more than others in it, because an ability to establish order which is done by
cognitive power, and an ability to execute it which is done by operative power, are
both required for providence, and rational creatures share in both types of power,
while the rest of creatures have operative powers only.[3] Therefore, all other creatures
are ruled by means of rational creatures under divine providence.

3. Besides, to whomever any power is given by God, the recipient is given the
power together with an ordination toward the effect of that power. For in that way all
things are arranged for the best, inasmuch as each thing is ordered to all the goods
that can naturally come from it. Now, the intellectual power by itself is capable of
ordering and ruling; hence, we see that the operative power follows the direction of

the intellective power, when they are combined in the same subject. In man, for instance, we observe that the bodily members are moved at the command of the will. The same is evident even if they are in different subjects; for instance those men who excel in operative power must be directed by those who excel in intellectual power.[4] Therefore, the rational plan of divine providence demands that other creatures be ruled by intellectual creatures.

4. Moreover, particular powers are naturally adapted to be moved by universal powers; this is evident quite as much in the artistic as in the natural sphere. Now, it is obvious that intellectual power is more universal than any operative power, for the intellectual power contains universal forms, while each power is operative only because of some form proper to the agent. Therefore, all other creatures must be moved and regulated by means of intellectual powers.[5]

5. Furthermore, in all powers arranged in an order one is directive in relation to the next, and it knows the rational plan best. Thus, we see in the case of the arts that one art, which is concerned with the end from which the plan for the entire artistic production is derived, directs and commands another art which makes the product, as the art of navigation does in regard to shipbuilding. So, the one that introduces the form commands the one that prepares the matter. Instruments, on the other hand, which do not know the plan at all, are simply ruled. Since only intellectual creatures can know the rational plans for the ordering of creatures, it will therefore be their function to rule and govern all other creatures.[6]

6. Again, that which is of itself is the cause of that which is through another. But only intellectual creatures operate by themselves, in the sense that they are masters of their operations through free choice of their will. On the other hand, other creatures are involved in operation resulting from the necessity of nature, since they are moved by something else.[7] Therefore, intellectual creatures by their operation are motivating and regulative of other creatures.

Chapter 81: On the Ordering of Men among Themselves and to Other Things

1. As a matter of fact, human souls hold the lowest rank in relation to the other intellectual substances,[8] because, as we said above, at the start of their existence they receive a knowledge of divine providence, wherein they know it only in a general sort of way. But the soul must be brought to a perfect knowledge of this order, in regard to individual details, by starting from the things themselves in which the order of divine providence has already been established in detail. So, the soul had to have bodily organs by which it might draw knowledge from corporeal things. Yet, even with such equipment, because of the feebleness of its intellectual light, man's soul is not able to acquire a perfect knowledge of the things that are important to man unless it be helped by higher spirits, for the divine disposition requires this, that lower spirits acquire perfection through the higher ones, as we showed above. Nevertheless, since man does

participate somewhat in intellectual light, brute animals are subject to him by the order of divine providence for they participate in no way in understanding. Hence it is said: "Let us make man to our own image and likeness," namely, according as he has understanding,[9] "and let him have dominion over the fishes of the sea, and the fowls of the air, and the beasts of the earth" (Gen. 1:26).

2. Even brute animals, though devoid of understanding, have some knowledge;[10] and so, in accord with the order of divine providence, they are set above plants and other things that lack knowledge. Hence it is said: "Behold I have given you every herb bearing seed upon the earth, and all trees that have in themselves seed of their own kind, to be your meat, and to all the beasts of the earth" (Gen. 1:23).

3. Moreover, among things utterly devoid of knowledge one thing comes under another, depending on whether the one is more powerful in acting than the other. Indeed, they do not participate in anything of the disposition of providence, but only in its execution.

4. Now, since man possesses intellect, sense, and bodily power, these are interrelated within him by a mutual order, according to the disposition of divine providence, in a likeness to the order which is found in the universe. In fact, corporeal power is subject to sense and intellectual power, as carrying out their command, and the sensitive power is subject to the intellectual and is included under its command.

5. On the same basis, there is also found an order among men themselves. Indeed, those who excel in understanding naturally gain control, whereas those who have defective understanding, but a strong body, seem to be naturally fitted for service, as Aristotle says in his *Politics*. The view of Solomon is also in accord with this, for he says: "The fool shall serve the wise" (Prov. 11:29); and again: "Provide out of all the people wise men such as fear God ... who may judge the people at all times" (Exod. 18:21–22).

Chapter 111: That Rational Creatures Are Subject to Divine Providence in a Special Way

1. From the points which have been determined above, it is manifest that divine providence extends to all things. Yet we must note that there is a special meaning for providence in reference to intellectual and rational creatures, over and above its meaning for other creatures.

For they do stand out above other creatures, both in natural perfection and in the dignity of their end. In the order of natural perfection, only the rational creature holds dominion over his acts, moving himself freely in order to perform his actions. Other creatures, in fact, are moved to their proper workings rather than being the active agents of these operations, as is clear from what has been said. And in the dignity of their end, for only the intellectual creature reaches the very ultimate end of the whole of things through his own operation, which is the knowing and loving of God;[11]

whereas other creatures cannot attain the ultimate end except by a participation in its likeness. Now, the formal character of every work differs according to the diversity of the end and of the things which are subject to the operation; thus, the method of working in art differs according to the diversity of the end and of the subject matter. For instance, a physician works in one way to get rid of illness and in another way to maintain health, and he uses different methods for bodies differently constituted. Likewise, in the government of a state, a different plan of ordering must be followed, depending on the varying conditions of the persons subject to this government and on the different purposes to which they are directed. For soldiers are controlled in one way, so that they may be ready to fight; while artisans will be managed in another way, so that they may successfully carry out their activities. So, also, there is one orderly plan in accord with which rational creatures are subjected to divine providence, and another by means of which the rest of creatures are ordered.

Chapter 112: That Rational Creatures Are Governed for Their Own Sakes, While Others Are Governed in Subordination to Them

1. First of all, then, the very way in which the intellectual creature was made, according as it is master of its acts, demands providential care whereby this creature may provide for itself, on its own behalf; while the way in which other things were created, things which have no dominion over their acts, shows this fact, that they are cared for, not for their own sake, but as subordinated to others. That which is moved only by another being has the formal character of an instrument, but that which acts of itself has the essential character of a principal agent. Now, an instrument is not valued for its own sake, but as useful to a principal agent. Hence it must be that all the careful work that is devoted to instruments is actually done for the sake of the agent, as for an end, but what is done for the principal agent either by himself or by another, is for his own sake, because he is the principal agent. Therefore, intellectual creatures are so controlled by God, as objects of care for their own sakes, while other creatures are subordinated, as it were, to the rational creatures.[12]

2. Again, one who holds dominion over his own acts is free in his activity, "for the free man is he who acts for his own sake."[13] But one who is acted upon by another, under necessity is subject to slavery. So, every other creature is naturally subject to slavery; only the intellectual creature is by nature free. Now, under every sort of government, provision is made for free men for their own sakes, but for slaves in such a way that they may be at the disposal of free men. And so, through divine providence provision is made for intellectual creatures on their own account, but for the remaining creatures for the sake of the intellectual ones.

3. Besides, whenever things are ordered to any end, and some of these things cannot attain the end through their own efforts, they must be subordinated to things which do achieve the end and which are ordered to the end for their own sakes.

Thus, for instance, the end of an army is victory, and this the soldiers may achieve through their own act of fighting; that is why only soldiers are needed for their own sake in an army. All others, who are assigned to different tasks—for instance, caring for the horses and supplying the weapons—are needed for the sake of the soldiers in the army. Now, from what has been seen earlier, it is established that God is the ultimate end of the whole of things; that an intellectual nature alone attains to Him in Himself, that is, by knowing and loving Him, as is evident from what has been said. Therefore, the intellectual nature is the only one that is required in the universe, for its own sake, while all others are for its sake.[14]

4. Moreover, in any whole the principal parts are needed in themselves in order to constitute the whole, but the other parts are for the preservation or for some betterment of the principal ones. Now, of all the parts of the universe the more noble are intellectual creatures, since they come closer to the divine likeness. Therefore, intellectual creatures are governed by divine providence for their own sakes, while all others are for the intellectual ones. ...

6. Again, as a thing is acted upon in the course of nature, so is it disposed to action by its natural origin. Now, we see that things do go on in the course of nature in such a way that intellectual substance uses all others for itself:[15] either for the perfecting of its understanding, since it contemplates the truth in them; or for the exercise of its power and the development of its knowledge, in the fashion of an artist who develops his artistic conception in bodily matter; or even for the support of his body which is united with the intellectual soul, as we see in the case of men. Therefore, it is clear that all things are divinely ruled by providence for the sakes of intellectual substances. ...

8. Nor is what was shown in earlier arguments opposed to this, namely, that all parts of the universe are ordered to the perfection of the whole. For all parts are ordered to the perfection of the whole, inasmuch as one is made to serve another. Thus, in the human body it is apparent that the lungs contribute to the perfection of the body by rendering service to the heart; hence, it is not contradictory for the lungs to be for the sake of the heart, and also for the sake of the whole organism. Likewise, it is not contradictory for some natures to be for the sake of the intellectual ones, and also for the sake of the perfection of the universe. For, in fact, if the things needed for the perfection of intellectual substance were lacking, the universe would not be complete.

9. Similarly, too, the foregoing is not opposed by the fact that individuals are for the sake of their proper species.[16] Because they are ordered to their species, they possess a further ordination to intellectual nature. For a corruptible[17] thing is not ordered to man for the sake of one individual man only, but for the sake of the whole human species. A corruptible thing could not be of use to the whole human species except by virtue of the thing's entire species. Therefore, the order whereby corruptible things are ordered to man requires the subordination of individuals to their species. ...

11. Hence it is said in Deuteronomy (4:19): "Lest thou see the sun and the moon and the other stars, and being deceived by error, thou adore and serve them, which the Lord thy God created for the service of all the nations are under heaven"; and again in the Psalm (8:8): "Thou hast subjected all things under his feet, all sheep and oxen, moreover the beasts of the field"; and in Wisdom (12:18) it is said: "Thou, being Master of power, judgest with tranquillity and with great favor disposest of us."

12. Through these considerations we refute the error of those who claim it is a sin for man to kill brute animals.[18] For animals are ordered to man's use in the natural course of things, according to divine providence. Consequently, man uses them without any injustice, either by killing them or by employing them in any other way. For this reason, God said to Noah: "As the green herbs, I have delivered all flesh to you" (Gen. 9:3).

13. Indeed, if any statements are found in Sacred Scripture prohibiting the commission of an act of cruelty against brute animals, for instance, that one should not kill a bird accompanied by her young (Deut. 22:6), this is said either to turn the mind of man away from cruelty which might be used on other men, lest a person through practicing cruelty on brutes might go on to do the same to men; or because an injurious act committed on animals may lead to a temporal loss[19] for some man, either for the agent or for another man; or there may be another interpretation of the text, as the Apostle (I Cor. 9:9) explains it, in terms of "not muzzling the ox that treadeth the corn" (Deut. 25:4).[20]

ST. THOMAS AQUINAS
Summa Theologica
TR. BY THE FATHERS OF THE ENGLISH DOMINICAN PROVINCE

II-II, 23, 1

Whether charity[21] is friendship[22]
... Objection 2. Further, there is no friendship without return of love (Ethic. viii, 2).[23] But charity extends even to one's enemies, according to Mt. 5:44: "Love your enemies." Therefore charity is not friendship.

Objection 3. Further, according to the Philosopher (Ethic. viii, 3) there are three kinds of friendship, directed respectively towards the delightful, the useful, or the virtuous.[24] Now charity is not the friendship for the useful or delightful; for Jerome says in his letter to Paulinus which is to be found at the beginning of the Bible: "True friendship cemented by Christ, is where men are drawn together, not by household interests, not by mere bodily presence, not by crafty and cajoling flattery, but by the fear of God, and the study of the Divine Scriptures." No more is it friendship for the virtuous, since by charity we love even sinners, whereas friendship based on the virtuous is only for virtuous men (Ethic. viii). Therefore charity is not friendship.

On the contrary, It is written (Jn. 15:15): "I will not now call you servants ... but My friends." Now this was said to them by reason of nothing else than charity. Therefore charity is friendship.

I answer that, According to the Philosopher (Ethic. viii, 2,3) not every love has the character of friendship, but that love which is together with benevolence, when, to wit, we love someone so as to wish good to him. If, however, we do not wish good to what we love, but wish its good for ourselves (thus we are said to love wine, or a horse, or the like), it is love not of friendship, but of a kind of concupiscence. For it would be absurd to speak of having friendship for wine or for a horse.[25]

Yet neither does well-wishing suffice for friendship, for a certain mutual love is requisite, since friendship is between friend and friend: and this well-wishing is founded on some kind of communication.

Accordingly, since there is a communication between man and God, inasmuch as He communicates His happiness to us, some kind of friendship must needs be based on this same communication, of which it is written (1 Cor. 1:9): "God is faithful: by Whom you are called unto the fellowship of His Son." The love which is based on this communication, is charity: wherefore it is evident that charity is the friendship of man for God.

... Reply to Objection 2. Friendship extends to a person in two ways: first in respect of himself, and in this way friendship never extends but to one's friends: secondly, it extends to someone in respect of another, as, when a man has friendship for a certain person, for his sake he loves all belonging to him, be they children, servants, or connected with him in any way. Indeed so much do we love our friends, that for their sake we love all who belong to them, even if they hurt or hate us; so that, in this way, the friendship of charity extends even to our enemies, whom we love out of charity in relation to God, to Whom the friendship of charity is chiefly directed.

Reply to Objection 3. The friendship that is based on the virtuous is directed to none but a virtuous man as the principal person, but for his sake we love those who belong to him, even though they be not virtuous: in this way charity, which above all is friendship based on the virtuous, extends to sinners, whom, out of charity, we love for God's sake.[26]

II-II, 25, 3

Whether irrational creatures also ought to be loved out of charity

Objection 1. It would seem that irrational creatures also ought to be loved out of charity. For it is chiefly by charity that we are conformed to God. Now God loves irrational creatures out of charity, for He loves "all things that are" (Wis. 11:25), and whatever He loves, He loves by Himself Who is charity. Therefore we also should love irrational creatures out of charity.

Objection 2. Further, charity is referred to God principally, and extends to other things as referable to God. Now just as the rational creature is referable to God, in as much as it bears the resemblance of image, so too, are the irrational creatures, in as much as they bear the resemblance of a trace.[27] Therefore charity extends also to irrational creatures.

Objection 3. Further, just as the object of charity is God, so is the object of faith. Now faith extends to irrational creatures, since we believe that heaven and earth were created by God, that the fishes and birds were brought forth out of the waters, and animals that walk, and plants, out of the earth. Therefore charity extends also to irrational creatures.

On the contrary, The love of charity extends to none but God and our neighbor. But the word neighbor cannot be extended to irrational creatures, since they have no fellowship with man in the rational life.[28] Therefore charity does not extend to irrational creatures.

I answer that, According to what has been stated above (13, 1) charity is a kind of friendship. Now the love of friendship is twofold: first, there is the love for the friend to whom our friendship is given, secondly, the love for those good things which we desire for our friend. With regard to the first, no irrational creature can be loved out of charity; and for three reasons. Two of these reasons refer in a general way to friendship, which cannot have an irrational creature for its object: first because friendship is towards one to whom we wish good things, while, properly speaking, we cannot wish good things to an irrational creature, because it is not competent, properly speaking, to possess good, this being proper to the rational creature which, through its free-will, is the master of its disposal of the good it possesses.[29] Hence the Philosopher says (Phys. ii, 6) that we do not speak of good or evil befalling such like things, except metaphorically. Secondly, because all friendship is based on some fellowship in life; since "nothing is so proper to friendship as to live together," as the Philosopher proves (Ethic. viii, 5). Now irrational creatures can have no fellowship in human life which is regulated by reason. Hence friendship with irrational creatures is impossible, except metaphorically speaking. The third reason is proper to charity, for charity is based on the fellowship of everlasting happiness, to which the irrational creature cannot attain. Therefore we cannot have the friendship of charity towards an irrational creature.

Nevertheless we can love irrational creatures out of charity, if we regard them as the good things that we desire for others, in so far, to wit, as we wish for their preservation, to God's honor and man's use; thus too does God love them out of charity.

Wherefore the Reply to the First Objection is evident.

Reply to Objection 2. The likeness by way of trace does not confer the capacity for everlasting life, whereas the likeness of image does: and so the comparison fails.

Reply to Objection 3. Faith can extend to all that is in any way true, whereas the friendship of charity extends only to such things as have a natural capacity for everlasting life; wherefore the comparison fails.

Notes

1   Like Aristotle, St. Thomas Aquinas takes God to be the ultimate cause of all change. But Aquinas departs from Aristotle in attributing to the intelligence and will of God the existence of the various species that are found in the world. God determines which essences there will be. God also has the role of governing and controlling the course of events in the world. This is "divine providence."

2   We might use the term "analogy" instead of proportion. Just as 3 is to 6 as 6 is to 12 (as, in each case, the first term is half of the second), so God is to human beings as human beings are to nonhuman living things (as in each case the first term rules over the second).

3   Aquinas's point can be simply put as follows. Rational intelligence is able to determine what is best. In order to bring about what is seen to be best, one requires brute strength and other resources. God's intelligence is what ultimately determines what is best. But God has allowed human beings to "participate" in this intelligence, to some degree. That is to say, it is part of God's plan to allow human beings to plan things for themselves. To a certain extent, humans have the wherewithal to accomplish their goals. But animals have an even greater share of "operative power"; an ox or a horse are stronger than a human being. Accordingly, the operative power of living things other than human beings requires the guidance of human intelligence in order for it to be used to accomplish God's rational plan. Notice that this is a good argument only if it is established that the ultimate goal of the divine scheme of things involves the attaining of human goals, but not the attainment of the goals of those beings that have no share in reason. We will see Aquinas state this when, in Chapter 111, he posits the knowledge of God as the ultimate goal of the cosmos as a whole.

4   In other words, it is fitting, and conducive to order, to have intelligent people direct the actions of stronger, less intelligent people. The hierarchy in the realm of human society is taken to parallel the hierarchy of living things.

5   Aquinas is here appealing to his metaphysics of mind, which will not be summarized here. The basic idea is that whenever someone acts in order to achieve some goal, this is because a rational being has seen that, in general, a certain kind of goal ought to be pursued, and that, in general, it is to be attained in a certain way. But operative power does not deal with generalities; it deals with the here and now (for example, moving a certain rock to a certain spot, at a certain time). Animals, who are superior to us in operative power, are irrational, and hence cannot conceive of general principles, which determine when the operative power is to be employed. So what they do must be controlled by intelligent beings.

6   Drawing on a discussion by Aristotle, Aquinas points to how various techniques and arts are arranged in hierarchies. The captain tells the shipbuilder what sort of ship to make.

The chief shipbuilder tells each carpenter what sort of wood to cut or join. At the bottom of the hierarchy are the tools used by the carpenter, which control nothing at all and are totally controlled. Aquinas takes the role of the tool to be analogous to the role played by nonhuman living things.

7 Aquinas accepts the analysis of nature that we saw above in Aristotle, *Physics* 2.1. Living things other than human beings do what they do by themselves, insofar as they are natural beings. But in a sense, they are not in control of themselves, because their essence totally determines how they are going to move and change. They cannot alter their instinctive responses. Human beings can do so, through the exercise of their free will. Aquinas infers that this is why it is fitting that human beings, who can be in control of their own actions, rule other kinds of beings, who have no such control.

8 The other intellectual substances are God and the angels.

9 Aquinas interprets the Biblical teaching that human beings are made in the likeness of God as meaning that humans, like God, are rational (although our rationality is of a lower order).

10 The knowledge of animals is found in their perception and memory of particular things.

11 Like the Stoics (and unlike Aristotle) Aquinas takes the universe to be like a single substance, and, as such, to be a whole in its own right. The goal of this whole is the knowledge and love of God. But this knowledge and love belongs to the individual substances within the whole; the cosmos, as a whole, is not thought to have a single mind.

12 Only rational beings can directly contribute to the good of the whole cosmos, the knowledge of God. Accordingly, nonrational beings are good only insofar as they contribute to the welfare of rational beings, and indirectly contribute to the knowledge of God that there is in the cosmos.

13 The quotation is from Aristotle's *Metaphysics* 1.2 982b26.

14 In other words, of all things in the world created by God, only intellectual beings are valuable in and of themselves. The existence of all other beings is for the sake of intellectual beings.

15 Like Aristotle before him, Aquinas believes that the universe is basically orderly and well functioning. So the fact that rational beings make use of nonrational beings only for their own sake is taken to be evidence that it is right for rational beings to do so.

16 Aquinas holds that the individual has as its good not only its own good, but also the good of the species to which it belongs. Thus a rabbit has young, not only because that is part of what it is to lead a good rabbit life, but also because so doing ensures the survival of the species as a whole. Aquinas asserts that this species, too, is not a good in and of itself. Rather, the species of a nonhuman plant or animal is for the sake of the good of the whole human species.

17 A corruptible thing is one that can perish. Corruptible things are the form/matter composites found on Earth.

18 Aquinas has in mind the view of the Manicheans, a heretical sect prevalent in the third century, who held that the material world is created and governed by an evil principle, and that our conduct should aim at escaping the evil influence of materiality. This involves abstaining from the eating of animals and the cutting of plants, for, on their view, both plants and animals embody the divine principle of soul. Aquinas would have been

familiar with their views from having read the extensive written refutations of St. Augustine, himself a former Manichean. Such views were echoed by the Albigenses, a neo-Manichean heretical sect prevalent in the South of France in the twelfth and thirteenth centuries. Like Porphyry, they stressed how abstaining from animal products allowed the soul to disengage itself from the hold of the body.

19 A temporal loss is the loss of some temporal good. A temporal good is the sort of good thing that is subject to the passage of time; it can perish or change its character. Aquinas is saying that if I injure an animal or plant that belongs to someone else, I am taking away from the value of his or her possessions, or otherwise taking away from the things of this world that can benefit that person.

20 In I Corinthians 9:10–11, St. Paul defends his living at the expense of others by appealing to Deut. 25:4: "For it has been written in the law of Moses, 'thou shalt not muzzle the ox that treads out the corn.' God does not care about oxen, does he? Doesn't he rather say this entirely on our account? For it was written on our account, in order that the one who plows should plow in hope, and in order that the one who threshes (or 'treads') in hope should share in hope." Perhaps under the influence of Stoic ideas, Paul is convinced that the Jewish law could not have been framed for the benefit of animals, and interprets it as a metaphorical expression concerning the sharing among human beings of the fruits of human labor.

21 The Latin term is *caritas*, translated as "love" or "charity." This term (the same as that by which Hildegard names the feminine divine principle) refers to the sort of love that, according to Scripture, we are commanded to have toward our neighbors, whether we have any special bonds with them or not. Aquinas takes this to be a "theological virtue." This means that, although there is an ethical obligation to live in accordance with charity, this obligation falls outside of the "Natural Law," the basic principles of how to live well that are available to all human beings through rational reflection on human nature. We are obligated to show charity to others, not because our reason tells us that this is right, but because we accept by faith the divine authority of a book that reveals this obligation to us.

22 Within the *Summa Theologica*, Aquinas writes in a way that loosely parallels the classroom debates by which philosophy at that time was taught. First, there is a statement of the question to be answered. Next, arguments are presented in favor of the view that Aquinas holds to be incorrect. Following these, Aquinas responds with an assertion of his view, usually backed up by Scripture or some other Church authority. This is followed by an argument for the view taken to be correct. Each objection is then refuted in turn.

23 Aristotle had defined friendship as the state that holds between two people who wish each other well and recognize that this is so. Objection 2 points out that Christians are commanded to love their enemy. Hence, this love cannot be friendship, as Aristotle understands it.

24 Aristotle analyzes the various reasons why we might wish someone well. We may do so because that person is useful to us, or so that we may continue to enjoy that person's company, or because we appreciate that person's true character. Mutual good will based on one of the first two reasons cannot be the foundation of true friendship, because it is not the friend, as such, that is really cared about; it is the pleasure or use that the other provides. True friendship, which Aristotle takes to be something rare, must be based on

wishing someone well because of their true character. According to Aristotle ("the Philosopher"), this can be the case only if the other has an excellence of character or virtue that is truly admirable.

25 This would be the case for the first two varieties of friendship that Aristotle outlines.

26 Charity to one's enemies or the wicked remains friendship, but, properly speaking, it is God who is one's true friend. The enemies or the wicked are loved only on account of the relation that they have to the true object of love, which is God.

27 A trace is an effect that serves as evidence of the existence of a cause, but does not share a common character or serve as an image of that cause. For example, the sight of smoke would be a trace of fire, for one can infer the existence of fire from seeing smoke, but smoke is not itself the same sort of thing as is fire. On the other hand, the warm air near the fire is also evidence of the fire, but insofar as both it and fire share the characteristic of heat, it is not a trace. Animals are said to have the status of a trace of God, as from them one can infer God's existence as creator and the one who imparts existence; yet they (unlike human beings) are not rational, and hence do not have the status of being an image of God.

28 For Aquinas, our rationality not only makes us who we are as individuals; it also defines the basic character of our association with one another. A human community is a community of rational beings. Irrational animals are necessarily excluded from such a community. Accordingly, "love thy neighbor as thyself" cannot be understood as commanding us to have charity toward animals, because they cannot properly be considered as neighbors.

29 The good that we wish for ourselves is a distinctively human good: excellent rational activity and choice. This cannot be wished for those who are incapable of rationality. Aquinas does not here say why it is not possible for us to wish nonhumans to achieve the sort of good proper to them, for their own sake.

12. The logic now in use serves rather to fix and give stability to the errors which have their foundation in commonly received notions than to help the search after truth. So it does more harm than good.

13. The syllogism is not applied to the first principles of sciences, and is applied in vain to intermediate axioms; being no match for the subtlety of nature.[4] It commands assent therefore to the proposition, but does not take hold of the thing.[5]

14. The syllogism consists of propositions, propositions consist of words, words are symbols of notions. Therefore if the notions themselves (which is the root of the matter) are confused and over-hastily abstracted from the facts, there can be no firmness in the superstructure. Our only hope therefore lies in a true induction.[6]

15. There is no soundness in our notions, whether logical or physical. Substance, Quality, Action, Passion, Essence itself, are not sound notions:[7] much less are Heavy, Light, Dense, Rare, Moist, Dry, Generation, Corruption, Attraction, Repulsion, Element, Matter, Form, and the like;[8] but all are fantastical and ill defined.

16. Our notions of less general species, as Man, Dog, Dove, and of the immediate perceptions of the sense, as Hot, Cold, Black, White, do not materially mislead us; yet even these are sometimes confused by the flux and alteration of matter and the mixing of one thing with another. All the others which men have hitherto adopted are but wanderings, not being abstracted and formed from things by proper methods.

17. Nor is there less of willfulness and wandering in the construction of axioms than in the formations of notions; not excepting even those very principles which are obtained by common induction; but much more in the axioms and lower propositions educed by the syllogism.

18. The discoveries which have hitherto been made in the sciences are such as lie close to vulgar notions, scarcely beneath the surface. In order to penetrate into the inner and further recesses of nature, it is necessary that both notions and axioms be derived from things by a more sure and guarded way; and that a method of intellectual operation be introduced altogether better and more certain.

19. There are and can be only two ways of searching into and discovering truth. The one flies from the senses and particulars to the most general axioms, and from these principles, the truth of which it takes for settled and immovable, proceeds to judgment and to the discovery of middle axioms. And this way is now in fashion. The other derives axioms from the senses and particulars, rising by a gradual and unbroken assent, so that it arrives at the most general axioms last of all. This is the true way, but as yet untried. ...

23. There is a great difference between the Idols of the human mind and the Ideas of the divine. That is to say, between certain empty dogmas, and the true signatures and marks set upon the works of creation as they are found in nature. ...

26. The conclusions of human reason as ordinarily applied in matters of nature, I call for the sake of distinction *Anticipations of Nature* (as a thing rash or premature).

That reason which is elicited from facts by a just and methodical process, I call *Interpretation of Nature.*

27. Anticipations are a ground sufficiently firm for consent; for even if men went mad all after the same fashion, they might agree one with another well enough.

28. For the winning of assent, indeed, anticipations are far more powerful than interpretations; because being collected from a few instances, and those for the most part of familiar occurrence, they straightway touch the understanding and fill the imagination; whereas interpretations on the other hand, being gathered here and there from very various and widely dispersed facts, cannot suddenly strike the understanding; and therefore they must needs, in respect of the opinions of the time, seem harsh and out of tune; much as the mysteries of faith do.

29. In sciences founded on opinions and dogmas, the use of anticipations and logic is good; for in them the object is to command assent to the proposition, not to master the thing.

30. Though all the wits of all the ages should meet together and combine and transmit their labors, yet will no great progress ever be made in science by means of anticipations; because radical errors in the first concoction of the mind are not to be cured by the excellence of functions and subsequent remedies. ...

31. It is idle to expect any great advancement in science from the superinducing and engrafting of new things upon old. We must begin anew from the very foundations, unless we would revolve forever in a circle with mean and contemptible progress. ...

51. The human understanding is of its own nature prone to abstractions and gives a substance and reality to things which are fleeting. But to resolve nature into abstractions is less to our purpose than to dissect her into parts; as did the school of Democritus,[9] which went further into nature than the rest. Matter rather than forms should be the object of our attention, its configurations and changes of configuration, and simple action, and law of action or motion; for forms are figments of the human mind, unless you will call those laws of action forms.[10] ...

71. The sciences which we possess come for the most part from the Greeks. For what has been added by Roman, Arabic, or later writers is not much nor of much importance; and whatever it is, it is built on the foundation of Greek discoveries. Now the wisdom of the Greeks was professorial and much given to disputations; a kind of wisdom most adverse to the inquisition of truth. Thus that name of Sophists, which by those who would be thought philosophers was in contempt cast back upon and so transferred to the ancient rhetoricians, Gorgias, Protagoras, Hippias, Polus, does indeed suit the entire class, Plato, Aristotle, Zeno, Epicurus, Theophrastus, and their successors Chrysippus, Carneades, and the rest. There was this difference only, that the former class was wandering and mercenary, going about from town to town, putting up their wisdom to sale, and taking a price for it; while the latter was more

pompous and dignified, as composed of men who had fixed abodes, and who opened schools and taught their philosophy without reward. Still both sorts, though in other respects unequal, were professorial; both turned the matter into disputations, and set up and battled for philosophical sects and heresies; so that their doctrines were for the most part (as Dionysius not unaptly rallied Plato) "the talk of idle old men to ignorant youths." But the elder of the Greek philosophers, Empedocles, Anaxagoras, Leucippus, Democritus, Parmenides, Heraclitus, Xenophanes, Philolaus, and the rest (I omit Pythagoras as a mystic), did not, so far as we know, open schools; but more silently and severely and simply—that is, with less affectation and parade—betook themselves to the inquisition of truth. And therefore they were in my judgment more successful; only that their works were in the course of time obscured by those slighter persons who had more which suits and pleases the capacity and tastes of the vulgar; time, like a river, bringing down to us things which are light and puffed up, but letting weighty matters sink. Still even they were not altogether free from the failing of their nation; but leaned too much to the ambition and vanity of founding a sect and catching popular applause. But the inquisition of truth must be despaired of when it turns aside to trifles of this kind. Nor should we omit that judgment, or rather divination, which was given concerning the Greeks by the Egyptian priest— that "they were always boys, without antiquity of knowledge or knowledge of antiquity."[11] Assuredly they have that which is characteristic of boys; they are prompt to prattle, but cannot generate; for their wisdom abounds in words but is barren of works. And therefore the signs which are taken from the origin and birth-place of the received philosophy are not good. ...

73. Of all signs there is none more certain or more noble than that taken from fruits. For fruits and works are as it were sponsors and sureties for the truth of philosophies. Now, from all these systems of the Greeks, and their ramifications through particular sciences, there can hardly after the lapse of so many years be adduced a single experiment which tends to relieve and benefit the condition of man, and which can with truth be referred to the speculations and theories of philosophy. And Celsus[12] ingenuously and wisely owns as much, when he tells us that the experimental part of medicine was first discovered, and that afterwards men philosophized about it, and hunted for and assigned causes; and not by an inverse process that philosophy and the knowledge of causes led to the discovery and development of the experimental part. And therefore it was not strange that among the Egyptians, who rewarded inventors with divine honours and sacred rites, there were more images of brutes than of men; inasmuch as brutes by their natural instinct have produced many discoveries, whereas men by discussion and the conclusions of reason have given birth to few or none.

Some little has indeed been produced by the industry of chemists; but it has been produced accidentally and in passing, or else by a kind of variation of experiments, such as mechanics use; and not by any art or theory; for the theory which they have devised rather confuses the experiments than aids them. They too who have busied themselves with natural magic, as they call it, have but few discoveries to show, and those trifling and imposture-like. Wherefore, as in religion we are warned to show our faith by works, so in philosophy by the same rule the system should be judged of by its fruits, and pronounced frivolous if it be barren; more especially if, in place of fruits of grape and olive, it bear thorns and briers of dispute and contention.

74. Signs also are to be drawn from the increase and progress of systems and sciences. For what is founded on nature grows and increases; while what is founded on opinion varies but increases not. If therefore those doctrines had not plainly been like a plant torn up from its roots, but had remained attached to the womb of nature and continued to draw nourishment from her, that could never have come to pass which we have seen now for twice a thousand years; namely, that the sciences stand where they did and remain almost in the same condition, receiving no noticeable increase, but on the contrary, thriving most under their first founder, and then declining. Whereas in the mechanical arts, which are founded on nature and the light of experience, we see the contrary happen, for these (as long as they are popular) are continually thriving and growing, as having in them a breath of life; at the first rude, then convenient, afterwards adorned, and at all times advancing. ...

81. Again there is another great and powerful cause why the sciences have made but little progress, which is this. It is not possible to run a course aright when the goal itself has not been rightly placed. Now the true and lawful goal of the sciences is none other than this: that human life be endowed with new discoveries and powers. But of this the great majority have no feeling, but are merely hireling and professorial; except when it occasionally happens that some workman of acuter wit and covetous of honour applies himself to a new invention; which he mostly does at the expense of his fortunes. But in general, so far are men from proposing to themselves to augment the mass of arts and sciences, that from the mass already at hand they neither take nor look for anything more than what they may turn to use in their lectures, or to gain, or to reputation, or to some similar advantage. And if any one out of all the multitude court science with honest affection and for her own sake, yet even with him the object will be found to be rather the variety of contemplations and doctrines than the severe and rigid search after truth. And if by chance there be one who seeks after truth in earnest, yet even he will propose to himself such a kind of truth as shall yield satisfaction to the mind and understanding in rendering causes for things long since discovered, and not the truth which shall lead to new assurance of works and new light of axioms. If then the end of the sciences has not as yet been well placed, it is not strange that men have erred as to the means. ...

89. Neither is it to be forgotten that in every age Natural Philosophy has had a troublesome and hard to deal with adversary—namely, superstition, and the blind and immoderate zeal of religion. For we see among the Greeks that those who first

proposed to men's then uninitiated ears the natural causes for thunder and for storms, were thereupon found guilty of impiety. Nor was much more forbearance shown by some of the ancient fathers of the Christian church to those who on most convincing grounds (such as no one in his senses would now think of contradicting) maintained that the earth was round, and of consequence asserted the existence of the antipodes.

Moreover, as things now are, to discourse of nature is made harder and more perilous by the summaries and systems of the schoolmen; who having reduced theology into regular order as well as they were able, and fashioned it into the shape of an art, ended in incorporating the contentious and thorny philosophy of Aristotle, more than was fit, with the body of religion. ...

98. Now for grounds of experience—since to experience we must come—we have as yet had either none or very weak ones; no search has been made to collect a store of particular observations sufficient either in number, or in kind, or in certainty, to inform the understanding, or in any way adequate. ...

99. Again, even in the great plenty of mechanical experiments, there is yet a great scarcity of those which are of most use for the information of the understanding. For the mechanic, not troubling himself with the investigation of truth, confines his attention to those things which bear upon his particular work, and will not either raise his hand or stretch out his hand for anything else. But then only will there be good ground of hope for the further advance of knowledge, when there shall be received and gathered together into natural history a variety of experiments which are of no use in themselves, but simply serve to discover causes and axioms; which I call "*Experimenta lucifera*," experiments of *light*, to distinguish them from those which I call "*fructifera*," experiments of *fruit*. Now experiments of this kind have one admirable property and condition: they never miss or fail. For since they are applied, not for the purpose of producing any particular effect, but only of discovering the natural cause of some effect, they answer the end equally well whichever way they turn out; for they settle the question. ...

124. Again, it will be thought, no doubt, that the goal and mark of knowledge which I myself set up (the very point which I object to in others) is not the true or the best, for that the contemplation of truth is a thing worthier and loftier than all utility and magnitude of works; and that this long and anxious dwelling with experience and matter and the fluctuations of individual things, drags down the mind to earth, or rather sinks it to a very Tartarus of turmoil and confusion, removing and withdrawing it from the serene tranquility of abstract wisdom, a condition far more heavenly. Now to this I readily assent, and indeed this which they point at as so much to be preferred is the very thing of all others which I am about. For I am building in the human understanding a true model of the world, such as it is in fact, not such as a man's own reason would have it to be; a thing which cannot be done without a very diligent dissection and anatomy of the world. But I say that those

foolish and apish images of worlds which the fancies of men have created in philosophical systems must be utterly scattered to the winds. Be it known then how vast a difference there is (as I said above) between the Idols of the human mind[13] and the Ideas of the divine. The former are nothing more than arbitrary abstractions; the latter are the creator's own stamp upon creation, impressed and defined in matter by true and exquisite lines. Truth therefore and utility are here the very same things; and works themselves are of greater value as pledges of truth than as contributing to the comforts of life.[14] ...

127. It may also be asked (in the way of doubt rather than objection) whether I speak of natural philosophy only, or whether I mean that the other sciences, logic, ethics, and politics, should be carried on by this method. Now I certainly mean what I have said to be understood of them all; and as the common logic, which governs by the syllogism, extends not only to natural but to all sciences; so does mine also, which proceeds by induction, embrace everything. For I form a history and table of discovery for anger, fear, shame, and the like; for matters political; and again for the mental operations of memory, composition and division, judgment and the rest; not less than for heat and cold, or light, or vegetation, or the like. But nevertheless since my method of interpretation, after the history has been prepared and duly arranged, regards not the working and discourse of the mind only (as the common logic does) but the nature of things also, I supply the mind with such rules and guidance that it may in every case apply itself aptly to the nature of things. And therefore I deliver many and diverse precepts in the doctrine of Interpretation, which in some measure modify the method of invention according to the quality and condition of the subject of the inquiry.[15] ...

129. It remains for me to say a few words touching the excellency of the end in view. Had they been uttered earlier, they might have seemed like idle wishes; but now that hopes have been raised and unfair prejudices removed, they may perhaps have greater weight. Also if I had finished all myself, and had no occasion to call in others to help and take part in the work, I should even now have abstained from such language, lest it might be taken as a proclamation of my own deserts. But since I want to quicken the industry and rouse and kindle the zeal of others, it is fitting that I put men in mind of some things.

In the first place then, the introduction of famous discoveries appears to hold by far the first place among human actions; and this was the judgment of the former ages. For to the authors of inventions they awarded divine honors; while to those who did good service in the state (such as founders of cities and empires, legislators, saviors of their country from long endured evils, quellers of tyrannies, and the like) they decreed no higher honors than heroic. And certainly if a man rightly compare the two, he will find that this judgment of antiquity was just. For the benefits of discoveries may extend to the whole race of man, civil benefits only to particular places; the latter last not beyond a few ages, the former through all time. Moreover the reformation of a state in civil matters is seldom brought in without violence and confusion; but discoveries carry blessings with them, and confer benefits without causing harm or sorrow to any.

Again, discoveries are as it were new creations, and imitations of God's works, as the poet well sang:

> To man's frail race great Athens long ago
> First gave the seed whence waving harvests grow,
> And recreated all our life below.

And it appears worthy of remark in Solomon, that though mighty in empire and in gold, in the magnificence of his works, his court, his household, and his fleet, in the lustre of his name and the worship of mankind, yet he took none of these to glory in, but pronounced that "The glory of God is to conceal a thing; the glory of the king to search it out."

Again, let a man only consider what a difference there is between the life of men in the most civilized province of Europe, and in the wildest and most barbarous districts of New India; he will feel it be great enough to justify the saying that "man is a god to man," not only in regard of aid and benefit, but also by a comparison of condition. And this difference comes not from soil, not from climate, not from race but from the arts.

Again, it is well to observe the force and virtue and consequences of discoveries, and these are to be seen nowhere more conspicuously than in those three which were unknown to the ancients, and of which the origin, though recent, is obscure and inglorious; namely, printing, gunpowder, and the magnet. For these three have changed the whole face and state of things throughout the world; the first in literature, the second in warfare, the third in navigation; whence have followed innumerable changes, insomuch that no empire, no sect, no star seems to have exerted greater power and influence in human affairs than these mechanical discoveries.

Further, it will not be amiss to distinguish the three kinds and as it were grades of ambition in mankind. The first is of those who desire to extend their own power in their native country, which kind is vulgar and degenerate. The second is of those who labor to extend the power of their country and its dominion among men. This certainly has more dignity, though not less covetousness. But if a man endeavor to establish and extend the power and dominion of the human race itself over the universe, his ambition (if ambition it can be called) is without doubt both a more wholesome and a more noble thing than the other two. Now the empire of man over things depends wholly on the arts and sciences. For we cannot command nature except by obeying her.

Again, if men have thought so much of some one particular discovery as to regard him as more than man who has been able by some benefit to make the whole human race his debtor, how much higher a thing to discover that by means of which all things else shall be discovered with ease! And yet (to speak the whole truth), as the uses of light are infinite, in enabling us to walk, to ply our arts, to read, to recognize one another—and nevertheless the very beholding of the light is itself a more excellent and a fairer thing than all the uses of it—so assuredly the very contemplation of things, as they are, without superstition or imposture, error or confusion, is in itself more worthy than all the fruit of inventions.

Lastly, if the debasement of arts and sciences to purposes of wickedness, luxury, and the like, be made a ground of objection, let no one be moved thereby. For the same may be said of all earthly goods; of wit, courage, strength, beauty, wealth, light itself, and the rest. Only let the human race recover that right over nature which belongs to it by divine bequest, and let power be given it; the exercise thereof will be governed by sound reason and true religion.

Notes

1 The Latin here is actually to be translated "Nature to be conquered must be obeyed." There is a subtle distinction. The conquering of Nature is a single enterprise, like a victorious war. Only once victory has been achieved can there be the assurance that specific commands will be carried out.

2 On the Greek root for this term, see Xenophon, *Memorabilia* 4.3, n. 1.

3 The logic of Bacon's time was based on the logical writings of Aristotle, which together were commonly known by the title *Organon* (tool), on the (questionable) understanding that Aristotle had meant for all of them to serve as a tool or instrument for the use of human reason. In giving this work the title *The New Organon*, Bacon is presenting to the world a method intended to be a tool for the advancement of scientific research that is to be more effective than that of Aristotle.

4 On the Aristotelian account of science, a feature of the world is explained by showing how it logically follows from the fundamental truths about the world. The most fundamental truths are expressed in "first principles"; general principles that are derived from these are "intermediate axioms." Bacon argues that such principles cannot be arrived at by means of Aristotelian syllogistic reasoning.

5 For Aristotle, the syllogism is the basic unity of deduction. Given two premises of the appropriate form (such as "all trees are plants" and "all plants are alive") one can complete the syllogism with a conclusion ("all trees are alive"). Bacon argues that in actual scientific practice nothing is ever learned by following such a path of reasoning; at best, it can be employed as a tool for convincing others.

6 Although deduction allows one to come to derive a conclusion from certain premises, induction allows one to reason upwards to more basic premises. Bacon argues that the basic principles of the sciences are as yet unknown, for lack of a suitable method of induction. This is why he advocates a new inductive method.

7 These are some of the fundamental notions of Aristotelian metaphysics.

8 These are some of the fundamental notions employed by the Aristotelians in their explanations of the physical world.

9 Democritus (470?–366? BC) was an important presocratic philosopher, who attempted to explain all natural processes as resulting from the combination and separation of minimal bits of stuff, called "atoms" ("unsplittables").

10 With this assertion one should compare Aristotle, *Physics* 2.1, in which it is asserted that nature (the source of motion and rest) in the primary sense is form, rather than matter.

11 The reference is to a conversation between the Greek sage Solon and certain Egyptian priests, related in the beginning of Plato's *Timaeus.*

12 Aulus Cornelius Celsus, a Roman of the first century AD, wrote a history of medicine, to which Bacon refers.

13 In an omitted part of the text, Bacon distinguishes four kinds of mistaken doctrines, or "Idols which beset men's minds." The Idols of the Tribe come from the inherent limitations of the human mind. The Idols of the Cave are errors that come from an individual's particular limitations. The Idols of the Market-place come from the limitations of language. The Idols of the Theatre are errors that come from mistaken philosophical and scientific systems.

14 Bacon usually takes the main purpose of science to be technological innovation, leading to a better satisfaction of human needs and desires. Here, in contrast, he grants some credence to the ancient view that contemplation of the truth is to be valued for its own sake, and is a good of higher value than any practical application it may have. Bacon nonetheless insists that it is practical application that assures one of the truth of a scientific theory.

15 Bacon here argues that what we now call the social sciences are to follow the methods of the physical sciences. He does not go so far as to suggest that all of the sciences are to be unified, or that the social sciences are to be ultimately understood in the light of the physical sciences.

CHAPTER 12

René Descartes

ALTHOUGH Francis Bacon was the herald of modern science, it was René Descartes (1596–1650) who, more than anyone else, can be credited with having taken the first decisive steps along its path. Descartes believed that progress in scientific inquiry could be made only if it followed a method, by which complex entities and states of affairs were analyzed into their simple units, which would (Descartes was convinced), like mathematical axioms, be immediately intelligible. As part of this project, Descartes invented analytic geometry, which allowed scientists to employ algebraic formulae to analyze the geometrical form of bodies, as well as their motions through space. Thus modern science, unlike that of the Aristotelian tradition, makes extensive use of mathematics in its understanding of the natural world, and in this way tends to be removed from the everyday ways in which it is experienced by human beings.

In the following selections, Descartes sketches the "meditations" by which he analyzes the contents of his own mind in order to arrive at the metaphysical basis of his scientific world view. According to this metaphysics, there are two kinds of substances in the world: minds (or souls) and bodies. Because he clearly and distinctly perceives his own thought, Descartes grasps that there must be a thing whose fundamental character is to think. Bodies, on the other hand, are clearly and distinctly perceived to have spatial extension. Human beings are to be understood as complexes of soul and body. On the other hand, because they are incapable of speech, there is no reason to attribute thought to animals other than human beings. Because Descartes understands all consciousness as involving thought, he is led to deny consciousness to all animals other than human beings. Descartes' view held sway among many philosophers and scientists of the early modern period, and, at least indirectly, led to certain scientific experiments and agricultural practices that, in hindsight, have been re-evaluated as inhumane.

RENÉ DESCARTES
Discourse on Method
TR. PATRICIA KILROE

Part 4

... I do not know if I should let you know about the first meditations I made there; because they are so metaphysical and so uncommon, that they will perhaps not be to everyone's taste. Yet, in order that it can be judged whether the foundations I have laid are solid enough, I find myself somehow compelled to speak of them. I had for a long time noticed that, as far as morality goes, it is sometimes necessary to follow opinions that one knows are highly uncertain, just as if they were indubitable, as has been said above; but, because at that time I wanted to devote myself only to the pursuit of truth, I thought that it was necessary for me to do quite the opposite, and that I cast aside, as absolutely false, everything in which I could imagine the least doubt, in order to see if there would not remain, after that, something among my beliefs which was entirely indubitable. So, because our senses sometimes deceive us, I wanted to suppose that there was not a single thing which was such as they make us imagine. And because there are men who are mistaken in their reasoning, even concerning the simplest matters of geometry, and who fall prey to paralogisms, judging that I was subject to being wrong as much as anyone else, I rejected as false all the reasonings I had formerly taken as demonstrations.[1] And finally, considering that all the same thoughts which we have while awake could also come to us while we are sleeping, without a single one of them being true, I resolved to pretend that everything that had ever entered my mind was no more true than the illusions of my dreams. But, immediately afterward, I became mindful that, during the time I wanted to think that everything was false, it was necessarily the case that I, who thought this, be something. And observing that this truth: *I think, therefore I am*, was so firm and so certain that all the most extravagant assumptions of the skeptics were not capable of shaking it, I decided that I could take it, without scruple, as the first principle of the philosophy that I was seeking.

Then, examining carefully what I was, and seeing that I could suppose that I had no body, and that there was no world nor any place where I might be, but that I could not suppose, for all that, that I did not exist; and that on the contrary, for the very reason that I thought of doubting the truth of other things, it followed very clearly and most assuredly that I existed. Whereas, if I had merely ceased to think, even if all the rest of what I had ever imagined had been true, I would have no reason to believe that I existed. From that I knew that I was a substance, the entire essence or nature of which was only to think, and which, to exist, has need of no place, nor depends on any material thing. So that this I, that is, the soul by which I am what I am, is entirely distinct from the body, and the former is even easier to know than the latter, and that even if the body did not exist, the soul would not cease to be all that it is. ...

Part 5

... I did not want to conclude from all these things, however, that this world has been created in the way that I described, because it is much more likely that, since the beginning, God has made it as it was supposed to be. But it is certain, and it is an opinion commonly held among theologians, that the action by which he now conserves it is the same as that by which he created it; so that even if he had not given it, in the beginning, a form other than that of chaos, provided that, having established the laws of nature, he made his contribution, so that it might act in its usual way, we may believe, without detracting from the miracle of creation, that by that means alone all the things which are purely material would have been able, with time, to become such as we see them at present. And their nature is quite a bit easier to conceive of when we see them come into this world gradually in this way, than when we only consider them when fully formed.[2]

From the description of inanimate bodies and of plants, I passed to that of animals and in particular to that of human beings. But because I was not yet familiar enough with these to speak of them in the same way as of the rest, that is, in demonstrating effects on the basis of causes, and showing from what seeds and in what way nature must produce them, I contented myself with supposing that God must have formed the body of a man entirely similar to one of ours, as much in the outer shape of his members as in the internal structure of his organs, without forming it of other matter than that which I had described, and without putting in it, at the beginning, any rational soul, nor any other thing to serve as a vegetative or sensitive soul,[3] except that he stirred up in his heart one of those fires without light, which I had already explained, and that I did not conceive of as having any other nature than that which heats up hay when it has been bundled up before it has dried, or which makes new wines boil when they are left to ferment on the vine.[4] For, examining the functions which could be in this body as a result of that, I found contributing to them precisely all those which can be in us without our thinking about them, and consequently without our soul, that is, this part distinct from the body whose nature it has been said above is only to think, and these are all the same functions in which we can say that nonrational animals resemble us, without my being able to find among them any of those which, since they are dependent on thought, are the only ones which belong to us insofar as we are human beings; rather I did find them all there afterwards, when I supposed that God created a rational soul, and that he joined it to this body in the particular way I have described ...

I had explained in enough detail all of these things in the treatise which I had previously intended to publish.[5] And then I had shown what the fabric of nerves and muscles of the human body must be, in order for animal spirits, being within, to have the power to move its members, in the same way that we see that heads, a little after being cut off, still move and bite the earth, although they are no longer animated; what changes must occur in the brain to cause wakefulness, and sleepiness, and dreams; how light, sounds, odors, tastes, heat, and all the other qualities of external objects can imprint on it various ideas through the medium of the senses; how hunger, thirst, and the other internal passions can also send their ideas to it; what must be taken for the common sense, where these ideas are received; for memory, which conserves them; and for fantasy, which can variously alter them and form new ones from them, and which, by the same means, distributing animal spirits through the muscles, can make the members of this body move in as many diverse ways, and in a manner suitable to the objects which appear to its senses and internal passions, as our own bodies can move without the guidance of the will. This will not seem at all strange to those who, knowing how many different *automata*, or moving machines, human industry can make, without using more than a very few parts, by comparison with the great multitude of bones, muscles, nerves, arteries, veins, and all the other parts which are in the body of each animal, will consider this body as a machine, which, having been made by the hands of God, is incomparably better ordered, and has in itself movements more admirable than any of those which can be devised by human beings.

And I was here particularly set on showing that, if there were such machines, which had the organs and the shape of a monkey or some other nonrational animal, we would have no way to recognize that they would not be in every way of the same nature as these animals; whereas, if there were some who resembled our bodies and imitated our actions as much as would be morally possible, we would still have two very certain means for recognizing that they were not for all that real human beings. The first is that they could never use words or other signs by putting them together, as we do for making known our thoughts to others. For we could well conceive of a machine being made such that it utters words, and even that it utters several regarding bodily actions which will cause some change in its organs, as, if we touch it in some place, it asks what we want to say to it; if in another, it cries out that we are hurting it, and so on; but not that it orders them differently, in order to reply sensibly to everything that is said to it in its presence, as even the most feeble-minded human beings can do. And the second is that, even though they do some things as well, or perhaps better, than any of us, they would inevitably fall short in others, by which we would discover that they would not act from knowledge, but only from the disposition of their organs. For, whereas reason is a universal instrument, which can serve in all sorts of situations, these organs need some particular arrangement for each particular action; hence it is morally impossible that there be enough diversity in a machine to make it act in all of life's circumstances, in the same way that our reason makes us act.

Now, by these two same means, we can also know the difference between men and beasts. For it is most remarkable that there are no human beings so feeble-minded and so stupid, without excluding even idiots, that they are not capable of putting different words together, and of making a discourse out of them by which they make their thoughts understood; and that on the other hand, there is no other animal, however perfect and however fortunate its birth, which can do the like. This does not occur for lack of organs, because we see that magpies and parrots can utter words just as we can, and yet cannot speak as we can, that is, in giving evidence that they are thinking about what they are saying; whereas people born deaf and mute, who as much or more than the beasts are deprived of organs which serve others for speaking, are in the habit of inventing their own signs, by which they make themselves understood by those who are usually with them and have the leisure to learn their language. And this not only proves that beasts have less reason than human beings, but that they have none at all. For we see that only a very little of it is needed to be able to speak; and since we notice the inequality between animals of a same species, just as we do among human beings, and that some are easier to train than others, it is not likely that a monkey or a parrot, which might be the most perfect of its species, would not equal in that the stupidest of children, or at least a child with a disturbed brain, if their soul was not of a completely different nature from ours. And we must not confuse words with natural movements, which are a sign of passions, which can be imitated by machines as well as by animals; nor think, as some of the ancients did,[6] that beasts speak, although we do not understand their language; for if it were true, since they have several organs which correspond to ours, they could just as well make themselves be understood by us as by their fellow creatures. It is also very notable that, even though there are animals who show more industry than us in some of their actions, we see, however, that these same animals do not show any at all in many others; so that what they do better than us does not prove that they have a mind; for, in that case they would have more reason than any of us and would do better in everything; but rather they have no reason at all and it is Nature which acts in them, according to the arrangement of their organs. In the same way we see that a clock, which is composed only of wheels and springs, can calculate the hours and measure the time more precisely than we can with all our intelligence.

I had described, after that, the rational soul, and had shown that it can in no way be derived from the power of matter, in the same way as the other things I had spoken about, but that it must be expressly created; and how it is not enough that it be housed in the human body, as a pilot in his ship, except perhaps to move its members, but that it is necessary that it be joined and connected more closely with it to have, in addition to that, sensations and appetites resembling our own, and in this manner to form a true human being. And so, I have elaborated a little on the subject of the soul, because it is one of the most important; for, next to the error of those who deny the existence of God, which I think I have above adequately refuted, there is none that leads weak minds away from the straight path of virtue more than to imagine that the soul of the beasts is of the same nature as our own, and that, consequently, we have nothing to fear or to hope for following this life, any more than the flies and the ants; whereas, when we know how different they are, we understand much better the reasons which prove that ours is of a nature entirely independent of the body and, consequently, that it is not subject to die with it. And insofar as we see no other causes which can destroy it, we are naturally led to judge from that that it is immortal.

Notes

1 In the Aristotelian tradition (against which Descartes is rebelling) a "demonstration" is a proof based on first principles, which the mind immediately grasps as true and certain.

2 Descartes has just sketched a materialistic cosmogony, indicating how it is that the world attained its present form and characteristics through a sequence of material interactions. He is careful not to run afoul of religious authorities by indicating that the alternative account of Genesis, interpreted literally, is more likely: the world was created such as it now is. He adds that (a) even the scientific cosmogony he has sketched has as its metaphysical foundation the existence of matter, with certain characteristics, and this, in turn depends on God's creating and preserving matter, and (b) even if false as history, the scientific cosmogony serves to isolate the various causal factors that are concurrently operative in making the world as it is.

3 In Aristotle's biology, the first actuality of eating, growing, and reproducing, shared by plants and animals alike, is the vegetative (or nutritive) soul. The first actuality of sensation is the sensitive soul. (On this see Aristotle, *On the Soul* 2.1–3, included in this volume.) These first actualities cannot be wholly understood as processes undergone by the underlying material stuffs.

4 Descartes is alluding to the Aristotelian account of life, which is expressed in some of the selections from *Physics* and *On the Soul* included in the present volume. In the Aristotelian tradition, life processes are made possible by special *natures*, which are special forms that inhere in certain varieties of matter that have the potentiality to accept these forms. For Descartes, on the other hand, all matter has the same essence, which is merely to take up space. The processes within the human body, like all material processes, can be wholly understood as geometrical extension in motion. This includes the production of bodily heat, by means of a kind of fire that does not produce light.

5 Descartes is referring to the book *The World*, in which he sketched out in full the main lines of his physics, chemistry, and biology. When he learned that Galileo had been put on trial by the Inquisitor of the Holy Office of Rome for having argued that Earth is not in the center of the cosmos, Descartes decided against having *The World* published.

6 Cf. Porphyry, *On Abstaining from Animals* 3.3, in this volume.

CHAPTER 13

Baruch Spinoza

BARUCH SPINOZA (1632–1677) set out to develop the project of Descartes, but, in his hands, Descartes' metaphysical speculations took a radically different turn. From the notion that a substance is the ultimate cause of all of its attributes, Spinoza infers that there is only one substance, and this is God. All other beings are "modes" of God, who causes them. God possesses two sorts of infinite attributes: thought and extension. While for Descartes these two are constitutive of two different sorts of substances, for Spinoza they are different infinite attributes of the single substance, which is God. It is by virtue of these that we become aware of the modes of God.

From Spinoza's argument that a conscious, sentient being is not a different kind of substance than a material being, it follows that there is no fundamental metaphysical distinction between human beings, who can think, and other beings, both living and not living. All have some sort of inner life. Some environmental philosophers have been influenced by this idea, arguing that it forms the foundation of an ethic of concern for the nonhuman world.

But perhaps it is Spinoza's monism that is of greater importance to today's environmental philosophy. Like the Stoics centuries before him, Spinoza takes the universe to be a single, self-sufficient organism. This organism is God, the true substance, which is causally responsible for all particular things and events. Particular organisms may appear independent, but they are in fact merely parts of a greater, interdependent whole. This idea is strikingly expressed in the following letter, which compares the existence of an individual organism with that of a microscopic "worm" living in the blood of a human being. The limited perspective of the worm prevents it from being able to see that it is part of a single great mass of blood, each part of which has its contribution to the functioning of the whole. Spinoza points out that this is an imperfect example, as the blood itself is merely a part of some greater unity.

BARUCH SPINOZA
Letter 32 *Spinoza to Henry Oldenburg*
TR. EDWIN CURLEY

... When you ask me what I think about the question which concerns *how we know how each part of Nature agrees with the whole to which it belongs and how it coheres with the others,* I think you are asking for the reasons by which we are persuaded that each part of Nature agrees with the whole to which it belongs and coheres with the others.

For I said in my preceding letter that I do not know absolutely how they really cohere and how each part agrees with its whole. To know this would require knowing the whole of Nature and all its parts.[1] So I shall try to show as briefly I can the reason which forces me to affirm this. But first I should like to warn that I attribute to Nature neither beauty nor ugliness, neither order nor confusion. For things can only be called beautiful or ugly, orderly or confused, in relation to our imagination.

By the coherence of parts, then, I understand nothing but that the laws *or* nature of the one part so adapt themselves to the laws *or* nature of the other part that they are opposed to each other as little as possible. Concerning whole and parts, I consider things as parts of some whole insofar as the nature of the one so adapts itself to the nature of the other that so far as possible they are all in harmony with one another. But insofar as they are out of harmony with one another, to that extent each forms an idea distinct from the others in our mind, and therefore it is considered as a whole and not as a part.

For example, when the motions of the particles of lymph, chyle, and the like, so adapt themselves to one another, in relation to their size and shape, that they are completely in harmony with one another, and they all constitute one fluid together, to that extent only the chyle, lymph, and the like are considered as parts of the blood. But insofar as we conceive the particles of lymph, by reason of their shape and motion, to differ from the particles of chyle, to that extent we consider them as a whole and not as a part.

Let us conceive now, if you please, that there is a little worm living in the blood which is capable of distinguishing by sight the particles of the blood, of lymph, of chyle, and the like, and capable of observing by reason how each particle, when it encounters another, either bounces back, or communicates a part of its motion, and so on. Indeed, it would live in this blood as we do in this part of the universe, and would consider each particle of the blood as a whole, not as a part. Nor could it know how all the parts of the blood are restrained by the universal nature of the blood, and compelled to adapt themselves to one another, as the universal nature of the blood requires, so that they harmonize with one another in a certain way.

For if we should suppose that there are no causes outside the blood which would communicate new motions to the blood, and no space outside the blood, nor any other bodies to which the particles of blood could transfer their motion, it is certain that the blood would always remain in the same state, and its particles would undergo no other variations than those which can be conceived from the given relation of the motion of the blood to those of the lymph, chyle, and the like. Thus the blood would always have to be considered as a whole and not as a part. But because there are a great many other causes which restrain the laws of the nature of the blood in a certain way, and which in turn are restrained by the blood, it happens that other motions and other variations arise in the particles of the blood which follow not simply from the relation of the motion of its parts to one another, but from the relation of the motion of the blood as a whole and of the external causes to one another. In this way the blood has the nature of a part and not of a whole. This is what I say concerning whole and part.[2]

Now all bodies in Nature can and must be conceived as we have here conceived the blood, for all bodies are surrounded by others, and are determined by one another to existing and producing an effect in a certain and determinate way, the same ratio of motion to rest always being preserved in all of them at once, that is, in the whole universe. From this it follows that every body, insofar as it exists modified in a certain way, must be considered as a part of the whole universe, must agree with the whole to which it belongs, and must cohere with the remaining bodies. And since the nature of the universe is not limited, as the nature of the blood is, but is absolutely infinite, its parts are restrained in infinite ways by the nature of the infinite power, and compelled to undergo infinitely many variations.

But in relation to substance I conceive each part to have a closer union with its whole. For as I previously strove to demonstrate in my first letter, which I wrote to you while I was still living in Rijnsburg, since it is of the nature of substance to be infinite, it follows that each part pertains to the nature of corporeal substance, and can neither be nor be conceived without it.

You see, therefore, how and why I think that the human body is a part of Nature. But as far as the human mind is concerned, I think it is a part of Nature too. For I maintain that there is also in Nature an infinite power of thinking, which, insofar as it is infinite, contains in itself objectively the whole of Nature, and whose thoughts proceed in the same way as Nature itself, its object, does.

Next, I maintain that the human mind is this same power, not insofar as it is infinite and perceives the whole of Nature, but insofar as it is finite and perceives only the human body. For this reason I maintain that the human mind is a part of a certain infinite intellect.

But it would take too long here to explain accurately and demonstrate all these things, along with the things which are connected with them. And I do not think you expect this of me at present. Indeed, I wonder whether I have sufficiently grasped your intention, and have not answered a different question than the one you were asking. Please let me know.

    Yours with all affection,

    B. de Spinoza

    Voorburg, 20 November 1665

Notes

1 Because the world is an interdependent unity, to know how any particular part depends on any other is to know the bonds of interdependence among all things. Spinoza says that this is beyond his power. The best that he can do is present considerations that ought to persuade one that it is in fact the case that all things contribute to such a unity.

2 In reality, the blood is not a single independent organism, for its motions are dependent on causes lying outside the blood. For Spinoza, a true whole would comprehend every cause of anything that happens to it or within it. It follows that no particular thing can be considered a true whole, except for the universe itself.

CHAPTER 14

John Ray

DURING THE new era of scientific discovery heralded by Bacon's writings, many scientists successfully explained various phenomena on the basis of general principles concerning the motion and change undergone by inanimate matter. It was easy for philosophers to generalize, and say that all motion and change can be accounted for on the basis of the interactions among microscopic bits of stuff. We have seen Descartes make such a move, with the prominent exception of only those changes occurring within human consciousness. We have already mentioned that the materialistic account of animal life led to a denial that animals other than humans are sentient, which in turn led to a number of inhumane practices.

The English naturalist, priest, and philosopher John Ray (1627?–1705) took such a materialistic account of life to be both incorrect and dangerous. He took it to be incorrect, first, because he was convinced that there can be no adequate materialistic account of life processes, and second, because he was convinced of the absurdity of the Cartesian view that nonhuman animals lack sentience. He took it to be dangerous because in his view there is only a short step from a materialistic science to a denial of the religious teachings of God's action in the world and the existence of an immortal human soul.

In *The Wisdom of God Manifested in the Creation*, Ray argues that a proper scientific study of nature confirms Christian teachings concerning the role of God in the world. Because interactions among inanimate stuffs cannot explain life processes, Ray appeals to either soul or a "plastic nature" that shapes and guides organic material processes. Ray was greatly influenced by a group of philosophers known as the Cambridge Platonists, who argued, against the followers of Bacon, that the metaphysics of Plato's *Timaeus* is fundamentally correct. The soul to which Ray appeals can be seen as a variation of soul as understood by Plato (although he is careful not to commit himself on the issue of the immortality of animal souls). To those for whom the existence of soul is a metaphysical extravagance, Ray suggests that appeal can be made to a "plastic nature," a mysterious stuff whose workings are in fact that of soul, in the Platonic sense. In the passage presented here, Ray also argues against Descartes' denial of the sentience of animals other than human beings. He goes so far as to follow the ancient Platonic tradition in attributing a rational soul to (at least some) nonhuman animals.

JOHN RAY
The Wisdom of God Manifested in the Creation

... I am difficult to believe, that the bodies of animals can be formed by matter
divided and moved by what laws you will or can imagine, without the immediate
presidency, direction and regulation of some intelligent being. In the generation or
first formation of, suppose the human body, out of (though not an homogeneous[1]
liquor, yet) a fluid substance, the only material agent or mover is a moderate heat.[2]
Now how this, by producing an intestine motion in the particles of the matter, which
can be conceived to differ in nothing else but figure, magnitude and gravity, should
by virtue thereof, not only separate the heterogeneous[3] parts, but assemble the homogeneous into masses or systems, and that not each kind into one mass, but into
many and disjoined ones, as it were so many troops; and that in each troop the
particular particles should take their places, and cast themselves into such a figure; as
for example, the bones being about 300 are formed of various sizes and shapes, so
situate and connected, as to be subservient to many hundred intentions and uses,
and many of them conspire to one and the same action, this, I say, I cannot by any
means conceive. I might instance in all the homogeneous parts of the body, their sites
and figures; and ask by what imaginable laws of motion their bulk, figure, situation
and connexion can be made out? What account can be given of the valves, of the
veins and arteries of the heart, and of the veins elsewhere, and of their situation; of
the figure and consistency of all the humours and membranes of the eye, all conspiring and exactly fitted to the use of seeing; but I have touched upon that already, and
shall discourse of it largely afterward. You will ask me who or what is the operator in
the formation of the bodies of man and other animals? I answer, the sensitive soul
itself, if it be a spiritual and immaterial substance, as I am inclinable to believe: but if
it be material, and consequently the whole animal but a mere machine or automa-
ton, as I can hardly admit, then must we have recourse to a plastic nature.

   That the soul of brutes is material, and the whole animal, soul and body, but a
mere machine is the opinion publicly owned and declared, of Descartes, Gassendus,
Dr. Willis and others; the same is also necessarily consequent upon the doctrine of
the Peripatetics, viz. that the sensitive soul is educed out of the power of the matter.[4]
For nothing can be educed out of the matter, but what was there before, which must
be either matter or some modification of it. And therefore they cannot grant it to be
a spiritual substance, unless they will assert it to be educed out of nothing. This
opinion, I say, I can hardly digest. I should rather think animals to be endued with a
lower degree of reason, than that they are mere machines. I could instance in many
actions of brutes that are hardly to be accounted for without reason and argumenta-
tion; as that commonly noted of dogs, that running before their masters they will
stop at a divarication of the way, till they see which hand their masters will take; and

that when they have gotten a prey, which they fear their masters will take from them, they will run away and hide it, and afterwards return to it; and many the like actions, which I shall not spend time to relate. Should this be true, that beasts were automata or machines, they could have no sense or perception of pleasure or pain, and consequently no cruelty could be exercised towards them; which is contrary to the doleful significations they make when beaten or tormented, and contrary to the common sense of mankind, all men naturally pitying them as apprehending them to have such a sense and feeling of pain and misery as themselves have; whereas no man is troubled to see a plant torn, or cut, or stamped, or mangled how you please. Besides, having the same members and organs of sense as we have, it is very probable they have the same sensations and perceptions with us. To this Descartes answers or indeed sayeth, he hath nothing to answer; but that if they think as well as we, they have an immortal soul as well as we: which is not at all likely, because there is no reason to believe it of some animals without believing it of all, whereas there are many too too imperfect to believe it of them such as our oysters and sponges and the like. To which I answer that there is no necessity they should be immortal, because it is possible they may be destroyed or annihilated.

Notes

1 A homogeneous stuff is one that is of a single uniform kind throughout, e.g. water.

2 Cf. Descartes, Chapter 5 of *Discourse on Method* (in the present volume), in which it is argued that the bodies of animals, including human beings, are formed and animated by a kind of fire that gives off no light.

3 A heterogeneous stuff is one that is not of a single kind throughout; it is not homogeneous. Water is homogeneous, but a mixture of oil and water, or an animal body, is heterogeneous.

4 The Peripatetics are the followers of Aristotle. This is a misunderstanding of Aristotle's teachings: Aristotle did not explain sensation wholly on the basis of inorganic material motions.

CHAPTER 15

John Locke

JOHN LOCKE (1632–1704) was among the most important philosophers of the modern period. His political thought has been especially influential; echoes of it can be found in the ideas of liberal or revolutionary political theorists of the last three hundred years. For example, Thomas Jefferson's *Declaration of Independence* reflects the fundamentally Lockean principles that human beings are naturally at liberty to pursue their own welfare, that governments are instituted by the consent of the governed (not directly by God), and that a government continues to be accountable to the governed. Locke's idea that human beings have a claim to the goods that they have worked through their own labor is a key element of the economic teachings of Marx and Engels, and can be clearly discerned in the selection from Engels included in this volume. More recently, opponents of some environmental legislation have appealed to Locke's views that property rights are natural and that, except in a very few cases, one's right to employ one's property as one sees fit is not to be infringed upon by governmental regulation. Recent philosophical discussion of this issue has often turned to exactly how Locke justified natural property rights. This, as well as his account of the relation between human beings and their natural environment, makes Locke's discussion of the nature of property worthy of close study.

Locke's political views were primarily formulated in opposition to those of political theorist Robert Filmer (?–1653), whose political thought, which endorsed the divine right of kings, was grounded on what was at that time an orthodox reading of Biblical Scripture. For Filmer, God granted possession of the earth to Adam, and mandated a patrilineal line of succession for political rule. The rights of such a ruler are absolute, including the arrangements of property.

Locke devoted many pages of his *Two Treatises of Government* toward developing an alternative account of Scripture. Yet at bottom his own political philosophy does not rely on theological support. Locke's starting point is the basic liberty of individuals to provide for their own survival and comfort and that of their families. This presupposes freedom to take natural resources from the earth, and to develop the earth so that it might be more fruitful in producing these resources. This can be accomplished only if the individual contributes his or her own labor. When this happens, a bit of the individual and a bit of the earth are somehow mixed together, which enables the individual to have an exclusive claim on the mixture. The mixture thus becomes private property. One is free to do as one pleases with the property, unless doing so diminishes the natural freedom of others to provide for their survival and comfort. As an example of the illegitimate exercise of one's freedom over property, Locke asks us to consider one who harvests a store of goods from nature, and then leaves it to rot, so that it can benefit no one.

For Locke, natural property rights are prior to political communities. On his account, individuals come together to institute governments largely in order to protect their basic property rights.

It is a matter of great contention how Locke's theories are to be applied today. Locke presupposed that there would always be land in its natural state to which the individual would be free to turn and exert his or her labor; this no longer seems true, as in nearly every country all arable land is owned by either individuals or the state, and there may well be good reasons for leaving undeveloped certain lands under common ownership. It has also been called into question whether Locke's account of property rights can justify squandering natural resources, so that they cannot benefit future generations.

JOHN LOCKE
Second Treatise of Government

Chapter 5: Of Property

25. Whether we consider natural reason,[1] which tells us that men, being once born, have a right to their preservation, and consequently to meat and drink, and such other things as nature affords for their subsistence; or revelation, which gives us an account of those grants God made of the world to Adam, and to Noah, and his sons, it is very clear that God, as King David says (Psal. cxv. 16), "has given the earth to the children of men," given it to mankind in common. But this being supposed, it seems to some a very great difficulty, how any one should ever come to have a property in any thing. I will not content my self to answer, that if it be difficult to make out property, upon a supposition that God gave the world to Adam and his posterity in common, it is impossible that any man, but one universal monarch, should have any property, upon a supposition that God gave the world to Adam, and his heirs in succession, exclusive of all the rest of his posterity. But I shall endeavour to shew how men might come to have a property in several parts of that which God gave to mankind in common, and that without any express compact of all the commoners.

26. God, who hath given the world to men in common, hath also given them reason to make use of it to the best advantage of life, and convenience. The earth, and all that is therein, is given to men for the support and comfort of their being.[2] And though all the fruits it naturally produces, and beasts it feeds, belong to mankind in common, as they are produced by the spontaneous hand of nature; and no body has originally a private dominion, exclusive of the rest of mankind, in any of them, as they are thus in their natural state; yet being given for the use of men, there

must of necessity be a means to appropriate them some way or other before they can be of any use, or at all beneficial to any particular man. The fruit, or venison, which nourishes the wild Indian, who knows no enclosure, and is still a tenant in common, must be his, and so his, i.e., a part of him, that another can no longer have any right to it, before it can do him any good for the support of his life.

27. Though the earth, and all inferior creatures be common to all men, yet every man has a property in his own person. This no body has any right to but himself. The labour of his body, and the work of his hands, we may say, are properly his. Whatsoever then he removes out of the state that nature hath provided, and left it in, he hath mixed his labour with, and joined to it something that is his own, and thereby makes it his property. It being by him removed from the common state nature hath placed it in, it hath by this labour something annexed to it, that excludes the common right of other men. For this labour being the unquestionable property of the labourer, no man but he can have a right to what that is once joined to, at least where there is enough, and as good left in common for others.

28. He that is nourished by the acorns he picked up under an oak, or the apples he gathered from the trees in the wood, has certainly appropriated them to himself. No body can deny but the nourishment is his. I ask then, when did they begin to be his? When he digested? Or when he ate? Or when he boiled? Or when he brought them home? Or when he picked them up? And it is plain, if the first gathering made them not his, nothing else could. That labour put a distinction between them and common. That added something to them more than nature, the common mother of all, had done; and so they became his private right. And will any one say he had no right to those acorns or apples he thus appropriated, because he had not the consent of all mankind to make them his? Was it a robbery thus to assume to himself what belonged to all in common? If such a consent as that was necessary, man had starved, notwithstanding the plenty God had given him. We see in commons, which remain so by compact, that it is the taking any part of what is common, and removing it out of the state nature leaves it in, which begins the property; without which the common is of no use. And the taking of this or that part does not depend on the express consent of all the commoners. Thus the grass my horse has bit; the turfs my servant has cut; and the ore I have digged in any place, where I have a right to them in common with others, become my property, without the assignation or consent of any body. The labour that was mine, removing them out of that common state they were in, hath fixed my property in them.

29. By making an explicit consent of every commoner, necessary to any one's appropriating to himself any part of what is given in common, children or servants could not cut the meat which their father or master had provided for them in common, without assigning to every one his peculiar part. Though the water running in the fountain be every one's, yet who can doubt, but that in the pitcher is his only

who drew it out? His labour hath taken it out of the hands of nature, where it was common, and belonged equally to all her children, and hath thereby appropriated it to himself.

30. Thus this law of reason makes the deer that Indian's who hath killed it; it is allowed to be his goods who hath bestowed his labour upon it, though before, it was the common right of every one. And amongst those who are counted the civilized part of mankind, who have made and multiplied positive laws to determine property, this original law of nature for the beginning of property, in what was before common, still takes place; and by virtue thereof, what fish any one catches in the ocean, that great and still remaining common of mankind; or what ambergris[3] any one takes up here, is by the labour that removes it out of that common state nature left it in, made his property who takes that pains about it. And even amongst us the hare that any one is hunting is thought his who pursues her during the chase. For being a beast that is still looked upon as common, and no man's private possession, whoever has employed so much labour about any of that kind, as to find and pursue her, has thereby removed her from the state of nature, wherein she was common, and hath begun a property.

31. It will perhaps be objected to this, that if gathering the acorns, or other fruits of the earth, etc. makes a right to them, then any one may engross as much as he will. To which I answer, not so. The same law of nature, that does by this means give us property, does also bound that property too. "God has given us all things richly" (1 Tim. vi. 17) is the voice of reason confirmed by inspiration.[4] But how far has he given it us? To enjoy. As much as any one can make use of to any advantage of life before it spoils, so much he may by his labour fix a property in. Whatever is beyond this is more than his share, and belongs to others. Nothing was made by God for man to spoil or destroy. And thus considering the plenty of natural provisions there was a long time in the world, and the few spenders, and to how small a part of that provision the industry of one man could extend it self, and engross it to the prejudice of others; especially keeping within the bounds, set by reason of what might serve for his use; there could be then little room for quarrels or contentions about property so established.

32. But the chief matter of property being now not the fruits of the earth, and the beasts that subsist on it, but the earth itself; as that which takes in and carries with it all the rest; I think it is plain that property in that too is acquired as the former. As much land as a man tills, plants, improves, cultivates, and can use the product of, so much is his property. He by his labour does, as it were, enclose it from the common. Nor will it invalidate his right to say, every body else has an equal title to it; and therefore he cannot appropriate, he cannot enclose, without the consent of all his fellow-commoners, all mankind. God, when he gave the world in common to all mankind, commanded man also to labour, and the penury of his condition re-

quired it of him. God and his reason commanded him to subdue the earth, i.e., improve it for the benefit of life, and therein lay out something upon it that was his own, his labour. He that in obedience to this command of God subdued, tilled and sowed any part of it, thereby annexed to it something that was his property, which another had no title to, nor could without injury take from him.

33. Nor was this appropriation of any parcel of land, by improving it, any prejudice to any other man, since there was still enough, and as good left; and more than the yet unprovided could use. So that in effect, there was never the less left for others because of his enclosure for himself. For he that leaves as much as another can make use of, does as good as take nothing at all. No body could think himself injured by the drinking of another man, though he took a good draught, who had a whole river of the same water left him to quench his thirst. And the case of land and water, where there is enough of both, is perfectly the same.

34. God gave the world to men in common; but since he gave it them for their benefit, and the greatest conveniences of life they were capable to draw from it, it cannot be supposed he meant it should always remain common and uncultivated. He gave it to the use of the industrious and rational (and labour was to be his title to it), not to the fancy or covetousness of the quarrelsome and contentious. He that had as good left for his improvement, as was already taken up, needed not complain, ought not to meddle with what was already improved by another's labour; if he did, it is plain he desired the benefit of another's pains, which he had no right to, and not the ground which God had given him in common with others to labour on, and whereof there was as good left, as that already possessed, and more than he knew what to do with, or his industry could reach to.

35. It is true, in land that is common in England, or any other country, where there are plenty of people under government, who have money and commerce, no one can enclose or appropriate any part, without the consent of all his fellow commoners; because this is left common by compact, i.e., by the law of the land, which is not to be violated. And though it be common, in respect of some men, it is not so to all mankind; but is the joint property of this country, or this parish. Besides, the remainder, after such enclosure, would not be as good to the rest of the commoners as the whole was, when they could all make use of the whole; whereas in the beginning and first peopling of the great common of the world, it was quite otherwise. The law man was under was rather for appropriating. God commanded, and his wants forced him to labour. That was his property which could not be taken from him wherever he had fixed it. And hence subduing or cultivating the earth, and having dominion, we see are joined together. The one gave title to the other. So that God, by commanding to subdue, gave authority so far to appropriate. And the condition of human life, which requires labour and materials to work on, necessarily introduces private possessions.

36. The measure of property, nature has well set, by the extent of men's labour and the conveniences of life. No man's labour could subdue or appropriate all; nor could his enjoyment consume more than a small part; so that it was impossible for any man, this way, to entrench upon the right of another, or acquire, to himself, a property, to the prejudice of his neighbour, who would still have room for as good and as large a possession (after the other had taken out his) as before it was appropriated. This measure did confine every man's possession to a very moderate proportion, and such as he might appropriate to himself, without injury to anybody in the first ages of the world, when men were more in danger to be lost by wandering from their company in the then vast wilderness of the earth, than to be straitened for want of room to plant in. And the same measure may be allowed still, without prejudice to any body, as full as the world seems. For supposing a man, or family, in the state they were at first peopling of the world by the children of Adam, or Noah; let him plant in some inland, vacant places of America, we shall find that the possessions he could make himself upon the measures we have given would not be very large, nor, even to this day, prejudice the rest of mankind, or give them reason to complain, or think themselves injured by this man's encroachment, though the race of men have now spread themselves to all the corners of the world, and do infinitely exceed the small number [which] was at the beginning. Nay, the extent of ground is of so little value, without labour, that I have heard it affirmed that in Spain itself a man may be permitted to plough, sow, and reap, without being disturbed, upon land he has no other title to but only his making use of it. But, on the contrary, the inhabitants think themselves beholden to him, who, by his industry on neglected, and consequently waste land, has increased the stock of corn, which they wanted. But be this as it will, which I lay no stress on; this I dare boldly affirm, that the same rule of propriety, (viz.) that every man should have as much as he could make use of, would hold still in the world, without straitening any body, since there is land enough in the world to suffice double the inhabitants had not the invention of money, and the tacit agreement of men to put a value on it, introduced (by consent) larger possessions, and a right to them; which, how it has done, I shall, by and by, shew more at large.

37. This is certain, that in the beginning, before the desire of having more than man needed had altered the intrinsic value of things, which depends only on their usefulness to the life of man; or had agreed that a little piece of yellow metal, which would keep without wasting or decay, should be worth a great piece of flesh, or a whole heap of corn; though men had a right to appropriate, by their labour, each one of himself, as much of the things of nature as he could use; yet this could not be much, nor to the prejudice of others, where the same plenty was still left, to those who would use the same industry. To which let me add, that he who appropriates land to himself by his labour, does not lessen, but increase the common stock of mankind. For the provisions serving to the support of human life, produced by one

acre of enclosed and cultivated land, are (to speak much within compass) ten times more than those which are yielded by an acre of land of an equal richness, lying waste in common. And therefore he that encloses land and has a greater plenty of the conveniences of life from ten acres than he could have from an hundred left to nature, may truly be said to give ninety acres to mankind. For his labour now supplies him with provisions out of ten acres, which were but the product of an hundred lying in common. I have here rated the improved land very low in making its product but as ten to one, when it is much nearer an hundred to one. For I ask whether in the wild woods and uncultivated waste of America left to nature, without any improvement, tillage or husbandry, a thousand acres will yield the needy and wretched inhabitants as many conveniences of life as ten acres of equally fertile land do in Devonshire where they are well cultivated?

Before the appropriation of land, he who gathered as much of the wild fruit, killed, caught, or tamed, as many of the beasts as he could; he that so employed his pains about any of the spontaneous products of nature, as any way to alter them from the state which nature put them in, by placing any of his labour on them, did thereby acquire a propriety in them. But if they perished in his possession, without their due use; if the fruits rotted, or the venison putrefied, before he could spend it, he offended against the common law of nature, and was liable to be punished; he invaded his neighbour's share, for he had no right, farther than his use called for any of them, and they might serve to afford him conveniences of life.

38. The same measures governed the possession of land too: Whatsoever he tilled and reaped, laid up and made use of, before it spoiled, that was his peculiar right; whatsoever he enclosed, and could feed, and make use of, the cattle and product was also his. But if either the grass of his enclosure rotted on the ground, or the fruit of his planting perished without gathering, and laying up, this part of the earth, notwithstanding his enclosure, was still to be looked on as waste, and might be the possession of any other. Thus, at the beginning, Cain might take as much ground as he could till, and make it his own land, and yet leave enough to Abel's sheep to feed on; a few acres would serve for both their possessions. But as families increased, and industry enlarged their stocks, their possessions enlarged with the need of them; but yet it was commonly without any fixed property in the ground they made use of, till they incorporated, settled themselves together, and built cities; and then, by consent, they came in time to set out the bounds of their distinct territories, and agree on limits between them and their neighbours, and by laws within themselves, settled the properties of those of the same society. For we see that in that part of the world which was first inhabited, and therefore like to be best peopled, even as low down as Abraham's time, they wandered with their flocks, and their herds, which was their substance, freely up and down; and this Abraham did, in a country where he was a stranger. Whence it is plain that at least a great part of the land lay in common; that

the inhabitants valued it not, nor claimed property in any more than they made use of. But when there was not room enough in the same place for their herds to feed together, they, by consent, as Abraham and Lot did (Gen. xiii. 5), separated and enlarged their pasture, where it best liked them. And for the same reason Esau went from his father, and his brother, and planted in Mount Seir (Gen. xxxvi. 6).

39. And thus, without supposing any private dominion, and property in Adam, over all the world, exclusive of all other men, which can in no way be proved, nor any one's property be made out from it; but supposing the world given as it was to the children of men in common, we see how labour could make men distinct titles to several parcels of it, for their private uses; wherein there could be no doubt of right, no room for quarrel.

40. Nor is it so strange, as perhaps before consideration it may appear, that the property of labour should be able to overbalance the community of land. For it is labour indeed that puts the difference of value on everything; and let any one consider what the difference is between an acre of land planted with tobacco, or sugar, sown with wheat or barley, and an acre of the same land lying in common, without any husbandry upon it, and he will find that the improvement of labour makes the far greater part of the value. I think it will be but a very modest computation to say that of the products of the earth useful to the life of man nine-tenths are the effects of labour; nay, if we will rightly estimate things as they come to our use, and cast up the several expenses about them, what in them is purely owing to nature, and what to labour, we shall find that in most of them ninety-nine hundredths are wholly to be put on the account of labour.

41. There cannot be a clearer demonstration of any thing, than several nations of the Americans are of this, who are rich in land, and poor in all the comforts of life; whom nature having furnished as liberally as any other people, with the materials of plenty, i.e., a fruitful soil, apt to produce in abundance, what might serve for food, raiment, and delight; yet for want of improving it by labour, have not one hundredth part of the conveniences we enjoy; and a king of a large and fruitful territory there feeds, lodges, and is clad worse than a day labourer in England.

42. To make this a little clearer, let us but trace some of the ordinary provisions of life through their several progresses before they come to our use, and see how much they receive of their value from human industry. Bread, wine and cloth are things of daily use and great plenty; yet notwithstanding, acorns, water, and leaves, or skins, must be our bread, drink and clothing, did not labour furnish us with these more useful commodities. For whatever bread is more worth than acorns, wine than water, and cloth or silk than leaves, skins, or moss, that is wholly owing to labour and industry. The one of these being the food and raiment which unassisted nature furnishes us with; the other provisions which our industry and pains prepare for us, which how much they exceed the other in value, when any one hath computed, he

will then see how much labour makes the far greatest part of the value of things we enjoy in this world. And the ground which produces the materials is scarce to be reckoned in, as any, or at most, but a very small, part of it; so little, that even amongst us, land that is left wholly to nature, that hath no improvement of pasturage, tillage, or planting, is called, as indeed it is, waste; and we shall find the benefit of it amount to little more than nothing. This shews how much numbers of men are to be preferred to largeness of dominions, and that the increase of lands and the right employing of them is the great art of government. And that prince who shall be so wise and godlike as by established laws of liberty to secure protection and encouragement to the honest industry of mankind against the oppression of power and narrowness of party will quickly be too hard for his neighbours. But this by the bye. To return to the argument in hand.

43. An acre of land that bears here twenty bushels of wheat, and another in America, which, with the same husbandry, would do the like, are without doubt of the same natural, intrinsic value. But yet the benefit mankind receives from the one in a year, is worth £5 and from the other possibly not worth a penny, if all the profit an Indian received from it were to be valued, and sold here; at least, I may truly say, not one-thousandth. It is labour then which puts the greatest part of value upon land, without which it would scarcely be worth any thing; it is to that we owe the greatest part of all its useful products; for all that the straw, bran, bread, of that acre of wheat is more worth than the product of an acre of as good land, which lies waste, is all the effect of labour. For it is not barely the ploughman's pains, the reaper's and thresher's toil, and the baker's sweat [that] is to be counted into the bread we eat; the labour of those who broke the oxen, who digged and wrought the iron and stones, who felled and framed the timber employed about the plough, mill, oven, or any other utensils, which are a vast number, requisite to this corn, from its being seed to be sown to its being made bread, must all be charged on the account of labour, and received as an effect of that; nature and the earth furnished only the almost worthless materials, as in themselves. It would be a strange catalogue of things that industry provided and made use of, about every loaf of bread, before it came to our use, if we could trace them; iron, wood, leather, bark, timber, stone, bricks, coals, lime, cloth, dyeing drugs, pitch, tar, masts, ropes, and all the materials made use of in the ship that brought any of the commodities made use of by any of the workmen to any part of the work; all which it would be almost impossible, at least too long, to reckon up.

44. From all which it is evident, that though the things of nature are given in common, yet man (by being master of himself, and proprietor of his own person, and the actions or labour of it) had still in himself the great foundation of property; and that which made up the great part of what he applied to the support or comfort of his being, when invention and arts had improved the conveniences of life, was perfectly his own, and did not belong in common to others.

Notes

1 Natural reason is the reason human beings have, apart from any divine revelation. Locke is making clear that his account of property rights does not depend on the reader's acceptance of Scriptural authority.

2 Locke grounds this view in Scripture. Section 32 ("God and his reason commanded him to subdue the earth ..." indicates that for Locke this teleological view could be justified on the basis of "natural reason" as well.

3 Ambergris is a waxy substance, found in the intestines of some sperm whales, formerly used in the production of fine perfumes.

4 "Inspiration" here refers to divine guidance through Biblical revelation.

IV

Order, Hierarchy, and Struggle

CHAPTER 16

Carolus Linnaeus

SWEDISH BOTANIST Carolus Linnaeus (1707–1778) is best known for having pioneered a comprehensive system of biological classification by genus and species. From a philosophical point of view, however, his most significant contribution was perhaps not his scheme of classification but rather the way in which he gave a scientific grounding to the notion of the world as a single, interconnected whole. This notion was put forward in his 1749 essay *The Economy of Nature*, of which the 1759 translation by Benjamin Stillingfleet is excerpted below.

The term "economy" is derived from the Greek for "law of the household."[1] "Economics" was a body of knowledge concerning the expenditures and delegation of labor that were required to properly run a household. In a well-managed household, everyone would attend to their proper tasks, and everyone's needs would be met, in a manner that is indefinitely sustainable. Later, the term "economy" began to be applied to other sorts of expenditure, but the root idea of a sustainable, interconnected system remained. In referring to the economy of Nature, then, Linnaeus is pointing to how the world is organized analogously to a well-run household. The German biologist Ernst Haeckel (1834–1919), a prominent exponent of Darwin's ideas, had the same idea in mind when he coined the term "ecology" (which, also based on the Greek root *oikia*, household, means "account of the household") to refer to the branch of biology that deals with the interrelationships of living things to each other and to their environment.

We have seen that for Christian biologists such as Ray, the complex arrangement of the parts of a single living being was powerful evidence for divine providence. Linnaeus continues this line of thinking, arguing that the complex interdependence of living beings on each other as well as on the climate and other features of their habitat is an indication that God arranged things so that every region on earth could provide a suitable habitat for a number of living beings. Further, God has so arranged things that death and destruction have their place in Nature as a whole: the soil is enriched when dead organisms decompose. Thus, for Linnaeus, the study of biology has great spiritual value, insofar as it provides powerful evidence for the perfection of God's work. Linnaeus does not, however, depart from the traditional Christian view that the entire natural world is directly or indirectly for the sake of human beings. For Linnaeus, the study of the economy of nature provides further evidence of the care with which God designed the world for human benefit.

CAROLUS LINNAEUS
The Economy of Nature
TR. BENJAMIN J. STILLINGFLEET

1. By the Economy of Nature we understand the all-wise disposition of the Creator in relation to natural things, by which they are fitted to produce general ends, and reciprocal uses.

All things contained in the compass of the universe declare, as it were, with one accord the infinite wisdom of the Creator. For whatever strikes our senses, whatever is the object of our thoughts, are so contrived, that they concur to make manifest the divine glory, i.e., the ultimate end which God proposed in all his works. Whoever duly turns his attention to the things on this our terraqueous[2] globe, must necessarily confess, that they are so connected, so chained together, that they all aim at the same end, and to this end a vast number of intermediate ends are subservient. But as the intent of this treatise will not suffer me to consider them all, I shall at present only take notice of such as relate to the preservation of natural things. In order therefore to perpetuate the established course of nature in a continued series, the divine wisdom has thought fit, that all living creatures should constantly be employed in producing individuals; that all natural things should contribute and lend a helping hand to preserve every species; and lastly, that the death and destruction of one thing should always be subservient to the restitution of another. It seems to me that a greater subject than this cannot be found, nor one on which laborious men may more worthily employ their industry, or men of genius their penetration.

I am very sensible, being conscious of my own weakness, how vast and difficult a subject it is, and how unable I am to treat it as it deserves; a subject which would be too great a task for the ability of the most experienced and sagacious men, and which properly performed would furnish materials for large volumes. My design therefore is only to give a summary view of it, and to set forth to the learned world, as far I am able, whatever curious, worthy to be known, and not obvious to every observer occurs in the triple kingdom of nature. Thus if what the industry of others shall in future times discover in this way be added to these observations, it is to be hoped that a common stock may thence grow, and come to be of some importance. But before I examine these three kingdoms of nature, it will not, I think, be amiss to say something concerning the earth in general, and its changes. ...

8. The great Author and Parent of all things decreed that the whole earth should be covered with plants, and that no place should be void, none barren. But since all countries have not the same changes of seasons, and every soil is not equally fit for every plant, He therefore, that no place should be without some, gave to every one of them such a nature, as might be chiefly adapted to the climate; so that some of them can bear an intense cold, others an equal degree of heat; some delight in dry ground,

others in moist, etc. Hence the same plants grow only where there are the same seasons of the year and the same soil.

The *alpine* plants live only in high, and cold situations, and therefore often on the *Alps* of Armenia, Switzerland, the Pyreneans, etc. whose tops are equally covered with eternal snows, as those of the Lapland *Alps*, plants of the same kind are found, and it would be in vain to seek for them any where else. It is remarkable in relation to the *alpine* plants, that they blow, and ripen their *seeds* very early, otherwise the winter would steal upon them on a sudden, and destroy them.

Our northern plants, although they are extremely rare everywhere else, yet are found in Siberia, and about Hudson's Bay, as the *arbutus, Flor.* 339. *bramble,* 412. *wintergreen,* &c.

Plants impatient of cold live within the torrid zones; hence both the Indies though at such a distance from one another have plants in common. The Cape of Good Hope, I know not from what cause, produces plants peculiar to itself, as all the *mesembryanthema,* and almost all the species of *aloes. Grasses,* the most common of all plants, can bear almost any temperature of air, in which the good providence of the Creator particularly appears; for all over the globe they above all plants are necessary for the nourishment of cattle, and the same thing is seen in relation to our most common grains.

Thus neither the scorching sun, nor the pinching cold hinders any country from having its vegetables. Nor is there any soil, which does not bring forth many kinds of plants; the *pond-weeds,* the *water-lily, lobelia* inhabit the waters. The *fluviales, fuci, conservæ* cover the bottoms of rivers, and sea. The *sphagna* fill the marshes. The *brya* clothe the plains. The driest woods and places scarce ever illuminated by the rays of the sun are adorned with the *hypna.* Nay stones and the trunks of trees are not excepted, for these are covered with various kinds of *liverwort.*

The desert, and most sandy places have their peculiar trees, and plants; and as rivers or brooks are very seldom found there, we cannot without wonder observe that many of them distill water, and by that means afford the greatest comfort both to man, and beasts that travel there. Thus the *tillandfia,* which is a *parasitical plant,* and grows on the tops of trees in the deserts of America, has its leaves turned at the base into the shape of a pitcher, with the extremity expanded; in these the rain is collected, and preserved for thirsty men, birds, and beasts.

The *water-tree* in Ceylon produces cylindrical bladders, covered with a lid; into these is secreted a most pure, and refreshing water, that tastes like nectar to men, and other animals. There is a kind of *cuckow-pint* in New France, that if you break a branch of it, will afford you a pint of excellent water. How wise, how beautiful is the agreement between the plants of every country, and its inhabitants, and other circumstances! ...

10. Daily experience teaches us, that all *plants* as well as all living things, must submit to death.

They spring up, they grow, they flourish, they ripen their fruit, they wither, and at last, having finished their course, they die, and return to the dust again, from whence they first took their rise. Thus all black mold,[3] which everywhere covers the earth, for the greatest part is owing to dead *vegetables*. For all roots descend into the sand by their branches, and after a *plant* has lost its stem the root remains; but this too rots at last, and changes into mold. By this means this kind of earth is mixed with sand, by the contrivance of nature, nearly in the same way as dung thrown upon fields is wrought into the earth by the industry of the husbandman. The earth thus prepared offers again to *plants* from its bosom, what it has received from them. For when seeds are committed to the earth, they draw to themselves, accommodate to their nature, and turn into *plants*, the more subtle parts of this mold by the cooperation of the sun, air, clouds, rains, and winds; so that the tallest tree is, properly speaking, nothing but mold wonderfully compounded with air, and water, and modified by a virtue communicated to a small seed by the Creator. From these plants, when they die, just the same kind of mold is formed, as gave birth to them originally; but in such a manner, that it is in greater quantity than before. *Vegetables* therefore increase the black mold, whence fertility remains continually uninterrupted. Whereas the earth could not make good its annual consumption, unless it were constantly recruited by new supplies. ...

15. As soon as animals come to maturity, and want no longer the care of their parents, they attend with the utmost labor, and industry, according to the law and economy appointed for every species, to the preservation of their lives. But that so great a number of them, which occur everywhere, may be supported, and a certain and fixed order may be kept up amongst them, behold the wonderful disposition of the Creator, in assigning to each species certain kinds of food, and in putting limits to their appetites. So that some live on particular species of plants, which particular regions, and soils only produce. Some on particular animalcula, others on carcases, and some even on mud and dung. For this reason, Providence has ordained, that some should swim in certain regions of the watery element, others should fly; some should inhabit the torrid, the frigid, or the temperate zones, and others should frequent deserts, mountains, woods, pools or meadows, according as the food proper to their nature is found in sufficient quantity. By this means there is no terrestrial tract, no sea, no river, no country, but what contains, and nourishes various kinds of animals. Hence also an animal of one kind cannot rob those of another kind of its aliment; which, if it happened, would endanger their lives or health; and thus the world at all times affords nourishment to so many, and so large inhabitants, at the same time that nothing which it produces, is useless or superfluous. ...

20. Lastly, all these treasures of nature so artfully contrived, so wonderfully propagated, so providentially supported throughout her three kingdoms, seem intended by the Creator for the sake of man. Every thing may be made subservient to his use, if not immediately, yet mediately, not so to that of other animals. By the help of reason

man tames the fiercest animals, pursues and catches the swiftest, nay he is able to reach even those which lie hid in the bottom of the sea.

By the help of reason he increases the number of vegetables immensely, and does that by art, which nature, left to herself, could scarcely effect. By ingenuity, he obtains from vegetables whatever is convenient or necessary for food, drink, clothing, medicine, navigation, and a thousand other purposes.

He has found the means of going down into the abyss of the earth, and almost searching its very bowels. With what artifice has he learned to get fragments from the most rocky mountains, to make the hardest stones fluid like water; to separate the useful metal from the useless dross, and to turn the finest sand to some use! In short when we follow the series of created things, and consider how providentially one is made for the sake of another, the matter comes to this, that all things are made for the sake of man; and for this end more especially, that he by admiring the works of the Creator should extol his glory, and at once enjoy all those things, of which he stands in need, in order to pass his life conveniently and pleasantly.

21. This subject concerning the economy of nature, a very final part of which I have lightly touched upon, is of such importance and dignity, that if it were to be properly treated in all its parts, men would find wherewithal to employ almost all the powers of the mind. Nay time itself would fail before even the most acute human sagacity would be able to discover the amazing economy, laws, and exquisite structure of the least structure, since as Pliny[4] observes, nature no where appears more herself, than in her most minute works. Every species of created beings deserves to engross one examiner.

If according to gross calculation we reckon in the world 20,000 species of *vegetables*, 3,000 of *worms*, 12,000 of *insects*, 200 of *amphibious animals*, 2,600 of *fishes*, 2,000 of *birds*, 200 of *quadrupeds*; the whole sum of the species of living creatures will amount to 40,000. Out of these our country has scarcely 3,000, for we have discovered only about 1,200 native plants, and about 1,400 species of animals. We of the human race, who were created to praise and adore our Creator, unless we choose to be mere idle spectators, should and in duty ought to be affected with nothing so much as the pious consideration of this glorious palace. Most certainly if we were to improve and polish our minds by the knowledge of these things; we should, besides the great use which would accrue to our economy, discover the more excellent economy of nature, and more strongly admire it when discovered.

> Omnium elementorum alterni recursi sunt,
> Quicquid alteri perit in alterum transit.
> Seneca Nat. III. 10.[5]

Notes

1 See n. 11 of the Xenophon selection included in this volume.

2 "Terraqueous" means "consisting of both land and water."

3 Mold is topsoil that is rich in organic matter.

4 Pliny the Elder (23–79) was an important Roman botanist.

5 These lines from Seneca's *Natural Questions* can be translated as "Reciprocal changes occur in the case of all elements. Whatever is lost to one thing moves on to another."

CHAPTER 17

Immanuel Kant

WE HAVE SEEN a number of respects in which philosophers of the modern period called into question traditional teachings. The efforts of philosophers such as Bacon or Descartes to devise a method that would lead to new, certain knowledge of the natural world were not entirely successful. There continued to be new challenges from skeptics, who questioned the extent to which it is possible to acquire certain knowledge at all. Some empiricist philosophers argued that ultimately, all we can really know with certainty is the immediate contents of our own minds.

Immanuel Kant (1724–1804) appreciated the force of such skeptical challenges, but argued that human reason is such that it *must* structure human experience in certain fixed ways. Thus, although we can never know what the external world is *really* like, we can know quite a bit about the structure and workings of the world as given to us by the experiences that we happen to have, and as structured by the inevitable operations of our own minds. Kant presented complex and detailed accounts of how this is so for almost all areas of human knowledge.

There are three main areas in which the work of Kant has importance for the issues discussed in the present volume.

First, Kant derives moral law not from certain feelings that people happen to have, but from the necessary workings of reason itself. He argues that all rational beings necessarily impose on themselves a single moral law. This law requires them to consider every other rational being as intrinsically important, or, what for Kant comes to the same thing, to always act in a manner in which one, as a rational being, could wish all rational beings to act. From this it follows that there are no direct moral obligations to anything that is not rational, such as ecosystems, plants, or nonrational animals, as is clearly stated in the first selection that follows. Kant develops the point we have seen made by St. Thomas Aquinas, that cruelty to animals is ethically reprehensible only because it may lead to cruelty to human beings. Although Kant took only rational beings to be moral subjects, a number of environmental ethicists have argued for such direct obligations by employing reasoning that owes a great debt to the arguments in Kant's ethical writings.

Second, Kant suggests that certain landscapes and natural events have great aesthetic power insofar as they are perceived as threatening, and thus indirectly call to mind the freedom of human reason to choose to act morally, in spite of great danger to physical well-being. This is called an experience of the "sublime." Kant's ideas here are predecessors of arguments for defending wilderness on the grounds of how the wilderness experience builds human character in a unique and important way.

Third, Kant argues against biological explanations that rely on external teleology, positing the goal of one organism as lying in the good of another. (Recall that such explanations were central to the anthropomorphic world views of the Stoics and St. Thomas Aquinas, among others.) But, Kant argues, biology must accept explanations that rely on internal teleology, explaining the characteristic of an organism by showing how it contributes to the goal of that organism, its good. Kant agrees with Aristotle that a complete reductive explanation of life processes on the basis of the material interactions of material constituents cannot be forthcoming. But while Aristotle asserts that this is because the world itself is in fact teleologically organized, Kant again suggests that human reason is unable to fathom the true organization of the world. Nonetheless, our minds are so constituted that we cannot help but understand the characteristics of a living thing as contributing to the well-being of that organism. Likewise, insofar as we are naturally led to consider the world as a single whole, we cannot help but follow Linnaeus and posit teleological explanations, according to which each individual organism contributes to the good of the whole. This is not the sort of appeal to extrinsic teleology that Kant thinks is illegitimate, for here each organism is considered as an integral part of the whole that it benefits; it is not a matter of explaining one organism on the basis of the good that it does to another, totally independent, organism.

IMMANUEL KANT
Lectures on Ethics
TR. LOUIS INFIELD

Duties Toward Animals and Spirits

Baumgarten[1] speaks of duties towards beings which are beneath us and beings which are above us. But so far as animals are concerned, we have no direct duties. Animals are not self-conscious and are there merely as a means to an end. That end is man. We can ask, "Why do animals exist?" But to ask, "Why does man exist?" is a meaningless question.[2] Our duties towards animals are merely indirect duties towards humanity. Animal nature has analogies to human nature, and by doing our duties to animals in respect of manifestations which correspond to manifestations of human nature, we indirectly do our duty towards humanity. Thus, if a dog has served his master long and faithfully, his service, on the analogy of human service, deserves reward, and when the dog has grown too old to serve, his master ought to keep him until he dies. Such action helps to support us in our duties towards human beings, where they are bounden duties. If then any acts of animals are analogous to human acts and spring from the same principles, we have duties towards the animals because thus we cultivate the corresponding duties towards human beings. If a man shoots his dog because the animal is no longer capable of service, he does not fail in his duty to the dog, for the dog cannot judge, but his act is inhuman and damages in himself that humanity which it is his duty to show towards mankind. If he is not to stifle his human feelings, he must practice kindness towards animals, for he who is cruel to animals becomes hard also in his dealings with men. We can judge the heart of a man by his treatment of animals. Hogarth depicts this in his engravings. He shows how cruelty grows and develops. He shows the child's cruelty to animals, pinching the tail of a dog or a cat; he then depicts the grown man in his cart running over a child; and lastly, the culmination of cruelty in murder. He thus brings home to us in a terrible fashion the rewards of cruelty, and this should be an impressive lesson to children. The more we come in contact with animals and observe their behavior, the more we love them, for we see how great is their care for their young.[3] It is then difficult for us to be cruel in thought even to a wolf. Leibniz used a tiny worm for purposes of observation, and then carefully replaced it with its leaf on the tree so that it should not come to harm through any act of his. He would have been sorry—a natural feeling for a humane man—to destroy such a creature for no reason. Tender feelings towards dumb animals develop humane feelings towards mankind. In England butchers and doctors do not sit on a jury because they are accustomed to the sight of death and hardened. Vivisectionists, who use living animals for their experiments, certainly act cruelly, although their aim is praiseworthy, and they can justify their cruelty, since animals must be regarded as man's instruments; but any such cruelty for sport cannot be justified. A master who turns out his ass or his dog because the animal can no longer earn its keep manifests a small mind. The Greeks' ideas in this respect were high-minded, as can be seen from the fable of the ass and the bell of ingratitude. Our duties towards animals, then, are indirect duties towards mankind.

Critique of Judgment
TR. WERNER S. PLUHAR

"On the Dynamically Sublime in Nature"

28. On Nature as a Might
Might is an ability that is superior to great obstacles. It is called *dominance* [*Gewalt*] if it is superior even to the resistance of something that itself possesses might. When in an aesthetic judgment we consider nature as a might that has no dominance over us, then it is *dynamically sublime*.

If we are to judge nature as sublime dynamically, we must present it as arousing fear. (But the reverse does not hold: not every object that arouses fear is found sublime when we judge it aesthetically.) For when we judge something aesthetically (without a concept),[4] the only way we can judge a superiority over obstacles is by the magnitude of the resistance. But whatever we strive to resist is an evil, and it is an object of fear if we find that our ability [to resist it] is no match for it. Hence nature can count as a might, and so as dynamically sublime, for aesthetic judgment only insofar as we consider it as an object of fear.

We can, however, consider an object *fearful* without being afraid *of* it, namely, if we judge it in such a way that we merely *think* of the case where we might possibly want to put up resistance against it, and that any resistance would in that case be utterly futile. Thus a virtuous person fears God without being afraid of him. For he does not think of wanting to resist God and his commandments as a possibility that should worry *him*. But for every such case, which he thinks of as not impossible intrinsically, he recognizes God as fearful.

Just as we cannot pass judgment on the beautiful if we are seized by inclination and appetite, so we cannot pass judgment at all on the sublime in nature if we are afraid. For we flee from the sight of an object that scares us, and it is impossible to like terror that we take seriously. That is why the agreeableness that arises from the cessation of a hardship is gladness. But since this gladness involves our liberation from a danger, it is accompanied by our resolve never to expose us to that danger again. Indeed, we do not even like to think back on that sensation, let alone actively seek out an opportunity for it.

On the other hand, consider boldly, overhanging and, as it was, threatening rocks, thunderclouds piling up in the sky and moving about accompanied by lightning and thunderclaps, volcanoes with all their destructive power, hurricanes with all the devastation they leave behind, the boundless ocean heaved up, the high waterfall of a mighty river, and so on. Compared to the might of any of these, our ability to resist becomes an insignificant trifle. Yet the sight of them becomes all the more attractive the more fearful it is, provided we are in a safe place. And we like to call these objects sublime because they raise the soul's fortitude above its usual middle range and allow us to discover in ourselves an ability to resist which is of a quite different kind, and which gives us the courage [to believe] that we could be a match for nature's seeming omnipotence.

For although we found our own limitation when we considered the immensity of nature and the inadequacy of our ability to adopt a standard proportionate to estimating aesthetically the magnitude of nature's domain, yet we also found, in our power of reason, a different and nonsensible standard that has this infinity itself under it as a unit; and since in contrast to this standard everything in nature is small, we found in our mind a superiority over nature itself in its immensity.[5] In the same way, though the irresistibility of nature's might makes us, considered as natural beings, recognize our physical impotence, it reveals in us at the same time an ability to judge ourselves independent of nature, and reveals in us a superiority over nature that is the basis of a self-preservation quite different in kind from the one that can be assailed and endangered by nature outside us. This keeps the humanity in our person from being degraded, even though a human being would have to succumb to that dominance [of nature]. Hence if in judging nature aesthetically we call it sublime, we do so not because nature arouses fear, but because it calls forth our strength (which does not belong to nature [within us]), to regard as small the [objects] of our [natural] concerns: property, health, and life, and because of this we regard nature's might (to which we are indeed subjected in these [natural] concerns) as yet not having such dominance over us, as persons, that we should have to bow to it if our highest principles were at stake and we had to choose between upholding or abandoning them.[6] Hence nature is here called sublime [*erhaben*] merely because it elevates [*erhebt*] our imagination, [making] it exhibit those cases where the mind can come to feel its own sublimity, which lies in its vocation and elevates it even above nature.

This self-estimation loses nothing from the fact that we must find ourselves safe in order to feel this exciting liking, so that (as it might seem), since the danger is not genuine, the sublimity of our intellectual ability might also not be genuine. For here the liking concerns only our ability's vocation, revealed in such cases, insofar as the predisposition to this ability is part of our nature, whereas it remains up to us, as our obligation, to develop and exercise this ability. And there is truth in this, no matter how conscious of his actual present impotence man may be when he extends his reflection thus far. ...

Hence sublimity is contained not in any thing of nature, but only in our mind, insofar as we can become conscious of our superiority to nature within us, and thereby also to nature outside us (as far as it influences us). Whatever arouses this feeling in us, and this includes the *might* of nature that challenges our forces, is then (although improperly) called sublime. And it is only by presupposing this idea within us, and by referring to it, that we can arrive at the idea of the sublimity of that being who arouses deep respect in us, not just by his might as demonstrated in nature, but even more by the ability, with which we have been endowed, to judge nature without fear and to think of our vocation as being sublimely above nature.

63. On Relative, as Distinguished from Intrinsic, Purposiveness of Nature

Only in one case does experience lead our power of judgment to the concept of a purposiveness that is both objective and material or real, i.e., to the concept of a purpose of nature—namely, when we have to judge a relation of cause to effect which is such that we can see it as law-governed only if we regard the cause's action as based on the idea of the effect, with this idea as the underlying condition under which the cause itself can produce that effect. We can do this in two ways: we may regard the effect either as directly the product of art, or as only the material that other possible natural beings employ in their art; in other words, we may regard the effect either as a purpose, or as a means that other causes employ purposively.[7] The second purposiveness is called either usefulness (for human beings) or benefit (for any other creature), and this second purposiveness is merely relative, whereas the first is an intrinsic purposiveness of the natural being.[8]

For example, rivers carry along all sorts of soil on which plants can grow. Sometimes they deposit it inland, but often also at their mouths. On some coasts the high tide carries this mud over the land, or deposits it along the shore. And if the low tide is kept, above all by people, from carrying the mud off again, then the fertile land expands and the vegetable kingdom takes over where fish and crustaceans used to live. Probably in most cases it is nature itself that extended the land in this way, and is doing so still, even if slowly. Here the question arises whether we should judge this [process] to be a purpose of nature, since it is useful to human beings. (That it is useful for the vegetable kingdom itself does not count, since the sea creatures lose as much as the land gains.)

An example of how certain natural things benefit other creatures as a means (if we presuppose that these creatures are purposes) is the following: There is no better soil for spruces than a sandy soil. Now as the ancient sea withdrew from the land, it left behind so many tracts of sand in these northern regions that this soil, so useless for any cultivation otherwise, enabled extensive spruce forests to establish themselves, for whose unreasonable destruction we often blame our ancestors. And so we may ask: did nature pursue a purpose in depositing these very ancient layers of sand, namely, to make spruce forests possible there? This much is clear: if we assume that the spruce forests are a purpose of nature, then we must also grant that the sand is a purpose, though only a relative one, for which in turn the beach and the withdrawal [of the ancient sea] were the means. For in the series of mutually subordinated links in a connection of purposes, each intermediate link must be regarded as a purpose (though, by the same token, not as a final purpose), and its proximate cause is the means to it. Thus if there were to be cattle, sheep, horses, etc. in the world one day, then grass had to grow on the earth. And alkaline plants [*Salzkraüter*] had to grow in the deserts if camels were to thrive. Again, camels and other herbivorous animals had to abound if there were to be wolves, tigers, and lions. Hence objective purposiveness that is based on benefit is not an objective purposiveness of things themselves; for in that case it would have to be impossible for us to grasp how the sand, considered by itself, could be an effect caused by the sea without our regarding the sea as having acted on a purpose, and without our regarding the sand—its effect—as a work of art. Rather, it is a purposiveness that is merely relative and that the thing to which we attribute this purposiveness has merely contingently; and although, among the examples just mentioned, the various kinds of grass, considered by themselves, must be judged as organized products of nature and hence as artistic, nevertheless in relation to the animals that feed on them they [must] be regarded as mere raw material.

But man, because of the freedom he has in his causality, seems to consider all natural things beneficial: many of them for foolish aims (such as colorful bird feathers to adorn his clothes, or colored earths or plant juices for makeup), but others for reasonable aims, such as horses for riding, oxen and—in Minorca—even donkeys and pigs for plowing. Yet in these cases we cannot even assume a relative purpose of nature (directed to these uses). For man's own reason knows how to make things harmonize with the notions [*Einfälle*] that were his own choice, notions to which even nature did not predestine him. Only *if* we assume that human beings were [meant] to live on the earth, then there had to be at least the means without which they could not subsist as animals, or even as (to however low a degree) rational animals. In that case, however, those natural things that would be indispensable for this would also have to be regarded as natural purposes.

We can easily see from this that extrinsic purposiveness (a thing's being beneficial to others) can be regarded as an extrinsic natural purpose only under the condition that the existence of what it benefits proximately or remotely is a purpose of nature in its own right. This, however, we can never tell by merely examining nature; and hence it follows that, although relative purposiveness points hypothetically to natural purposes, it does not justify any absolute teleological judgment.

In cold lands, snow protects crops from the frost. It makes it easier for people to get together (by means of sleighs). In Lapland, the people find animals (reindeer) that they use to get together. These animals find adequate nourishment in a dry moss that they have to scrape out for themselves from under the snow. But they are also easily tamed, and willingly permit people to deprive them of their freedom even though they could easily support themselves on their own. For other peoples in the same frigid zone, the sea holds rich supplies of animals that provide them not only with food and clothing, and with timber that the sea floats to them, as it were, as building material for their homes, but also with fuel for heating their huts. So here we have an admirable collection of cases where nature relates to a purpose; that purpose is the Greenlander, the Lapp, the Samoyed, the Yakut, etc. And yet it is not clear why people should have to live in those regions at all. Therefore it would be hazardous and arbitrary indeed if we judged that vapors fall from the air as snow, that currents in the sea bring timber grown in warmer lands, and that large marine animals replete with oil are there *because* the cause providing all these natural products acts on the idea of an advantage for certain wretched creatures. For even if there were none of that natural utility, we would find that natural causes are fully adequate to make [things] come out this way; rather, we ourselves would then consider it impudent and rash even to demand that there be such a predisposition and to require nature to pursue such a purpose (on the ground that otherwise only people's extreme inability to get along with one another could have scattered them all the way to such inhospitable regions).

66. On the Principle for Judging Intrinsic Purposiveness in Organized Beings

This principle, which is also the definition of organized beings, is: *An organized product of nature is one in which everything is a purpose and reciprocally also a means.* In such a product nothing is gratuitous, purposeless, or to be attributed to a blind natural mechanism.

Now in a way this principle must be derived from experience: experience must prompt us to [adopt] it, namely, the kind of experience in which we engage methodically and which we call observation. But because of the universality and necessity which that principle claims [*aussagen*] for such purposiveness, it cannot rest merely on empirical bases but must be based on some a priori principle, even if this principle turns out to be merely regulative and those purposes turn out to reside merely in the idea of the judging person and in no efficient cause. Hence we may call the above principle a *maxim* for judging the intrinsic purposiveness of organized beings.[9]

It is a familiar fact that those who dissect plants and animals in order to investigate their structure and gain insight into the reasons why and to what end these plants and animals were given those very parts, their position and combination, and were given precisely that internal form assume this maxim as inescapably necessary—i.e., the maxim that nothing in such a creature is *gratuitous*. They appeal to it just as they appeal to the principle of universal natural science—viz., that *nothing* happens by *chance*.[10] Indeed, they can no more give up that teleological principle than they can this universal physical principle. For just as abandoning this physical principle would leave them without any experience whatsoever, so would abandoning that teleological principle leave them without anything for guidance in observing the kind of natural things that have once been thought teleologically, under the concept of natural purposes.

For the concept of natural purposes leads reason into an order of things that is wholly different from that of a mere natural mechanism, which we no longer find adequate when we deal with such natural products. And hence the possibility of such a product is to be based on an idea.[11] But an idea is an absolute unity of presentation, whereas matter is a plurality of things that cannot itself supply a determinate unity for its combination. Therefore if the unity of the idea is to serve as the very basis that determines a priori a natural law of the causality [responsible] for a product with such a form in its combination, then the purpose [the idea] of nature has to be extended to *everything* that is in this product of nature. For once we take such an effect *as a whole* beyond the blind mechanism of nature and refer it to a supersensible basis as determining it, then we must also judge this effect wholly in terms of that principle. There would be no basis for assuming that the form of such a thing still depends in part on blind mechanism, since we would then be mixing heterogeneous principles and hence be left without any safe rule by which to judge.[12]

Now it is entirely possible that some parts in (say) an animal body (such as skin, bone, or hair) could be grasped as accumulations governed by merely mechanical laws. Still the cause that procures the appropriate matter, that modifies and forms it in that way, and that deposits it in the pertinent locations must always be judged teleologically. Hence everything in such a body must be regarded as organized; and everything, in a certain relation to the thing itself, is also an organ in turn.

67. On the Principle by Which We Teleologically Judge Nature in General as a System of Purposes

We said above that *extrinsic* purposiveness of natural things does not give us adequate justification for also considering them to be purposes of nature so as to explain their existence, and for treating—in thought—their contingently purposive effects as the bases [responsible] for their existence in terms of the principle of final causes. For example, though *rivers* further communication among peoples who live inland, that does not yet entitle us to regard them as natural purposes; nor may we so regard *mountains* because they contain the sources of these rivers and the supply of snow required to sustain them during rainless periods; nor again the *slope* of the land, which carries that water away and allows the land to dry. For although these features of the earth's surface were very necessary in order that the vegetable and animal kingdoms could arise and be sustained, still there is nothing about these features that forces us to assume a causality in terms of purposes so as to account for their possibility. The same holds for plants that man employs for his needs or his enjoyment; it also holds for animals, such as camels, cattle, horses, dogs, etc., for which man has such varied uses, sometimes as food and sometimes to do work for him, that for the most part he finds them quite indispensable. If things are such that we have no cause to regard any of them as itself a purpose, then the extrinsic relation between them can be judged purposive only hypothetically.

Judging a thing to be a natural purpose on account of its intrinsic form is some-thing quite different from considering the existence of that thing to be a purpose of [i.e., pursued by] nature. To make the latter assertion we would need more than the concept of a possible purpose; we would have to cognize the final purpose (*scopus*) of nature. To do that, we would have to refer nature to something supersensible, for the purpose of the existence of nature itself must be sought beyond nature; and yet refer-ring nature to something supersensible far surpasses all our teleological cognition of nature. The internal form of a mere blade of grass suffices to prove to our human judging ability that the blade can have originated only under the rule of purposes. But we arrive at no categorical [but only at a hypothetical] purpose[13] if we disregard the internal form and organization, and consider instead extrinsic purposive relations as to what use other natural beings make of the grass: how cattle need grass, and how people need cattle as a means for their existence. We cannot arrive at a categorical purpose in this way because, after all, we cannot see why people should have to exist (a question it might not be so easy to answer if we have in mind, say, the New Hollanders or the Fuegians); rather, each such purposive relation rests on a condition that we have to keep putting off: this condition (namely, the existence of a thing as a final purpose) is unconditioned and hence lies wholly outside a physicoteleological consideration of the world. But such a thing is also not a natural purpose, since it (or its entire species) is not to be regarded as a natural product.

Hence only as far as matter is organized does it necessarily carry with it the concept of it as a natural purpose, because the specific [purposive] form it has is at the same time a product of nature. But this concept of a natural purpose leads us necessarily to the idea of all of nature as a system in terms of the rule of purposes, and we must subordinate all mechanism of nature to this idea according to principles of reason (at least in order to test nature's appearance against this idea). The principle of reason applies to this idea only subjectively, namely, as this maxim: Everything in the world is good for something or other; nothing in it is gratuitous; and the example that nature offers us in its organic products justifies us, indeed calls upon us, to expect nothing from it and its laws except what is purposive [in relation] to the whole.[14]

It goes without saying that this principle [for judging nature teleologically] holds only for reflective but not for determinative judgment, that it is regulative and not constitutive.[15] It only serves us as a guide that allows us to consider natural things in terms of a new law-governed order by referring them to an already given basis [a purpose] as that which determines them. Thus we expand natural science [*Naturkunde*] in terms of a different principle, that of final causes, yet without detracting from the principle of mechanism in the causality of nature. That is all the principle does; it does not in any way allow us to decide whether anything we judge in terms of it is an *intentional* purpose of nature: whether grass is there for cattle or sheep, and these and all other natural things are there for man. It is helpful to consider from this point of view even things that we find disagreeable and contrapurposive in particular respects. For example, we might say that the vermin that plague people in their clothes, hair, or beds are there by a wise provision of nature, namely, as an incentive to keep clean, which even by itself is an important means for preserving our health. Or we might say that the mosquitoes and other stinging insects that make the wilderness areas of America so troublesome for the savages are so many prods to stir these primitive people to action, such as draining the marshes and clearing the dense forests that inhibit the flow of air, so that in this way, as well as by tilling the soil, they will also make the place where they live healthier. There are features in man's internal organization that seem to us to be contrary to nature; but even these, if dealt with in this manner, provide an entertaining and sometimes also instructive outlook into a teleological order of things to which we would not be led if we used no such principle as this but considered them merely in physical terms. Some say that when people or animals have a tapeworm, they were given it to compensate, as it were, for some deficiency in their vital organs. I would ask, similarly, whether dreams (there is no sleep without dreams, even though we rarely remember them) might not be a purposive arrangement made by nature. For when all the motive forces of the bodily kind relax, dreams serve to thoroughly agitate the vital organs by means of imagination and its great activity (which in dreams usually reaches the level of an affect). Imagination frequently does the same when we have gone to sleep with an overloaded stomach; we then need this agitation all the more, and the imagination's play is all the more lively. Therefore if no such force moved us inwardly and made us restless and tired, for which we then blame the dreams (though in fact these consequences of them may be conducive to our health), sleep would even in a healthy person probably be a complete extinction of life.

Moreover, once nature has been judged teleologically, and the natural purposes that we find in organized beings have entitled us to the idea of a vast system of purposes of nature, then even beauty in nature, i.e., nature's harmony with the free play of our cognitive powers as we apprehend and judge its appearance,[16] can similarly be considered an objective purposiveness, namely, of the whole of nature [regarded] as a system that includes man as a member. We may regard nature as having held us in favor when it distributed not only useful things but a wealth of beauty and charms as well; and we may love it for this, just as its immensity may lead us to contemplate it with respect and to feel that we ourselves are ennobled in this contemplation—just as if nature had erected and decorated its splendid stage quite expressly with that aim.

The only point I want to make in this section is this: that once we have discovered that nature is able to make products that can be thought of only in terms of the concept of final causes, we are then entitled to go further; we may thereupon judge products as belonging to a system of purposes even if they (or the relation between them, though [perhaps] purposive) do not require us, [so as to account] for their possibility, to look for a different principle beyond the mechanism of blind efficient causes. For the idea of nature as a system of nature already leads us, as concerns its basis, beyond the world of sense, so that the unity of the supersensible principle must be considered valid not merely for certain species of natural beings, but just as much for the whole of nature as a system.

Notes

1 The present selection is from lectures delivered relatively early in Kant's career, before he had written his major ethical treatises. Kant was required to teach from a textbook; he chose texts by Alexander Baumgarten, an author otherwise little remembered today. Kant mentions Baumgarten's chapter headings, and then immediately proceeds to develop his own thoughts on the matter.

2 Kant takes reason to be an end in itself. The goal of human life is rationality, which is precisely what is constitutive of humanity.

3   For Kant, morality is a matter of rational choice. A feeling, even one of compassion or pity, has no moral worth in and of itself, as it does not involve the exercise of rational choice. Nonetheless, we ought to encourage certain feelings (such as compassion), for when people experience them they are more likely to act in accordance with the moral law laid down by reason.

4   Kant is exploring the various *aesthetic* ways of regarding the natural world. He here clarifies what it is to regard the world aesthetically: one is not engaged in the intellectual act of classifying the object to which one attends; rather, the object is given to our experience before this occurs, and our minds can have certain responses to it even on this level. Such responses are aesthetic.

5   This is an allusion to Kant's ethical theory. According to Kant, the "sensible" world of physical objects within our experience *must* be experienced in such a way that every event is necessitated by some cause. This is not true for reason itself, however, which is always free to choose to act rightly or to choose not to do so. There are no limits to its freedom in this regard; it is infinite.

6   For Kant, a truly moral action is never done merely to satisfy some material need. It is always done because it is the right thing to do. Hence, in Kant's view, the indirect experience of the immense power of nature allows us to recognize that within all of us there is reason, which always freely wills that we should do what is right, regardless of any danger this power should pose. Ultimately, then, this sort of aesthetic appreciation of nature (the experience of the "sublime") is an appreciation of ourselves, as rational beings.

7   Kant is here distinguishing varieties of teleology. In a teleological judgment, an effect is seen to have been caused by virtue of something having some purpose. Either the effect is itself the purpose to be attained, or it is only a means for attaining some purpose that lies beyond it.

8   Kant is about to present an argument that human reason is on shaky ground in appealing to relative, or extrinsic, teleology in its explanations of the natural world.

9   In contrast to relative or extrinsic teleology, human reason legitimately attributes intrinsic teleology to natural beings. As in Aristotelian biology, each part of an organism is for the sake of the flourishing of the whole. Kant adds that the whole is, in a sense, for the sake of the good of each of the parts. For Kant, biological research provides much evidence of this sort of teleology. But its basis is even deeper: the human mind is so structured that it *must* regard natural organisms that it experiences as organized according to a principle of intrinsic teleology.

10   This is an allusion to the principle, mentioned in n. 5, above, that the physical world must be regarded as having each of its events necessitated by some other event, which causes it. Kant argues that the principle of intrinsic teleology is just as binding on human reason as the principle that every physical event is necessitated by a cause.

11   For Kant, an "idea" is a mental entity that the mind employs to make sense of an object of experience, but is not itself the concept by virtue of which an object is to be classified. A dog is explained by virtue of the idea of intrinsic teleology. But the dog is not itself understood as an intrinsic teleology; it is understood as a dog.

12   Human reason is on safe ground in assuming that any particular physical event is necessitated by some other particular physical event. But it cannot extend this line of thinking

to the whole of the natural world, for the whole and the part are "heterogenous" (of different kinds). (A particular physical thing is "sensible," for it can be sensed. But the whole is "supersensible"; as such, it cannot be sensed.) Hence the principle that all nature is organized teleologically is not inconsistent with the principle that each particular natural event is necessitated by the sorts of physical interactions explainable by modern physics.

13 A categorical purpose is one that holds categorically, that is, without exceptions or qualifications.

14 We may find it useful to hold that everything in the natural world is of some benefit to us (or other things), but this principle has no objective basis in our experience of the world.

15 I.e., the principle of intrinsic teleology is the basis on which biologists are convinced that further research will reveal the teleology behind every feature of a living organism. As such, it regulates the course of further research. But these teleological relations are not directly given to the human mind by the world as first experienced. They do not constitute the concept of the object itself.

16 Kant takes the beauty of an object to be a matter of the free play of reason that comes about by virtue of the experience of that object. This account holds in regard to the experience of beauty in both works of art and in natural objects.

CHAPTER 18

T.R. Malthus

Dᴜʀɪɴɢ ᴛʜᴇ time of the English economist T. R. Malthus (1766–1834), there was a great surge in the sort of political thought that has become known as "liberal": espousing the view that social institutions can and should be changed to allow all citizens, including the poor, to have the liberty to achieve their own happiness. In the first edition of his *An Essay on Population as It Affects the Future Improvement of Society* (1798) Malthus argued against well-meaning liberal policies, on the grounds that poverty and hunger were inevitable parts of the human condition. His argument was that population, which increases geometrically (being multiplied by a certain number, *y*, at certain intervals, that is, every *x* years), will always far outstrip advances in food production, which, at best, can increase at a linear rate (having a certain amount, *z*, added to itself every *x* years).

Malthus was roundly criticized as being hard-hearted and cruel. In response, he espoused a less harsh position in later editions of the *Essay*. The poor can have a better life, he subsequently wrote, but it is up to them to improve it. They need to practice "moral restraint," refraining from sexual activity until they are economically self-sufficient and fairly advanced in their child-bearing years.

Malthus's predictions concerning widespread hunger in Europe did not come true, thanks to unforeseen advances in agricultural productivity. Nonetheless, he remains a highly influential figure in environmental circles. He was the first to draw attention to the problem of overpopulation, and advanced the notion of limits to growth. Those who today argue that the human species is fast approaching the ceiling of Earth's "carrying capacity" are often called neo-Malthusians.

T.R. MALTHUS
An Essay on Population as It Affects the Future Improvement of Society, 1st edition (1798), Ch. 1

I have read some of the speculations on the perfectibility of man and of society with great pleasure. I have been warmed and delighted with the enchanting picture which they hold forth. I ardently wish for such happy improvements. But I see great, and, to my understanding, unconquerable difficulties in the way to them. These difficulties it is my present purpose to state, declaring, at the same time, that so far from exulting in them, as a cause of triumph over the friends of innovation, nothing would give me greater pleasure than to see them completely removed ...

I think I may fairly make two postulata.

First, That food is necessary to the existence of man.

Secondly, That the passion between the sexes is necessary and will remain nearly in its present state.

These two laws, ever since we have had any knowledge of mankind, appear to have been fixed laws of our nature, and, as we have not hitherto seen any alteration in them, we have no right to conclude that they will ever cease to be what they now are, without an immediate act of power in that Being who first arranged the system of the universe, and for the advantage of his creatures, still executes, according to fixed laws, all its various operations.

I do not know that any writer has supposed that on this earth man will ultimately be able to live without food. But Mr. Godwin[1] has conjectured that the passion between the sexes may in time be extinguished. As, however, he calls this part of his work a deviation into the land of conjecture, I will not dwell longer upon it at present than to say that the best arguments for the perfectibility of man are drawn from a contemplation of the great progress that he has already made from the savage state and the difficulty of saying where he is to stop. But towards the extinction of the passion between the sexes, no progress whatever has hitherto been made. It appears to exist in as much force at present as it did two thousand or four thousand years ago. There are individual exceptions now as there always have been. But, as these exceptions do not appear to increase in number, it would surely be a very unphilosophical mode of arguing to infer, merely from the existence of an exception, that the exception would, in time, become the rule, and the rule the exception.

Assuming then my postulata as granted, I say, that the power of population is indefinitely greater than the power in the earth to produce subsistence for man.

Population, when unchecked, increases in a geometrical ratio. Subsistence increases only in an arithmetical ratio. A slight acquaintance with numbers will shew the immensity of the first power in comparison of the second.[2]

By that law of our nature which makes food necessary to the life of man, the effects of these two unequal powers must be kept equal.

This implies a strong and constantly operating check on population from the difficulty of subsistence. This difficulty must fall somewhere and must necessarily be severely felt by a large portion of mankind.

Through the animal and vegetable kingdoms, nature has scattered the seeds of life abroad with the most profuse and liberal hand. She has been comparatively sparing in the room and the nourishment necessary to rear them. The germs of existence contained in this spot of earth, with ample food, and ample room to expand in, would fill millions of worlds in the course of a few thousand years. Necessity, that imperious all pervading law of nature, restrains them within the prescribed bounds. The race of plants and the race of animals shrink under this great restrictive law. And the race of man cannot, by any efforts of reason, escape from it. Among plants and animals its effects are waste of seed, sickness, and premature death. Among mankind, misery and vice. The former, misery, is an absolutely necessary consequence of it. Vice is a highly probable consequence, and we therefore see it abundantly prevail, but it ought not, perhaps, to be called an absolutely necessary consequence. The ordeal of virtue is to resist all temptation to evil.

This natural inequality of the two powers of population and of production in the earth, and that great law of our nature which must constantly keep their effects equal, form the great difficulty that to me appears insurmountable in the way to the perfectibility of society. All other arguments are of slight and subordinate consideration in comparison of this. I see no way by which man can escape from the weight of this law which pervades all animated nature. No fancied equality, no agrarian regulations in their utmost extent, could remove the pressure of it even for a single century. And it appears, therefore, to be decisive against the possible existence of a society, all the members of which should live in ease, happiness, and comparative leisure; and feel no anxiety about providing the means of subsistence for themselves and families.

Consequently, if the premises are just, the argument is conclusive against the perfectibility of the mass of mankind.

Notes

1   William Godwin (1756–1836) was a minister and anarchistic communist political thinker; he is among the liberal thinkers to whom Malthus is addressing his argument. One of Godwin's responses to Malthus is reprinted in the present volume.

2   Malthus gives an example in the second chapter of the first edition: "... let us take the whole earth, instead of one spot, and suppose that the restraints to population were universally removed. If the subsistence for man that the earth affords was to be increased every twenty-five years by a quantity equal to what the whole world at present produces, this would allow the power of production in the earth to be absolutely unlimited, and its ratio of increase much greater than we can conceive that any possible exertions of mankind could make it.

   "Taking the population of the world at any number, a thousand millions, for instance, the human species would increase in the ratio of — 1, 2, 4, 8, 16, 32, 64, 128, 256, 512, etc. and subsistence as — 1, 2, 3, 4, 5, 6, 7, 8, 9, 10, etc. In two centuries and a quarter, the population would be to the means of subsistence as 512 to 10: in three centuries as 4096 to 13, and in two thousand years the difference would be almost incalculable, though the produce in that time would have increased to an immense extent.

   "No limits whatever are placed to the productions of the earth; they may increase for ever and be greater than any assignable quantity, yet still the power of population being a power of a superior order, the increase of the human species can only be kept commensurate to the increase of the means of subsistence by the constant operation of the strong law of necessity acting as a check upon the greater power."

CHAPTER 19

William Godwin

Though he is now seldom read, William Godwin (1756–1836) was one of the foremost English writers of his day. (He was also the husband of the early feminist Mary Wollstonecraft and the father of Mary Shelley, author of *Frankenstein.*) He wrote novels, economic treatises, and works in political philosophy. Godwin was convinced that a rationally organized system of education could provide sufficient moral training to render unnecessary centralized laws and the institutions of private property and the family. Malthus's warnings that disease and famine are inevitable were expressly directed against Godwin's cheery predictions of an anarchist utopia. Many readers were convinced by Malthus's arguments, so Godwin wrote *On Population* in response.

In this work Godwin makes the following major points: (1) Malthus did not adequately demonstrate, on the basis of existing evidence, that unchecked population does indeed increase geometrically. (2) Even if Malthus were right about this point, and even given the current state of agriculture, the earth could support a greater human population, and hence the need to worry is far off. (3) A greater population is to be welcomed, as human beings are good, and improve the earth. (4) It is likely that technological innovations will more than allow the food supply to keep up with population growth.

In recent years, Godwin's arguments have been echoed by those (such as Julian Simon and some representatives of the Catholic Church) who dismiss warnings that the earth is nearing its capacity for sustaining current levels of human life and consumption.

WILLIAM GODWIN
On Population

I am desirous, on the present occasion, of shutting out every thing conjectural, and which therefore by a certain class of reasoners might be called visionary. One practical way of looking at the subject is this. The habitable parts of the globe are computed to occupy a space of thirty-nine millions of square miles, and its human inhabitants to amount to six hundred millions. Of this surface China is said to constitute 1,300,000 square miles. Now, let us admit the present population of China to stand at three hundred millions of souls. How fully China is cultivated I do not know; but I have as little doubt as Mr. Malthus appears to have, that the soil of that empire might be made greatly more effective for the purposes of human subsistence, than it is at present.[1] But let us assume, for the sake of argument, the cultivation of

China for the standard of possible cultivation, and consequently its population for the standard of possible population. The earth then, if all its habitable parts could be made as fertile as China, is equal to the sustaining of a population of nine thousand millions of human beings.[2] In other words, wherever one human being is now found in existence, the earth is capable, not in theory only, and according to conceived improvements no where yet realised, but judging from approved facts, instead of that one, of subsisting fifteen.

The majority of men seem to have laboured under some deception as to the population of China. It is principally in the vast extent of an empire said to be everywhere so flourishing, that China is worthy of admiration. Taking from Pinkerton the dimensions of China on the one hand, and of England and Wales on the other, I find that, if the latter were as well stocked with citizens as the former, it would contain 13,461,923 inhabitants, that is about three millions beyond the returns to the population-act of 1811. Now it has been admitted by the most phlegmatic enquirers, that England and Wales might easily be made to maintain double their present number of inhabitants. Of course such enquirers proceed on the assumption, that there are tracts incapable of being profitably applied to the purposes of human subsistence. By parity of reason therefore the soil of China itself is very far from being turned to all the profit of which it is susceptible, for the subsistence of the human species.

The latter end of Mr. Malthus's system is of a character extremely discordant with the beginning. The author of the Essay on Population has been understood as proceeding upon the impression, that the surface of the earth was limited, containing only so many square miles, but that the power of population, upon the assumption of his geometrical ratio, was unlimited, and that the greater was at any time the actual number of human beings, the greater would be the power of increase.

I cannot but think that the first contemplation that would have suggested itself to an enlightened philanthropist, proceeding on these premises, would have been something like the following.

Man is an admirable creature, the beauty of the world, which, if he did not exist in it, would be "a habitation of dragons, and a court for owls; the wild beast of the desert would cry to the wild beast of the islands; baboons would dance there; and its pleasant places be filled with all doleful creatures."[3] How delightful a speculation then is it, that man is endowed by all-bountiful nature with an unlimited power of multiplying his species! I would look out upon the cheerless and melancholy world which has just been described, and imagine it all cultivated, all improved, all variegated with a multitude of human beings, in a state of illumination, of innocence, and of active benevolence, to which the progress of thought, and the enlargement of mind seem naturally to lead, beyond anything that has yet any where been realized. I would count up the acres and the square miles of the surface of the earth, and consider them all as the estate in fee simple of the human intellect. I would extend my view from China and England, countries already moderately, and but moderately peopled, to the plains of North America, of South America, of Africa, of many tracts of Asia, of the north of Europe, of Spain, and various other divisions of the prolific world. I should contemplate with delight the extensive emigrations that have taken place to North America,[4] and plan and chalk out, as far as my capacity and endowments of study would permit me, similar emigrations to other parts of the world, that should finally make the whole earth at least as populous as China is at present. ...

It is with some diffidence that I would enter upon the theoretical part of the question, and enquire how far the earth may be rendered more productive to the purposes of human subsistence than it is at present. This branch of the subject however would be left imperfect, if that consideration were wholly omitted.

To the improvements of man, more particularly in art, and the application of human industry, there is no end. No sooner therefore shall we have got rid of the geometrical ratio, and the still more absurd doctrine (if indeed there are any degrees between these) of "population necessarily and constantly pressing hard against the limits of subsistence, from the present moment to the time when the whole earth shall be cultivated like a garden," than our prospects will grow very cheering indeed. ...[5]

There is however one other circumstance that requires to be mentioned, before the subject can properly be considered as exhausted. Of all the sciences, natural or mechanical, which within the last half century have proceeded with such gigantic strides, chemistry is that which has advanced the most rapidly. All the substances that nature presents, all that proceeds from earth or air, is analyzed by us into its original elements. Thus we have discovered, or may discover, precisely what it is that nourishes the human body. And it is surely no great stretch of the faculty of anticipation to say that whatever man can decompose, man will be able to compound. The food that nourishes us, is composed of certain elements; and wherever these elements can be found, human art will hereafter discover the power of reducing them into a state capable of affording corporeal sustenance. No good reason can be assigned, why that which produces animal nourishment, must have previously passed through a process of animal or vegetable life. And, if a certain infusion of attractive exterior qualities is held necessary to allure us to our food, there is no reason to suppose that the most agreeable colors and scents and flavors may not be imparted to it, at a very small expense of vegetable substance. Thus it appears that, wherever earth, and water, and the other original chemical substances may be found, there human art may hereafter produce nourishment: and thus we are presented with a real infinite series of increase of the means of subsistence, to match Mr. Malthus's geometrical ratio for the multiplication of mankind.—This may be thought too speculative; but surely it is not more so, than Mr. Malthus's period, when the globe of earth, or, as he has since told us, the solar system, and all the "other planets circling other suns," shall be overcrowded with the multitude of their human inhabitants.

Notes

1 [Godwin's note] It has already been mentioned that there are large forests within the boundaries of China ...

2 The current human population is around five and a half billion, a bit greater than half of Godwin's proposal for the earth's carrying capacity. The World Bank predicts that human population will reach nine billion before 2050.

3 This is a translation of Isaiah 34.14.

4 [Godwin's note] Emigration becomes a less pleasing object, in proportion as we are induced to doubt of the increase of the numbers of mankind; and however agreeable it may prove to the country (North America for example) by which the emigrants are received, it would be sedulously counteracted by all means of benevolent and parental treatment in the enlightened statesmen of the country from which they proceeded.

5 In the section that has been omitted here, Godwin makes two major suggestions concerning how food production is to be increased. First, agriculture is to be decentralized; crops are to be raised on gardens, rather than in fields. Second, there is to be a greater dependence on food from the sea. Godwin's next suggestion is that it may soon be technologically feasible to synthesize all the food that is required.

CHAPTER 20

Priscilla Wakefield

WE HAVE SEEN that, in opposition to Plato, Aristotle argued that there is a fundamental distinction between human beings and the other animals; only the former are able to reason. Supported by certain interpretations of Genesis, Aristotle's point of view remained dominant until the time of Darwin, who argued for a fundamental continuity between human nature and that of the other primates.

One dissenting voice preceding Darwin's belonged to Priscilla Wakefield (1751–1832), a prominent English Quaker and author of edifying popular science books for the young. Her *An Introduction to Botany, in a Series of Familiar Letters* (1796) was the first introductory botany book written by a woman. Essentially an exposition of Linnaean botany, this work, along with numerous others authored by Wakefield, was also intended to improve the physical and moral health of older children and adolescents, especially girls.

Wakefield advocated the study of natural history to instill a sense of reverence and awe for God's work. This was one reason for the writing of *Instinct Displayed in a Collection of Well-Authenticated Facts*, in which evidence is provided for the substantial cognitive abilities of various animals. Another was to provide evidence that animals merit human kindness.

In the Preface to *Instinct Displayed,* excerpted here, Wakefield anticipates Darwin in suggesting that there are no sharp lines of division between basic natural kinds. There is no clear distinction, she maintains, between rational action and instinctive response. Such a view leads to a demotion of the privileged status of human beings, and an elevation of the status of other animals.

PRISCILLA WAKEFIELD

Instinct Displayed in a Collection of Well-Authenticated Facts, Exemplifying the Extraordinary Sagacity of Various Species of the Animal Creation

Preface

The distinctions between reason and instinct are difficult to ascertain: to define their exact limits has exercised the ingenuity of the most profound philosophers, hitherto without success. Nor can the learned agree as to the nature of that wonderful quality that guides every creature to take the best means of procuring its own enjoyment, and of preserving its species by the most admirable care of its progeny. Some degrade this hidden impulse to a mere mechanical operation;[1] while others exalt it to a level with reason; that proud prerogative of man.[2] There are, indeed, innumerable grada-tions of intelligence, as of the other qualities with which the animal kingdom is en-dowed, in like manner as the different orders of beings approach each other so closely, and are so curiously united by links, partaking of the nature of those above and those below, that it requires a discerning eye to know what rank to assign them. Thus, quadrupeds and birds are assimilated to each other by the bat: the inhabitants of the waters to those of the land, by amphibious animals; animals to vegetables, by the leaf insect, and by plants that appear to have sensation; and animate to inanimate, by the oyster, the moluscæ, and sea anemones.

Reason and instinct have obvious differences; yet the most intelligent animals, in some of their actions, approach so near to reason, that it is really surprising how small the distinction is. The great and most striking superiority of reason seems to consist in these two points: the capacity of knowing and acknowledging our Creator, and of rendering its owner responsible for his conduct. Without investigating further the metaphysical distinctions of reason and instinct, to which I am quite incompe-tent, I will proceed to make some apology for the following work.

The harmonious beauty of creation, and the interesting objects it presents, have been my delight from childhood; and the enjoyments, as well as the advantages, I have received from this taste, have made me desirous of communicating to others, by relating a few *well-authenticated facts* of the exact coincidence of the instinctive pow-ers with the necessities of the animal. My friends, aware of my intention, increased the stock of my materials by several curious communications, which I thought more likely to arrest the attention of the young, when combined in the form of letters, than a long string of detached anecdotes, following each other like horses in a team.

My motive has been to excite attention to the propensities of animals, as a pow-erful antidote to treating them with cruelty or neglect, so often practised by the igno-rant and thoughtless from inconsideration. Who can observe, without admiring them! Who can admire, without adoring that Power that has so eminently displayed his wisdom and goodness, in the endowments of every inhabitant of this globe, from man to the most minute insects that our microscopes discover!—each created for a certain portion of enjoyment, adapted to its nature; with organs and dispositions so exactly fitted to procure this peculiar enjoyment, that none can doubt its being the work of an all-powerful, infinitely wise, and benevolent Being.

Notes

1 Wakefield has in mind Descartes and his followers.

2 It is possible that Wakefield has Platonists like Porphyry in mind. More likely she is thinking of *The Apology for Raymond Sebond* of Michel Eyquem de Montaigne (1533–1592), who, to support his claim that theoretical knowledge is impossible, presented a number of arguments against the alleged superiority of human beings.

CHAPTER 21

Charles Darwin

UNTIL THE nineteenth century, there was no clear distinction between philosophy and the sciences. Scientists generally saw themselves as pursuing the truth about reality in general, and took pains to relate their work to broader issues of the nature of knowledge and reality.

This approach is clearly reflected in the writings of the English naturalist Charles Darwin (1809–1882), whose account of biological evolution directly addresses earlier philosophical accounts of the nature of living things and the species to which they belong.

Insofar as Darwin's work constituted a direct challenge to a biology that had been grounded on Aristotelian and theological presuppositions, its general acceptance by the intellectual world had an enormous and far-reaching effect on later philosophy, including current environmental philosophy.

For some time before Darwin, the discovery of fossils of extinct species had challenged the Aristotelian idea of species as stable kinds, whose essence is conveyed unchanged from generation to generation. The fossil evidence also indicated that species gradually changed in a way that made them better adapted to changes in their environment. What was missing was a theory that could explain how such changes could occur. For if the parents impart the form to the children, and this form includes the essential characteristics of a kind, how could this kind ever be altered by new circumstances? Could the endeavor to adjust to new circumstances change the bodily form of the individual organism, and thereby change the form that is conveyed to the next generation? This view, proposed by the Frenchman Chevalier de Lamarck (1744–1829), could not be confirmed by biological research.

Darwin's solution, in brief, was that the characteristics that biological organisms impart to their young are never exactly the ones that they themselves possess. Rather, all of the characteristics are subject to variation. The few organisms that possess a beneficial variation will be those that are the most successful in reaching reproductive maturity; their offspring, in turn, will be more successful in reaching maturity and propagating than other organisms of the same kind that do not have the new characteristic. Eventually, one finds in regions with similar conditions only those organisms of that kind that have the new characteristic. The species has evolved.

Some of the ramifications of Darwin's thought that are relevant to environmental philosophy include the following:

1. Darwin realized that a species can be truly understood only within a more general context of geographic features and living things. Darwin saw that be-

cause each individual species is adapted to the entire network of living things around it, this network, of which these living things are constituents, is a kind of self-regulating whole. So Darwin came very close to the notion of an eco-system, a key concept in current environmental philosophy. As we have seen, Linnaeus had already drawn attention to "the economy of nature," according to which living things and the main features of their environment are all dependent on each other. But for Linnaeus, this is an eternal, unexplained feature of God's providence; Darwin explains the mechanism by which such interdependence comes about. Further, Darwin, unlike Linnaeus, recognizes that any given system of biological interdependence is fragile, and can be disrupted.

2. Darwin's theory portrays the world as a ruthless battleground in which organisms are competing for a niche in which they can survive and propagate; most are unsuccessful. Evolution is based on massive amounts of death and frustration. The evolutionary process, in which certain less well-adapted kinds of organisms are weeded out, has become known as "the survival of the fittest," a phrase Darwin borrowed from the English philosopher Herbert Spencer.

3. Darwin's explanation of why living beings are organized as they are makes no appeal to teleology, whether internal, as for Aristotle and Kant, or external, as for the Stoics.

4. Darwin's theory constitutes a deep challenge to the traditional view of hierarchies of life forms. Because the process of human evolution can be accounted for along the same lines as can the evolution of any other organism, it is hard to see how human beings can be ranked above all other living beings, as they were by the Stoics and in philosophical accounts influenced by the Stoics and by Biblical teachings. Darwin replaced traditional hierarchical images with the notion of life forms being like the branches of a tree, each equally and adequately suited to its own niche. He argues against the view that to understand humans as descended from apes entails lessening our regard for human worth.

5. Darwin did not take the natural world to be without inherent value. For Darwin, what is to be valued in nature is not a certain activity performed by a certain kind of organism (such as, for example, reasoning, performed by human beings) but the goodness and richness of the whole biotic realm. The notion that the diversity and richness of a system is a good unto itself, fundamental to numerous contemporary environmental philosophies, is foreshadowed in Darwin's work.

CHARLES DARWIN
On the Origin of Species

Chapter 4: Natural Selection; or the Survival of the Fittest

How will the struggle for existence, briefly discussed in the last chapter, act in regard to variation? Can the principle of selection, which we have seen is so potent in the hands of man, apply under nature? I think we shall see that it can act most efficiently. ... Can it ... be thought improbable, seeing that variations useful to man have undoubtedly occurred, that other variations useful in some way to each being in the great and complex battle of life, should occur in the course of many successive generations? If such do occur, can we doubt (remembering that many more individuals are born than can possibly survive) that individuals having any advantage, however slight, over others, would have the best chance of surviving and of procreating their kind? On the other hand, we may feel sure that any variation in the least degree injurious would be rigidly destroyed. This preservation of favourable individual differences and variations, and the destruction of those which are injurious, I have called Natural Selection, or the Survival of the Fittest. Variations neither useful nor injurious would not be affected by natural selection, and would be left either a fluctuating element, as perhaps we see in certain polymorphic species, or would ultimately become fixed, owing to the nature of the organism and the nature of the conditions.[1]

Several writers have misapprehended or objected to the term Natural Selection. Some have even imagined that natural selection induces variability, whereas it implies only the preservation of such variations as arise and are beneficial to the being under its conditions of life. No one objects to agriculturists speaking of the potent effects of man's selection; and in this case the individual differences given by nature, which man for some object selects, must of necessity first occur. Others have objected that the term selection implies conscious choice in the animals which become modified; and it has even been urged that, as plants have no volition, natural selection is not applicable to them! In the literal sense of the word, no doubt, natural selection is a false term; but who ever objected to chemists speaking of the elective affinities of the various elements?—and yet an acid cannot strictly be said to elect the base with which it in preference combines. It has been said that I speak of natural selection as an active power or Deity; but who objects to an author speaking of the attraction of gravity as ruling the movements of the planets? Everyone knows what is meant and is implied by such metaphorical expressions; and they are almost necessary for brevity. So again it is difficult to avoid personifying the word Nature; but I mean by Nature, only the aggregate action and product of many natural laws, and by laws the sequence of events as ascertained by us. With a little familiarity such superficial objections will be forgotten. . . .

Extinction Caused by Natural Selection

... From these several considerations I think it inevitably follows, that as new species in the course of time are formed through natural selection, others will become rarer and rarer, and finally extinct. The forms which stand in closest competition with those undergoing modification and improvement will naturally suffer most. And we have seen in the chapter on the Struggle for Existence that it is the most closely-allied forms—varieties of the same species, and species of the same genus or of related genera—which, from having nearly the same structure, constitution, and habits, generally come into the severest competition with each other; consequently, each new variety or species, during the progress of its formation, will generally press hardest on its nearest kindred, and tend to exterminate them. ...

Divergence of Character

The principle, which I have designated by this term, is of high importance, and explains, as I believe, several important facts. In the first place, varieties, even strongly-marked ones, though having somewhat of the character of species—as is shown by the hopeless doubts in many cases how to rank them—yet certainly differ far less from each other than do good and distinct species. Nevertheless, according to my view, varieties are species in the process of formation, or are, as I have called them, incipient species. How, then, does the lesser difference between varieties become augmented into the greater difference between species? ...

... [T]he more diversified the descendants from any one species become in structure, constitution, and habits, by so much will they be better enabled to seize on many and widely diversified places in the polity of nature, and so be enabled to increase in numbers. ...

The truth of the principle that the greatest amount of life can be supported by great diversification of structure, is seen under many natural circumstances.[2] In an extremely small area, especially if freely open to immigration, and where the contest between individual and individual must be very severe, we always find great diversity in its inhabitants. For instance, I found that a piece of turf, three feet by four in size, which had been exposed for many years to exactly the same conditions, supported twenty species of plants, and these belonged to eighteen genera and to eight orders, which shows how much these plants differed from each other. So it is with the plants and insects on small and uniform islets: also in small ponds of fresh water. Farmers find that they can raise most food by a rotation of plants belonging to the most different orders: nature follows what may be called a simultaneous rotation. Most of the animals and plants which live close round any small piece of ground, could live on it (supposing its nature not to be in any way peculiar), and may be said to be striving to the utmost to live there; but, it is seen, that where they come into the closest competition, the advantages of diversification of structure, with the accompanying differences of habit and constitution, determine that the inhabitants, which thus jostle each other most closely, shall, as a general rule, belong to what we call different genera and orders. ...

On the Degree to which Organisation Tends to Advance[3]

Natural Selection acts exclusively by the preservation and accumulation of variations, which are beneficial under the organic and inorganic conditions to which each creature is exposed at all periods of life. The ultimate result is that each creature tends to become more and more improved in relation to its conditions. This improvement inevitably leads to the gradual advancement of the organisation of the greater number of living beings throughout the world. But here we enter on a very intricate subject, for naturalists have not defined to each other's satisfaction what is meant by an advance in organisation. Amongst the vertebrata the degree of intellect and an approach in structure to man clearly come into play. It might be thought that the amount of change which the various parts and organs pass through in their development from the embryo to maturity would suffice as a standard of comparison; but there are cases, as with certain parasitic crustaceans, in which several parts of the structure become less perfect, so that the mature animal cannot be called higher than its larva. Von Baer's standard seems the most widely applicable and the best, namely, the amount of differentiation of the parts of the same organic being, in the adult state as I should be inclined to add, and their specialisation for different functions; or, as Milne Edwards would express it, the completeness of the division of physiological labour. But we shall see how obscure this subject is if we look, for instance, to fishes, amongst which some naturalists rank those as highest which, like the sharks, approach nearest to amphibians; whilst other naturalists rank the common bony or teleostean fishes as the highest, inasmuch as they are most strictly fish-like and differ most from the other vertebrate classes. We see still more plainly the obscurity of the subject by turning to plants, amongst which the standard of intellect is of course quite excluded; and here some botanists rank those plants as highest which have every organ, as sepals, petals, stamens, and pistils, fully developed in each flower; whereas other botanists, probably with more truth, look at the plants which have their several organs much modified and reduced in number as the highest.

If we take as the standard of high organisation, the amount of differentiation and specialisation of the several organs in each being when adult (and this will include the advancement of the brain for intellectual purposes), natural selection clearly leads towards this standard: for all physiologists admit that the specialisation of organs, inasmuch as in this state they perform their functions better, is an advantage to each being; and hence the accumulation of variations tending towards specialisation is within the scope of natural selection. On the other hand, we can see, bearing in mind that all organic beings are striving to increase at a high ratio and to seize on every unoccupied or less well-occupied place in the economy of nature,[4] that it is quite possible for natural selection gradually to fit a being to a situation in which several organs would be superfluous or useless: in such cases there would be retrogression in the scale of organisation. Whether organisation on the whole has actually advanced from the remotest geological periods to the present day will be more conveniently discussed in our chapter on Geological Succession.

But it may be objected that if all organic beings thus tend to rise in the scale, how is it that throughout the world a multitude of the lowest forms still exist; and how is it that in each great class some forms are far more highly developed than others? Why have not the more highly developed forms everywhere supplanted and exterminated the lower? Lamarck, who believed in an innate and inevitable tendency towards perfection in all organic beings, seems to have felt this difficulty so strongly, that he was led to suppose that new and simple forms are continually being produced by spontaneous generation. Science has not as yet proved the truth of this belief, whatever the future may reveal. On our theory the continued existence of lowly organisms offers no difficulty; for natural selection, or the survival of the fittest, does not necessarily include progressive development—it only takes advantage of such variations as arise and are beneficial to each creature under its complex relations of life. And it may be asked what advantage, as far as we can see, would it be to an infusorian animalcule—to an intestinal worm—or even to an earthworm, to be highly organised. If it were no advantage, these forms would be left, by natural selection, unimproved or but little improved, and might remain for indefinite ages in their present lowly condition. And geology tells us that some of the lowest forms, as the infusoria and rhizopods, have remained for an enormous period in nearly their present state. But to suppose that most of the many now existing low forms have not in the least advanced since the first dawn of life would be extremely rash; for every naturalist who has dissected some of the beings now ranked as very low in the scale, must have been struck with their really wondrous and beautiful organisation. ...

Summary of Chapter

... The affinities of all the beings of the same class have sometimes been represented by a great tree. I believe this simile largely speaks the truth. The green and budding twigs may represent existing species; and those produced during former years may represent the long succession of extinct species. At each period of growth all the growing twigs have tried to branch out on all sides, and to overtop and kill the surrounding twigs and branches, in the same manner as species and groups of species have at all times overmastered other species in the great battle for life. The limbs, divided into great branches, and these into lesser and lesser branches, were themselves once, when the tree was young, budding twigs, and this connection of the former and present buds by ramifying branches may well represent the classification of all extinct and living species in groups subordinate to groups. Of the many twigs which flourished when the tree was a mere bush, only two or three, now grown into great branches, yet survive and bear the other branches; so with the species which lived during long-past geological periods very few have left living and modified descendants. From the first growth of the tree, many a limb and branch has decayed and dropped off; and these fallen branches of various sizes may represent those whole orders, families, and genera which have now no living representatives, and which are known to us only in a fossil state. As we here and there see a thin straggling branch springing from a fork low down in a tree, and which by some chance has been favoured and is still alive on its summit, so we occasionally see an animal like the Ornithorhynchus or Lepidosiren, which in some small degree connects by its affinities two large branches of life, and which has apparently been saved from fatal competition by having inhabited a protected station. As buds give rise by growth to fresh buds, and these, if vigorous, branch out and overtop on all sides many a feebler branch, so by generation I believe it has been with the great Tree of Life, which fills with its dead and broken branches the crust of the earth, and covers the surface with its everbranching and beautiful ramifications.

Chapter 15: Recapitulation and Conclusion

... It can hardly be supposed that a false theory would explain, in so satisfactory a manner as does the theory of natural selection, the several large classes of facts so specified.[5] It has recently been objected that this is an unsafe method of arguing, but it is a method used in judging of the common events of life, and has often been used by the greatest natural philosophers. The undulatory theory of light has thus been arrived at; and the belief in the revolution of the earth on its own axis was until lately supported by hardly any direct evidence. It is no valid objection that science as yet throws no light on the far higher problem of the essence or origin of life. Who can explain what is the essence of the attraction of gravity? No one now objects to following out the results consequent on this unknown element of attraction; notwithstanding that Leibniz formerly accused Newton of introducing "occult qualities and miracles into philosophy."

I see no good reason why the views given in this volume should shock the religious feelings of anyone. It is satisfactory, as showing how transient such impressions are, to remember that the greatest discovery ever made by man, namely, the law of the attraction of gravity, was also attacked by Leibniz, "as subversive of natural, and inferentially of revealed, religion." A celebrated author and divine has written to me that "he has gradually learnt to see that it is just as noble a conception of the Deity to believe that He created a few original forms capable of self-development into other and needful forms, as to believe that He required a fresh act of creation to supply the voids caused by the action of His laws." ...

Although I am fully convinced of the truth of the views given in this volume under the form of an abstract, I by no means expect to convince experienced naturalists whose minds are stocked with a multitude of facts all viewed, during a long course of years, from a point of view directly opposite to mine. It is so easy to hide our ignorance under such expressions as the "plan of creation" or "unity of design," etc., and to think that we give an explanation when we only restate a fact. Anyone whose disposition leads him to attach more weight to unexplained difficulties than to the explanation of a certain number of facts will certainly reject the theory. A few naturalists, endowed with much flexibility of mind, and who have already begun to doubt the immutability of species, may be influenced by this volume; but I look with confidence to the future—to young and rising naturalists, who will be able to view both sides of the question with impartiality. Whoever is led to believe that species are mutable will do good service by conscientiously expressing his conviction; for thus only can the load of prejudice by which this subject is overwhelmed be removed.

Authors of the highest eminence seem to be fully satisfied with the view that each species has been independently created. To my mind it accords better with what we know of the laws impressed on matter by the Creator, that the production and extinction of the past and present inhabitants of the world should have been due to secondary causes, like those determining the birth and death of the individual. When I view all beings not as special creations, but as the lineal descendants of some few beings which lived long before the first bed of the Cambrian system was deposited, they seem to me to become ennobled. Judging from the past, we may safely infer that not one living species will transmit its unaltered likeness to a distant futurity. And of the species now living very few will transmit progeny of any kind to a far distant futurity; for the manner in which all organic beings are grouped, shows that the greater number of species in each genus, and all the species in many genera, have left no descendants, but have become utterly extinct. We can so far take a prophetic glance into futurity as to foretell that it will be the common and widely-spread species, belonging to the larger and dominant groups within each class, which will ultimately prevail and procreate new and dominant species. As all the living forms of life are the lineal descendants of those which lived long before the Cambrian epoch, we may feel certain that the ordinary succession by generation has never once been broken, and that no cataclysm has desolated the whole world. Hence we may look with some confidence to a secure future of great length. And as natural selection works solely by and for the good of each being, all corporeal and mental endowments will tend to progress towards perfection.[6]

It is interesting to contemplate a tangled bank, clothed with many plants of many kinds, with birds singing on the bushes, with various insects flitting about, and with worms crawling through the damp earth, and to reflect that these elaborately constructed forms, so different from each other, and dependent upon each other in so complex a manner, have all been produced by laws acting around us. These laws, taken in the largest sense, being Growth with Reproduction; Inheritance which is almost implied by reproduction; Variability from the indirect and direct action of the conditions of life and from use and disuse: a Ratio of Increase so high as to lead to a Struggle for Life, and as a consequence to Natural Selection, entailing Divergence of Character and the Extinction of less-improved forms. Thus, from the war of nature, from famine and death, the most exalted object which we are capable of conceiving, namely, the production of the higher animals, directly follows. There is grandeur in this view of life, with its several powers, having been originally breathed by the Creator into a few forms or into one; and that, whilst this planet has gone cycling on according to the fixed law of gravity, from so simple a beginning endless forms most beautiful and most wonderful have been, and are being evolved.

The Descent of Man

Conclusion

... The main conclusion arrived at in this work, namely, that man is descended from some lowly organised form, will, I regret to think, be highly distasteful to many. But there can hardly be a doubt that we are descended from barbarians. The astonishment which I felt on first seeing a party of Fuegians on a wild and broken shore will never be forgotten by me, for the reflection at once rushed into my mind—such were our ancestors. These men were absolutely naked and bedaubed with paint, their long hair was tangled, their mouths frothed with excitement, and their expression was wild, startled, and distrustful. They possessed hardly any arts, and like wild animals lived on what they could catch; they had no government, and were merciless to everyone not of their own small tribe. He who has seen a savage in his native land will not feel much shame, if forced to acknowledge that the blood of some more humble creature flows in his veins. For my own part I would as soon be descended from that heroic little monkey, who braved his dreaded enemy in order to save the life of his keeper, or from that old baboon, who descending from the mountains, carried away in triumph his young comrade from a crowd of astonished dogs—as from a savage who delights to torture his enemies, offers up bloody sacrifices, practices infanticide without remorse, treats his wives like slaves, knows no decency, and is haunted by the grossest superstitions. Man may be excused for feeling some pride at having risen, though not through his own exertions, to the very summit of the organic scale; and the fact of his having thus risen, instead of having been aboriginally placed there, may give him hope for a still higher destiny in the distant future. But we are not here concerned with hopes or fears, only with the truth as far as our reason permits us to discover it; and I have given the evidence to the best of my ability. We must, however, acknowledge, as it seems to me, that man with all his noble qualities, with sympathy which feels for the most debased, with benevolence which extends not only to other men but to the humblest living creature, with his god-like intellect which has penetrated into the movements and constitution of the solar system—with all these exalted powers—Man still bears in his bodily frame the indelible stamp of his lowly origin.

Notes

1 In the years following the writing of *On the Origin of Species*, Darwin became increasingly impressed by the number of characteristics of living things, some quite conspicuous, that could not be directly accounted for as providing some advantage to the organisms that have them. He took them to be unexplained side-effects of those changes that are advantageous.

2 Here, in germ, is the principle of biodiversity: that a healthy ecosystem, allowed to take its natural course, will develop into one with the greatest variety of organisms, which, in turn, will be one with the greatest amount of biological activity.

3 In the section that follows this subheading, Darwin wrestles with the question of whether living things can be arranged in hierarchies. The most evolved organisms are not necessarily the ones that are higher up on the Aristotelian scale of living things (as a species may lose some sentience or intelligence as it evolves to more adequately fill its niche); likewise it happens that some of the more evolved species have body parts that are less complicated and differentiated. Darwin's solution is to rid the science of biology of the notion that some life forms are higher and lower than others. Indeed, at one point Darwin jotted the note "Never use the word 'higher' or 'lower'."

4 This is a reference to the teaching of Linnaeus's *The Economy of Nature*, excerpted in the present volume.

5 Darwin has just reviewed the kinds of facts for which the theory of natural selection provides an explanation.

6 This is a rare reference to "goodness" or "perfection" of natural kinds, the sort of appeal common in Aristotle's biological writings. But for Darwin, in contrast to Aristotle, the good of a kind is never determinate; it is always unfolding in time.

V

Transforming Nature:
Progress or Ruin?

CHAPTER 22

John Stuart Mill

JOHN STUART MILL (1806–1873) was one of a long line of English thinkers who
tried to free philosophical thinking from the excesses of metaphysical speculation.
As one of the British Empiricists, he held that all meaningful discourse must, at
bottom, be about sensations that people experience. Thus, in the realm of the
sciences, a theoretical account is to be understood as identifying and expressing
the regularities found in our experience of things, not, as for an Aristotelian, as
expressing the true inner workings of reality. One who holds such a view can hardly
ground an ethical theory on the true essence of human beings. Thus it is not surprising that Mill also takes an ethical theory to be at bottom concerned with feelings and sensations that are experienced.

As a utilitarian, Mill held that the ethical course of action is that whose consequences lead to the greatest pleasure and the least pain. Mill does take some
pleasures to have higher rank than others, so that one ought to seek to maximize
the quality of pleasure, as well as its quantity. Nonetheless all ranking is to be
done on the basis of the character of the experience as such, with no appeal to
any essences or natures. Such a line of thinking has two implications for environmental ethics.

First, any ethical appeal to "following nature" is either meaningless or wrong.
Human beings have an ethical obligation to actively change the way the world is in
order to maximize the totality of pleasure in the world and to minimize the totality
of pain. In the first essay that is excerpted here, the posthumously published *Nature*, Mill argues against several ways in which philosophers had taken nature to
be a guide for appropriate conduct. He tries to explain how the notion of what is
"natural" came to be associated with notions of ethical obligation. Mill's dismissal
of challenges to technological innovation on the basis of its being against nature
is highly reminiscent of how many current scientists dismiss the objections of those
who challenge genetic engineering as interference with nature.

Second, because animals other than human beings are able to feel pleasure
and pain, they are moral subjects, to which we have direct moral obligations. They
are not to be excluded from such a status on the grounds that they are not rational. It is therefore no accident that utilitarian ethicists have played, and continue to play, an important role in the campaign against cruelty to animals.

In the second selection included below, *Whewell on Moral Philosophy*, Mill
comes to a spirited defense of his utilitarian predecessor, Jeremy Bentham (1748–
1832), who was among the first to apply utilitarian principles to the question of
how it is appropriate for human beings to treat animals.

Mill thus shows himself to be sensitive to the moral standing of beings that are not human, but only insofar as they are subject to pleasure and pain, for he holds that as a moral society we ought to devote our energies toward the maximization of pleasure and the minimization of pain. There is no more basic standard of morality, and hence there is nothing in principle wrong with unleashing the full powers of human ingenuity to alter the world in pursuit of these goals.

JOHN STUART MILL
Nature

Nature, natural, and the group of words derived from them, or allied to them in etymology, have at all times filled a great place in the thoughts and taken a strong hold on the feelings of mankind. That they should have done so is not surprising, when we consider what the words, in their primitive and most obvious signification, represent; but it is unfortunate that a set of terms which play so great a part in moral and metaphysical speculation should have acquired many meanings different from the primary one, yet sufficiently allied to it to admit of confusion. The words have thus become entangled in so many foreign associations, mostly of a very powerful and tenacious character, that they have come to excite, and to be the symbols of, feelings which their original meaning will by no means justify, and which have made them one of the most copious sources of false taste, false philosophy, false morality, and even bad law.

... [T]he first thing to be done with so vague a term [as nature] is to ascertain precisely what it means. It is also a rule of the same method that the meaning of an abstraction is best sought for in the concrete—of an universal in the particular. Adopting this course with the word Nature, the first question must be, what is meant by the "nature" of a particular object? as of fire, of water, or of some individual plant or animal? Evidently the *ensemble* or aggregate of its powers or properties: the modes in which it acts on other things (counting among those things the senses of the observer) and the modes in which other things act upon it; to which, in the case of a sentient being, must be added, its own capacities of feeling, or being conscious. The Nature of the thing means all this; means its entire capacity of exhibiting phenomena.[1] And since the phenomena which a thing exhibits, however much they vary in different circumstances, are always the same in the same circumstances, they admit of being described in general forms of words, which are called the *laws* of the thing's nature. Thus it is a law of the nature of water that under the mean pressure of the atmosphere at the level of the sea, it boils at 212° Fahrenheit.

As the nature of any given thing is the aggregate of its powers and properties, so Nature in the abstract is the aggregate of the powers and properties of all things. Nature means the sum of all phenomena, together with the causes which produce them, including not only all that happens, but all that is capable of happening; the unused capabilities of causes being, as much a part of the idea of Nature, as those which take effect. Since all phenomena which have been sufficiently examined are found to take place with regularity, each having certain fixed conditions, positive and negative, on the occurrence of which it invariably happens, mankind have been able to ascertain, either by direct observation or by reasoning processes grounded on it, the conditions of the occurrence of many phenomena; and the progress of science mainly consists in ascertaining those conditions.[2] ...

Nature, then, in this its simplest acceptation, is a collective name for all facts, actual and possible or (to speak more accurately) a name for the mode, partly known to us and partly unknown, in which all things take place. ...

Such, then, is a correct definition of the word Nature. But this definition corresponds only to one of the senses of that ambiguous term. It is evidently inapplicable to some of the modes in which the word is familiarly employed. For example, it entirely conflicts with the common form of speech by which Nature is opposed to Art, and natural to artificial. For in the sense of the word Nature which has just been defined, and which is the true scientific sense, Art is as much Nature as anything else; and everything which is artificial is natural—Art has no independent powers of its own; Art is but the employment of the powers of Nature for an end.[3] Phenomena produced by human agency, no less than those which as far as we are concerned are spontaneous, depend on the properties of the elementary forces, or of the elementary substances and their compounds. The united powers of the whole human race could not create a new property of matter in general, or of any one of its species. We can only take advantage for our purposes of the properties which we find. A ship floats by the same laws of specific gravity and equilibrium, as a tree uprooted by the wind and blown into the water. The corn which men raise for food, grows and produces its grain by the same laws of vegetation by which the wild rose and the mountain strawberry bring forth their flowers and fruit. A house stands and holds together by the natural properties, the weight and cohesion of the materials which compose it; a steam engine works by the natural expansive force of steam, exerting a pressure upon one part of a system of arrangements, which pressure, by the mechanical properties of the lever, is transferred from that to another part where it raises the weight or removes the obstacle brought into connexion with it. In these and all other artificial operations the office of man is, as has often been remarked, a very limited one; it consists in moving things into certain places. We move objects, and by doing this, bring some things into contact which were separate, or separate others which were in contact: and by this simple change of place, natural forces previously dormant are called into action, and produce the desired effect. Even the volition which designs, the intelligence which contrives, and the muscular force which executes these movements, are themselves powers of Nature.

It thus appears that we must recognize at least two principal meanings in the word Nature. In one sense, it means all the powers existing in either the outer or the inner world and everything which takes place by means of those powers. In another sense, it means, not everything which happens, but only what takes place without the agency, or without the voluntary and intentional agency, of man. This distinction is far from exhausting the ambiguities of the word, but it is the key to most of those on which important consequences depend.

Such, then, being the two principal senses of the word Nature, in which of these is it taken, or is it taken in either, when the word and its derivatives are used to convey ideas of commendation, approval, and even moral obligation?

It has conveyed such ideas in all ages. *Naturam sequi*[4] was the fundamental principle of morals in many of the most admired schools of philosophy. Among the ancients, especially in the declining period of ancient intellect and thought,[5] it was the test to which all ethical doctrines were brought. The Stoics[6] and the Epicureans,[7] however irreconcilable in the rest of their systems, agreed in holding themselves bound to prove that their respective maxims of conduct were the dictates of nature. ...

Is it necessary to recognize in these forms of speech another distinct meaning of the word Nature? ... Those who set up Nature as a standard of action do not intend a merely verbal proposition; they do not mean that the standard, whatever it be, should be *called* Nature; they think they are giving some information as to what the standard of action really is. Those who say that we ought to act according to Nature do not mean the mere identical proposition that we ought to do what we ought to do. They think that the word Nature affords some external criterion of what we should do; and if they lay down as a rule for what ought to be, a word which in its proper signification denotes what is, they do so because they have a notion, either clearly or confusedly, that what is constitutes the rule and standard of what ought to be.

The examination of this notion is the object of the present Essay. It is proposed to inquire into the truth of the doctrines which make Nature a test of right and wrong, good and evil, or which in any mode or degree attach merit or approval to following, imitating, or obeying Nature. To this inquiry the foregoing discussion respecting the meaning of terms was an indispensable introduction. Language is as it were the atmosphere of philosophical investigation, which must be made transparent before anything can be seen through it in the true figure and position. ...

When it is asserted, or implied, that Nature, or the laws of Nature, should be conformed to, is the Nature which is meant, Nature in the first sense of the term, meaning all which is—the powers and properties of all things? But in this signification, there is no need of a recommendation to act according to nature, since it is what nobody can possibly help doing, and equally whether he acts well or ill. ... To bid people conform to the laws of nature when they have no power but what the laws of nature give them—when it is a physical impossibility for them to do the smallest thing otherwise than through some law of nature, is an absurdity. The thing they need to be told is what particular law of nature they should make use of in a particular case. When, for example, a person is crossing a river by a narrow bridge to which there is no parapet, he will do well to regulate his proceedings by the laws of equilibrium in moving bodies, instead of conforming only to the law of gravitation, and falling into the river.

Yet, idle as it is to exhort people to do what they cannot avoid doing, and absurd as it is to prescribe as a rule of right conduct what agrees exactly as well with wrong, nevertheless a rational rule of conduct *may* be constructed out of the relation which it ought to bear to the laws of nature in this widest acceptation of the term. Man necessarily obeys the laws of nature, or in other words the properties of things, but he does not necessarily *guide* himself by them. Though all conduct is in conformity to laws of nature, all conduct is not grounded on knowledge of them and intelligently directed to the attainment of purposes by means of them. Though we cannot emancipate ourselves from the laws of nature as a whole, we can escape from any particular law of nature, if we are able to withdraw ourselves from the circumstances in which it acts. Though we can do nothing except through laws of nature, we can use one law to counteract another. According to Bacon's maxim, we can obey nature in such a manner as to command it.[8] . . .

But however much of its authority the *Naturam sequi* doctrine may owe to its being confounded with the rational precept *Naturam observare*,[9] its favourers and promoters unquestionably intend much more by it than that precept. To acquire knowledge of the properties of things, and make use of the knowledge for guidance, is a rule of prudence, for the adaptation of means to ends; for giving effect to our wishes and intentions whatever they may be. But the maxim of obedience to Nature, or conformity to Nature, is held up not as a simply prudential but as an ethical maxim,[10] and by those who talk of *jus naturae*, even as a law, fit to be administered by tribunals and enforced by sanctions. Right action must mean something more and other than merely intelligent action, yet no precept beyond this last can be connected with the word Nature in the wider and more philosophical of its acceptations. We must try it therefore in the other sense, that in which Nature stands distinguished from Art, and denotes, not the whole course of the phenomena which come under our observation, but only their spontaneous course.

Let us then consider whether we can attach any meaning to the supposed practical maxim of following Nature, in this second sense of the word, in which Nature stands for that which takes place without human intervention. In Nature as thus understood, is the spontaneous course of things when left to themselves the rule to be followed in endeavouring to adapt things to our use? But it is evident at once that the maxim, taken in this sense, is not merely, as it is in the other sense, superfluous and unmeaning, but palpably absurd and self-contradictory. For while human action cannot help conforming to Nature in the one meaning of the term, the very aim and object of action is to alter and improve Nature in the other meaning. If the natural course of things were perfectly right and satisfactory, to act at all would be a gratuitous meddling, which as it could not make things better, must make them worse. Or if action at all could be justified, it would only be when in direct obedience to instincts, since these might perhaps be accounted part of the spontaneous order of Nature; but to do anything with forethought and purpose would be a violation of that perfect order. If the artificial is not better than the natural, to what end are all the arts of life? To dig, to plough, to build, to wear clothes, are direct infringements of the injunction to follow nature.

Accordingly it would be said by everyone, even of those most under the influence of the feelings which prompt the injunction, that to apply it to such cases as those just spoken of would be to push it too far. Everybody professes to approve and admire many great triumphs of Art over Nature: the junction by bridges of shores which Nature had made separate, the draining of Nature's marshes, the excavation of her wells, the dragging to light of what she has buried at immense depths in the earth; the turning away of her thunderbolts by lightning rods, of her inundations by embankments, of her ocean by breakwaters. But to commend these and similar feats is to acknowledge that the ways of Nature are to be conquered not obeyed, that her powers are often towards man in the position of enemies, from whom he must wrest, by force and ingenuity, what little he can for his own use, and deserves to be applauded when that little is rather more than might be expected from his physical weakness in comparison to those gigantic powers. All praise of Civilization, or Art, or Contrivance, is so much dispraise of Nature, an admission of imperfection, which it is man's business, and merit, to be always endeavouring to correct or mitigate.

The consciousness that whatever man does to improve his condition is in so much a censure and a thwarting of the spontaneous order of Nature, has in all ages caused new and unprecedented attempts at improvement to be generally at first under a shade of religious suspicion, as being in any case uncomplimentary, and very probably offensive to the powerful beings (or, when polytheism gave place to monotheism, to the all-powerful Being) supposed to govern the various phenomena of the universe, and of whose will the course of nature was conceived to be the expression. Any attempt to mold natural phenomena to the convenience of mankind might easily appear an interference with the government of those superior beings, and though life could not have been maintained, much less made pleasant, without perpetual interferences of the kind, each new one was doubtless made with fear and trembling, until experience had shown that it could be ventured on without drawing down the vengeance of the Gods. ... No one, indeed, asserts it to be the intention of the Creator that the spontaneous order of the creation should not be altered, or even that it should not be altered in any new way. But there still exists a vague notion that though it is very proper to control this or the other natural phenomenon, the general scheme of nature is a model for us to imitate; that with more or less liberty in details, we should on the whole be guided by the spirit and general conception of nature's own ways; that they are God's work, and as such perfect; that man cannot rival their unapproachable excellence, and can best show his skill and piety by attempting, in however imperfect a way, to reproduce their likeness; and that if not the whole, yet some particular parts of the spontaneous order of nature, selected according to the speaker's predilections, are in a peculiar sense manifestations of the Creator's will; a sort of finger posts pointing out the direction which things in general, and therefore our voluntary actions, are intended to take. Feelings of this sort, though repressed on ordinary occasions by the contrary current of life, are ready to break out whenever custom is silent, and the native promptings of the mind have nothing opposed to them but reason; and appeals are continually made to them by rhetoricians, with the effect, if not of convincing opponents, at least of making those who already hold the opinion which the rhetorician desires to recommend, better satisfied with it. For in the present day it probably seldom happens that any one is persuaded to approve any course of action because it appears to him to bear an analogy to the divine government of the world, though the argument tells on him with great force, and is felt by him to be a great support, in behalf of anything which he is already inclined to approve. ...

... [H]owever offensive the proposition may appear to many religious persons, they should be willing to look in the face the undeniable fact that the order of nature, in so far as unmodified by man, is such as no being, whose attributes are justice and benevolence, would have made, with the intention that his rational creatures should follow it as an example. If made wholly by such a Being, and not partly by beings of very different qualities, it could only be as a designedly imperfect work, which man, in his limited sphere, is to exercise justice and benevolence in amending. The best persons have always held it to be the essence of religion that the paramount duty of man upon earth is to amend himself; but all except monkish quietists have annexed to this in their inmost minds (though seldom willing to enunciate the obligation with the same clearness) the additional religious duty of amending the world, and not solely the human part of it but the material—the order of physical nature.

In considering this subject it is necessary to divest ourselves of certain preconceptions which may justly be called natural prejudices, being grounded on feelings which, in themselves natural and inevitable, intrude into matters with which they ought to have no concern. One of these feelings is the astonishment, rising into awe, which is inspired (even independently of all religious sentiment) by any of the greater natural phenomena. A hurricane; a mountain precipice; the desert; the ocean, either agitated or at rest; the solar system, and the great cosmic forces which hold it together; the boundless firmament, and to an educated mind any single star; excite feelings which make all human enterprises and powers appear so insignificant, that to a mind thus occupied it seems insufferable presumption in so puny a creature as man to look critically on things so far above him, or dare to measure himself against the grandeur of the universe. But a little interrogation of our own consciousness will suffice to convince us that what makes these phenomena so impressive is simply their vastness. The enormous extension in space and time, or the enormous power they exemplify, constitutes their sublimity; a feeling in all cases, more allied to terror than to any moral emotion.[11] And though the vast scale of these phenomena may well excite wonder, and sets at defiance all idea of rivalry, the feeling it inspires is of a totally different character from admiration of excellence. Those in whom awe produces admiration may be aesthetically developed, but they are morally uncultivated. It is one of the endowments of the imaginative part of our mental nature that conceptions of greatness and power, vividly realized, produce a feeling which though in its higher degrees closely bordering on pain, we prefer to most of what are accounted pleasures. But we are quite equally capable of experiencing this feeling towards maleficent power, and we never experience it so strongly towards most of the powers of the universe, as when we have most present to our consciousness a vivid sense of their capacity of inflicting evil. Because these natural powers have what we cannot imitate, enormous might, and overawe us by that one attribute, it would be a great error to infer that their other attributes are such as we ought to emulate, or that we should be justified in using our small powers after the example which Nature sets us with her vast forces.

For, how stands the fact? That next to the greatness of these cosmic forces, the quality which most forcibly strikes everyone who does not avert his eyes from it is their perfect and absolute recklessness. They go straight to their end, without regarding what or whom they crush on the road. Optimists, in their attempts to prove that "whatever is, is right," are obliged to maintain, not that Nature ever turns one step from her path to avoid trampling us into destruction, but that it would be very unreasonable in us to expect that she should. Pope's "Shall gravitation cease when you go by?"[12] may be a just rebuke to anyone who should be so silly as to expect common human morality from nature. But if the question were between two men, instead of between a man and a natural phenomenon, that triumphant apostrophe would be thought a rare piece of impudence. A man who should persist in hurling stones or firing cannon when another man "goes by" and having killed him should urge a similar plea in exculpation, would very deservedly be found guilty of murder.

In sober truth, nearly all the things which men are hanged or imprisoned for doing to one another, are nature's every day performances. Killing, the most criminal act recognized by human laws, Nature does once to every being that lives; and in a large proportion of cases, after protracted tortures such as only the greatest monsters whom we read of ever purposely inflicted on their living fellow-creatures. If, by an arbitrary reservation, we refuse to account anything murder but what abridges a certain term supposed to be allotted to human life, nature also does this to all but a small percentage of lives, and does it in all the modes, violent or insidious, in which the worst human beings take the lives of one another. Nature impales men, breaks them as if on the wheel, casts them to be devoured by wild beasts, burns them to death, crushes them with stones like the first Christian martyr, starves them with hunger, freezes them with cold, poisons them by the quick or slow venom of her exhalation, and has hundreds of other hideous deaths in reserve, such as the ingenious cruelty of a Nabis or a Domitian[13] never surpassed. All this, Nature does with the most supercilious disregard both of mercy and of justice, emptying her shafts upon the best and noblest indifferently with the meanest and worst; upon those who are engaged in the highest and worthiest enterprises, and often as the direct consequence of the noblest acts; and it might almost be imagined as a punishment for them. She mows down those on whose existence hangs the well-being of a whole people, perhaps the prospects of the human race for generations to come, with as little compunction as those whose death is a relief to themselves, or blessing to those under their noxious influence. Such are Nature's dealings with life. ... Even the love of "order" which is thought to be a following of the ways of Nature is in fact a contradiction of them. All which people are accustomed to deprecate as "disorder" and its consequences is precisely a counterpart of Nature's ways. Anarchy and the Reign of Terror are overmatched in injustice, ruin, and death by a hurricane and a pestilence.

But, it is said, all these things are for wise and good ends. On this I must first remark that whether they are so or not is altogether beside the point. Supposing it true that contrary to appearances these horrors when perpetuated by Nature promote good ends, still as no one believes that good ends would be promoted by our following the example, the course of Nature cannot be a proper model for us to imitate. Either it is right that we should kill because nature kills; to torture because nature tortures; ruin and devastate because nature does the like; or we ought not to consider at all what nature does, but what it is good to do. If there is such a thing as a *reductio ad absurdum*,[14] this surely amounts to one. If it is a sufficient reason for doing one thing, that nature does it, why not another thing? If not all things, why anything? ...

But even if it were true that every one of the elementary impulses of human nature has its good side,[15] and may by a sufficient amount of artificial training be made more useful than hurtful; how little would this amount to, when it must in any case be admitted that without such training all of them, even those which are necessary to our preservation, would fill the world with misery, making human life an exaggerated likeness of the odious scene of violence and tyranny which is exhibited by the rest of the animal kingdom, except in so far as tamed and disciplined by man. ...

It will be useful to sum up in a few words the leading conclusions of this Essay.

The word Nature has two principal meanings: it either denotes the entire system of things, with the aggregate of all their properties, or it denotes things as they would be, apart from human intervention.

In the first of these senses, the doctrine that man ought to follow nature is unmeaning, since man has no power to do anything else than follow nature; all his actions are done through, and in obedience to, some one or many of nature's physical or mental laws.

In the other sense of the term, the doctrine that man ought to follow nature, or in other words, ought to make the spontaneous course of things the model of his voluntary actions, is equally irrational and immoral.

Irrational, because all human action whatever, consists in altering, and all useful action in improving, the spontaneous course of nature.

Immoral, because the course of natural phenomena being replete with everything which when committed by human beings is most worthy of abhorrence, anyone who endeavored in his actions to imitate the natural course of things would be universally seen and acknowledged to be the wickedest of men.

The scheme of Nature regarded in its whole extent cannot have had, for its sole or even principal object, the good of human or other sentient beings. What good it brings to them is mostly the result of their own exertions. Whatsoever, in nature, gives indication of beneficent design, proves this beneficence to be armed only with limited power; and the duty of man is to cooperate with the beneficent powers, not by imitating but by perpetually striving to amend the course of nature—and bringing that part of it over which we can exercise control more nearly into conformity with a high standard of justice and goodness.

+≥—≤+

Whewell on Moral Philosophy

Dr. Whewell[16] puts the last hand to his supposed refutation of Bentham's principle[17] by what he thinks a crushing *reductio ad absurdum*. The reader might make a hundred guesses before discovering what this is. We have not yet got over our astonishment, not at Bentham, but at Dr. Whewell. See, he says, to what consequences your greatest-happiness principle leads! Bentham says that it is as much a moral duty to regard the pleasures and pains of other animals as those of human beings. We cannot resist quoting the admirable passage which Dr. Whewell cites from Bentham, with the most *naif* persuasion that everybody will regard it as reaching the last pitch of paradoxical absurdity:

> Under the Gentoo[18] and Mahometan religion, the interests of the rest of the animal kingdom seem to have met with some attention. Why have they not universally, with as much as those of human creatures, allowance made for the difference in point of sensibility? Because the laws that are have been the work of mutual fear; a sentiment which the less rational animals have not had the same means

as man has of turning to account. Why ought they not? No reason can be given. The day may come when the rest of the animal creation may acquire those rights which never could have been withheld from them but by the hand of tyranny. It may come one day to be recognized, that the number of the legs, the velocity of the skin, or the termination of the *os sacrum*[19] are reasons insufficient for abandoning a sensitive being to the caprice of a tormentor. What else is it that should trace the insuperable line? Is it the faculty of reason, or perhaps the faculty of discourse? But a full-grown horse or dog is beyond comparison a more rational as well as a more conversable animal than an infant of a day, a week, or even a month old. But suppose the case were otherwise, what would it avail? The question is not, Can they reason? nor, Can they speak? But, Can they suffer?

This noble anticipation in 1780, of the better morality of which a first dawn has been seen in the laws enacted nearly fifty years afterwards against cruelty to animals, is, in Dr. Whewell's eyes, the finishing proof that the morality of happiness is absurd!

The pleasures of animals are elements of a very different order from the pleasures of man. We are bound to endeavor to augment the pleasures of men, not only because they are pleasures, but because they are human pleasures. We are bound to men by the universal tie of humanity, of human brotherhood. We have no such tie to animals.

This, then, is Dr. Whewell's noble and disinterested ideal of virtue. Duties, according to him, are only duties to ourselves and our like.

We are to be *humane* to them, because we are *human*, not because we and they alike feel *animal* pleasures. ... The morality which depends upon the increase of pleasure alone would make it our duty to increase the pleasures of pigs or of geese, rather than that of men, if we were sure that the pleasures we could give them were greater than the pleasures of men. ... It is not only not an obvious, but to most persons not a tolerable, doctrine, that we may sacrifice the happiness of men, provided we can in that way produce an overplus of pleasure to cats, dogs, and hogs.

It is "to most persons" in the Slave States of America not a tolerable doctrine that we may sacrifice any portion of the happiness of white men for the sake of a greater amount of happiness to black men. It would have been intolerable five centuries ago, "to most persons" among the feudal nobility to hear it asserted, that the greatest pleasure or pain of a hundred serfs ought not to give way to the smallest of a nobleman. According to the standard of Dr. Whewell, the slave-masters and the nobles were right. They, too, felt themselves "bound" by a "tie of brotherhood" to the white men and to the nobility, and felt no such tie to the negroes and serfs. And, if a feeling on moral subjects is right because it is natural, their feeling was justifiable. Nothing is more natural to human beings, nor, up to a certain point in cultivation, more universal, than to estimate the pleasures and pains of others as deserving of regard exactly in proportion to their likeness to ourselves. These superstitions of selfishness had the characteristics by which Dr. Whewell recognizes his moral rules; and his opinion on the rights of animals shows, that, in this case at least, he is consistent. We are perfectly willing to stake the whole question on this one issue. Granted that any practice causes more pain to animals than it gives pleasure to man: is that practice moral or immoral? And if, exactly in proportion as human beings raise their heads out of the slough of selfishness, they do not with one voice answer, "Immoral," let the morality of the principle of utility be for ever condemned.

Notes

1   Mill's empiricism is clearly to the fore in this definition. The nature of a thing is to be considered neither an inner essence nor an internal source of energy, with or without teleological direction. The nature of a thing is simply the sum total of its observable properties, including the results that are observed when it is near other things.

2   This is a version of the conception of science we have seen in such modern thinkers as Bacon and Descartes. Science is the determination of the means for bringing about desired results. Here, the means are called "conditions," and the results are called "phenomena."

3   Cf. Aristotle's contrast between nature and art in *Physics* 2.1. The bed has certain properties by nature; these include the attributes that it has by virtue of being made up of a natural substance, wood. The bed can only function as a bed by virtue of the nature of its matter. But Aristotle will insist that a bed, considered as a bed, does not have a nature. This is because it lacks an essence that gives it a true unity, enabling it to do certain things that are done only by things of that same kind. Mill, on the other hand, would have no reason to deny that the bed has a nature just as does the wood that makes it up. So for Mill, unlike Aristotle, if one contrasts Nature with Art, this is only because one uses Nature in a new sense, different from its primary sense.

4   In English, "Follow Nature."

5   The philosophy of the Hellenistic period of Greek philosophy, which followed that of Aristotle, was for centuries generally considered to be vastly inferior to the philosophy that preceded it. Today, this view is still held by many, but is being challenged by a resurgence of interest in Hellenistic thought.

6   In the selection from Cicero we saw that for the Stoics, nature is a rational force permeating living things and governing their growth. Because the whole cosmos is a living thing,

it too has such a nature. This is to be identified with Zeus, a rational deity that directs all things to the good that is proper to them. Stoic ethics is based on the idea that the ways of this divine *logos* can be learned by us, and we can achieve happiness by accepting the fate that has been determined for us by this *logos*.

7 The Epicureans, as we have seen, used "nature" to refer to what they took to be the basic constituents of the cosmos: atoms and void. From the Epicurean point of view, atoms have been put together within the void in such a way that living beings cannot help but pursue pleasure and avoid pain. Hence, human beings, too, must pursue pleasure as an end. In order to be happy, we need to recognize this, and reflect on the sort of life that will in fact achieve the most pleasure. This involves various ethical precepts, and is why these precepts involve "following Nature."

8 See in this volume, Francis Bacon, *The New Organon* I, Aphorisms 3 and 129.

9 "Pay attention to Nature."

10 A prudential maxim tells one what one ought to do in order to achieve certain desires; it specifies means to an end that one happens to have. An ethical maxim tells what is morally right to do; as such, it specifies the end at which one aims.

11 Mill is alluding to Kant's notion of the sublime, as presented in Section 28 of the *Critique of Judgment*. Mill is willing to grant that Kant's analysis of sublimity is correct. Nonetheless, he insists that the awe inspired by the sublime in nature is not a matter of admiring any moral qualities within nature.

12 The quotation is from Alexander Pope's Epistle 4, "Of the State of Nature and State of Man with Respect to Happiness." Pope indicates that it is not for human beings to complain about or judge the actions of God, which proceed despite how they immediately affect us:

"When the loose mountain trembles from on high
Shall gravitation cease, if you go by?"

13 Nabis (?–193 BC) purportedly seized the kingship of Sparta by killing the young king Pelops, of whom he was the guardian. Domitian (51–96 AD) was a Roman emperor, notorious for the ruthless means by which he attempted to hold on to power.

14 To simplify, this is an argument that proves its conclusion by first assuming that its conclusion is false, and then showing how this assumption leads to contradictory consequences, which cannot both be true.

15 In the omitted section, Mill has been continuing his examination of the senses in which people think that morality is determined by what is "natural." He has been examining the view that people ought to trust their natural instincts, pointing out that acting on instinct often leads to very negative consequences. Here he grants that instincts have their good side, but insists that this good side can prevail only through moral education, a kind of human intervention in the course of things.

16 William Whewell (1794–1866) was one of the most prominent philosophers of his time, perhaps best known today for having coined the term "scientist." He argued against the utilitarian ethical theories that were becoming fashionable in his time.

17 This is the basic principle of utilitarianism: an action is right insofar as it leads to the greatest happiness of the greatest number. Here "happiness" is understood as pleasure.

18 This is another term for "Hindu."

19 Bentham points to the moral irrelevance of the issue of whether or not an animal has a tail.

CHAPTER 23

George Perkins Marsh

GEORGE PERKINS MARSH (1801–1882) was an American lawyer, politician, and diplomat, whose love of learning and broad interest led him to become one of the world's great geographers. In *Man and Nature*, first printed in 1864, Marsh surveyed the various ways in which human beings had altered the topography and biology of the earth. His verdict, supported by hundreds of pages of detailed reports, was that such change has been sweeping, and, in many (if not most) cases, has had disastrous long-term effects. Marsh's research greatly influenced some of the founders of the American conservation movement, such as Theodore Roosevelt and Gifford Pinchot.

The conclusions that Marsh reached led to a new view of human beings in relation to their environment: the natural environment, left to itself, provides a fitting home for human life. But human beings can and usually do exercise their power over the earth imprudently. This suggests that human beings are intruders in the natural world: their presence disrupts its balance, turning formerly fruitful lands to barren waste. Nonetheless, Marsh sees human beings as the rightful possessors and masters of the natural world. His objection is not to all human alteration of the land, but to such alteration as is destructive and short-sighted. He expresses hope that technological innovations, such as the harnessing of solar energy, will someday allow human beings to restore, or even enhance, the original health of lands altered by human settlement.

The following selections, which present Marsh's philosophical outlook in outline, are taken from the first chapter of the final edition of *Man and Nature*.

GEORGE PERKINS MARSH
The Earth as Modified by Human Action:
A Last Revision of "Man and Nature"

Destructiveness of Man

Man has too long forgotten that the earth was given to him for usufruct alone, not for consumption, still less for profligate waste. Nature has provided against the absolute destruction of any of her elementary matter, the raw material of her works; the thunderbolt and the tornado, the most convulsive throes of even the volcano and the earthquake, being only phenomena of decomposition and recomposition. But she has left it within the power of man irreparably to derange the combinations of inorganic matter and of organic life, which through the night of aeons she had been proportioning and balancing, to prepare the earth for his habitation, when in the fullness of time his Creator should call him forth to enter into its possession.

Apart from the hostile influence of man, the organic and the inorganic world are, as I have remarked, bound together by such mutual relations and adaptations as secure, if not the absolute permanence and equilibrium of both, a long continuance of the established conditions of each at any given time and place, or at least, a very slow and gradual succession of changes in those conditions. But man is everywhere a disturbing agent. Wherever he plants his foot, the harmonies of nature are turned to discords. The proportions and accommodations which insured the stability of existing arrangements are overthrown. Indigenous vegetable and animal species are extirpated, and supplanted by others of foreign origin, spontaneous production is forbidden or restricted, and the face of the earth is either laid bare or covered with a new and reluctant growth of vegetable forms and with alien tribes of animal life. These intentional changes and substitutions constitute, indeed, great revolutions; but vast as is their magnitude and importance, they are, as we shall see, insignificant in comparison with the contingent and unsought results which have flowed from them.

The fact that, of all organic beings, man alone is to be regarded as essentially a destructive power, and that he wields energies to resist which Nature—that nature whom all material life and all inorganic substance obey—is wholly impotent, tends to prove that, though living in physical nature, he is not of her, that he is of more exalted parentage, and belongs to a higher order of existences, than those which are born of her womb and live in blind submission to her dictates.

There are, indeed, brute destroyers, beasts and birds and insects of prey—all animal life feeds upon, and, of course, destroys other life—but this destruction is balanced by compensations. It is, in fact, the very means by which the existence of one tribe of animals or of vegetables is secured against being smothered by the encroachments of another; and the reproductive powers of species, which serve as the food of others are always proportioned to the demand they are destined to supply. Man pursues his victims with reckless destructiveness; and while the sacrifice of life by the lower animals is limited by the cravings of appetite, he unsparingly persecutes, even to extirpation, thousands of organic forms which he can not consume.[1]

The earth was not, in its natural condition, completely adapted to the use of man, but only to the sustenance of wild animals and wild vegetation. These live, multiply their kind in just proportion, and attain their perfect measure of strength and beauty, without producing or requiring any important change in the natural arrangements of surface or in each other's spontaneous tendencies, except such mutual repression of excessive increase as may prevent the extirpation of one species by the encroachments of another. In short, without man, lower animal and spontaneous vegetable life would have been practically constant in type, distribution and proportion, and the physical geography of the earth would have remained undisturbed for indefinite periods, and been subject to revolution only from slow development, from possible unknown cosmical causes, or from geological action.[2]

But man, the domestic animals that serve him, the field and garden plants the products of which supply him with food and clothing, can not subsist and rise to the full development of their higher properties, unless brute and unconscious nature be effectually combatted, and, in a great degree, vanquished by human art. Hence, a certain measure of transformation of terrestrial surface, of suppression of natural, and stimulation of artificially modified productivity becomes necessary. This measure man has unfortunately exceeded. He has felled the forests whose network of fibrous roots bound the mold to the rocky skeleton of the earth; but had he allowed here and there a belt of woodland to reproduce itself by spontaneous propagation, most of the mischiefs which his reckless destruction of the natural protection of the soil has occasioned would have been averted. He has broken up the mountain reservoirs, the percolation of whose waters through unseen channels supplied the fountains that refreshed his cattle and fertilized his fields; but he has neglected to maintain the cisterns and the canals of irrigation which a wise antiquity had constructed to neutralize the consequences of its own imprudence. While he has torn the thin glebe which confined the light earth of extensive plains, and has destroyed the fringe of semi-aquatic plants which skirted the coast and checked the drifting of the sea sand, he has failed to prevent the spreading of the dunes by clothing them with artificially propagated vegetation. He has ruthlessly warred on all the tribes of animated nature whose spoil he could convert to his own uses, and he has not protected the birds which prey on the insects most destructive to his own harvests.

Purely untutored humanity, it is true, interferes comparatively little with the arrangements of nature,[3] and the destructive agency of man becomes more and more energetic and unsparing as he advances in civilization, until the impoverishment, with which his exhaustion of the natural resources of the soil is threatening him, at last awakens him to the necessity of preserving what is left, if not of restoring what has been wantonly wasted. The wandering savage grows no cultivated vegetable, fells no forest, and extirpates no useful plant, no noxious weed. If his skill in the chase enables him to entrap numbers of the animals on which he feeds, he compensates this loss by destroying also the lion, the tiger, the wolf, the otter, the seal, and the eagle, thus indirectly protecting the feebler quadrupeds and fish and fowls, which would otherwise become the booty of beasts and birds of prey. But with stationary life, or at latest with the pastoral state, man at once commences an almost indiscriminate warfare upon all the forms of animal and vegetable existence around him, and as he advances in civilization, he gradually eradicates or transforms every spontaneous product of the soil he occupies.

Human and Brute Action Compared

It is maintained by authorities as high as any known to modern science, that the action of man upon nature, though greater in *degree*, does not differ in *kind* from that of wild animals. It is perhaps impossible to establish a radical distinction *in genere* between the two classes of effects, but there is an essential difference between the motive of action which calls out the energies of civilized man and the mere appetite which controls the life of the beast. The action of man, indeed, is frequently followed by unforeseen and undesired results, yet it is nevertheless guided by a self-conscious will aiming as often at secondary and remote as at immediate objects. The wild animal, on the other hand, acts instinctively, and, so far as we are able to perceive, always with a view to single and direct purposes. The backwoodsman and the beaver alike fell trees; the man, that he may convert the forest into an olive grove that will mature its fruit only for a succeeding generation; the beaver, that he may feed upon the bark of the trees or use them in the construction of his habitation. The action of brutes upon the material world is slow and gradual, and usually limited, in any given case, to a narrow extent of territory. Nature is allowed time and opportunity to set her restorative powers at work, and the destructive animal has hardly retired from the field of his ravages before nature has repaired the damages occasioned by his operations. In fact, he is expelled from the scene by the very efforts which she makes for the restoration of her dominion. Man, on the contrary, extends his action over vast spaces, his revolutions are swift and radical, and his devastations are, for an almost incalculable time after he has withdrawn the arm that gave the blow, irreparable. ...

... The earth is fast becoming an unfit home for its noblest inhabitant, and another era of equal human crime and human improvidence, and of like duration with that through which traces of that crime and that improvidence extend, would reduce it to such a condition of impoverished productiveness, of shattered surface, of climatic excess, as to threaten the depravation, barbarism and perhaps even extinction of the species.

Physical Improvement

True, there is a partial reverse to this picture. On narrow theatres, new forests have been planted; inundations of flowing streams restrained by heavy walls of masonry and other constructions; torrents compelled to aid, by depositing the slime with which they are charged, in filling up lowlands, and raising the level of morasses which their own overflows had created; ground submerged by the encroachments of the ocean, or exposed to be covered by its tides, has been rescued from its dominion by diking; swamps and even lakes have been drained, and their beds brought within the domain of agricultural industry; drifting coast dunes have been checked and made productive by plantation; seas and inland waters have been repeopled with fish, and even the sands of the Sahara have been fertilized by artesian fountains. These achievements are more glorious than the proudest triumphs of war, but, thus far, they give but faint hope that we shall yet make full atonement for our spendthrift waste of the bounties of nature.

Limits of Human Power

It is, on the one hand, rash and unphilosophical to attempt to set limits to the ultimate power of man over inorganic nature, and it is unprofitable, on the other, to speculate on what may be accomplished by the discovery of now unknown and unimagined natural forces, or even by the invention of new arts and new processes. ... Yet among the mysteries which science is hereafter to reveal, there may be still undiscovered methods of accomplishing even grander wonders than these. Mechanical philosophers have suggested the possibility of accumulating and treasuring up for human use some of the greater natural forces, which the action of the elements puts forth with such astonishing energy.[4]

Notes

1 [Marsh's note] The terrible destructiveness of man is remarkably exemplified in the chase of large mammalia and birds, for single products, attended with the entire waste of enormous quantities of flesh and of other parts of the animal which are capable of valuable uses. The wild cattle of South America are slaughtered by millions, for their hides and horns; the buffalo of North America, for his skin or his tongue; the elephant, the walrus, and the narwhal, for their tusks; the cetacea, and some other marine animals, for their whalebone and oil; the ostrich and other large birds, for their plumage. Within a few years, sheep have been killed in New England, by whole flocks, for their pelts and suet alone, the flesh being thrown away; and it is even said that the bodies of the same quadrupeds have been used in Australia as fuel for limekilns. What a vast amount of human nutriment, of bone, and of other animal products valuable in the arts, is thus recklessly squandered! In nearly all these cases, the part which constitutes the motive for this wholesale destruction, and is alone saved, is essentially of insignificant value as compared with what is thrown away. The horns and hide of an ox are not economically worth a tenth part as much as the entire carcass. During the present year, large quantities of Indian corn have been used as domestic fuel, and even for burning.

One of the greatest benefits to be expected from the improvements of civilization is, that increased facilities of communication will render it possible to transport to places of consumption much valuable material that is now wasted because the price at the nearest market will not pay freight. ...

A very important recent economy is the utilization of those portions of certain agricultural products that were formerly treated as mere refuse. ...

We are also beginning to learn a better economy in dealing with the inorganic world. The utilization—or, as the Germans more happily call it, the *Verwerthung*, the "beworthing"—of waste from metallurgical, chemical and manufacturing establishments, is among the most important results of the application of science to industrial purposes. The incidental products from the laboratories of manufacturing chemists often become more valuable than those for the preparation of which they were erected. The slags from silver refineries, and even from smelting houses of the coarser metals, have not unfrequently yielded to a second operator a better return than the first had derived from dealing with the natural ore; and the saving of lead carried off in the smoke of furnaces has, of itself, given a large profit on the capital invested in the works. ... A few years ago, an officer of an American mint was charged with embezzling gold committed to him for coinage. He insisted, in his defence, that much of the metal was volatilized and lost in refining and melting, and upon scraping the chimneys of the melting furnaces and the roofs of the adjacent houses, gold enough was found in the soot to account for no small part of the deficiency. ...

There are still, however, cases of enormous waste in many mineral and mechanical industries. ...

2   Marsh is of the view that, in the absence of human interference, the topographical and biological characteristics of the Earth's regions are in a state of stable equilibrium, which is altered only in highly unusual circumstances. For many years, classical ecology held a version of this view: one ecosystem is succeeded by another, in a lawlike fashion, until the system reaches its "climax," a point of stability and equilibrium. As more has been learned about geographical and ecological change, this view has been superseded. Even healthy ecosystems are undergoing change, at varying rates. On this view, human beings damage ecosystems, not merely in changing them, but in acting in a way that leads to sudden losses of relative stability and biodiversity.

3   [Marsh's note] It is an interesting and not hitherto sufficiently noticed fact, that the domestication of the organic world, so far as it has yet been achieved, belongs, not indeed to the savage state, but to the earliest dawn of civilization; the conquest of inorganic nature, almost as exclusively to the most advanced stages of artificial culture. ...

It is familiarly known to all who have occupied themselves with the psychology and habits of the ruder races, and of persons with imperfectly developed intellects in civilized life, that although these humble tribes and individuals sacrifice, without scruple, the lives of the lower animals to the gratification of their appetites and the supply of their other physical wants, yet they nevertheless seem to cherish with brutes, and even with vegetable life, sympathies which are much more feebly felt by civilized men. May we not ascribe to this sympathy the fact that Homer does not refer to the ass as a type of stupidity, nor to the swine as an example of uncleanness? The father of Ulysses is called the *god-like swineherd*. The popular traditions of the simpler peoples recognize a certain community of nature between man, brute animals, and even plants; and this serves to explain why the apologue or fable, which ascribes the power of speech and the faculty of reason to birds, quadrupeds, insects, flowers and trees, is one of the earliest forms of literary composition. ...

4   [Marsh's note] Some well-known experiments show that it is quite possible to accumulate the solar heat by a simple apparatus, and thus to obtain a temperature which might be economically important even in the climate of Switzerland. ... The reciprocal convertibility of the natural forces has suggested the possibility of advantageously converting the heat of the sun into mechanical power. ... I do not know that any attempts have been made to accumulate and store up for use at pleasure, force derived from this powerful source.

CHAPTER 24

Friedrich Engels

KARL MARX (1818–1883) and Friedrich Engels (1820–1895) jointly developed the economic and social philosophy that has come to be known as Marxism. There are two reasons why Marxist thought plays a very important role in the development of environmental philosophy. First, Marxist analyses have often been used to explain the tendency of capitalist economies to recklessly industrialize and develop lands, heedless of the environmental consequences. Second, the materialistic anthropocentrism found in traditional Marxist teachings has itself been thought to have been responsible for the environmental damage done by political regimes established on Marxist principles.

Marxist thought has developed in a number of highly diverse directions over the past century; the following principles, however, are accepted by most interpreters.

1. Marxism is a materialist philosophy. This means that it takes all existing things to be material, bodily things.
2. Among material things, human beings are uniquely able to understand the world. This understanding is a material process, but it is special in enabling people to freely choose the path of their lives. In the best society, there would be no societal impediments to people achieving the goals that they set for themselves.
3. The key to understanding what human beings do, however, is not to be found in thought or free choice, but in labor. This is the means by which human beings are able to change the world, and themselves.
4. Capitalist economies prevent people from living free lives, insofar as they condemn the working classes to view themselves and the world in terms that ensure the perpetuation of the economic system that exploits them and makes others rich.
5. History obeys certain laws that are grounded in the necessary operations of matter. These laws allow one to predict the downfall of the capitalist economies. They are to be replaced by a structure that allows the workers (or "proletariat") to achieve their freedom.

Some scholars point to important differences in the outlooks of Marx and Engels, but each saw himself as in basic agreement with the other, and the following selection from Engels is representative of Marxist thought. Engels presents his account of the development of the human species apart from the rest of the natural world. The selection shows Engels' materialism, anthropocentrism, and claim of the centrality of labor. This passage also reveals Engels' awareness of the potentially devastating environmental consequences of human labor, and provides his explanation for why capitalist economies are especially prone to such problems.

FRIEDRICH ENGELS
"The Part Played by Labor in the Transition from Ape to Man"
TR. CLEMENS DUTT

Just as man learned to consume everything edible, he learned also to live in any climate. He spread over the whole of the habitable world, being the only animal that by its very nature had the power to do so. The other animals that have become accustomed to all climates—domestic animals and vermin—did not become so independently, but only in the wake of man. And the transition from the uniformly hot climate of the original home of man to colder regions, where the year is divided into summer and winter, created new requirements: shelter and clothing as protection against cold and damp, new spheres for labor and hence new forms of activity, which further and further separated man from the animal.

By the cooperation of hands, organs of speech, and brain, not only in each individual, but also in society, human beings became capable of executing more and more complicated operations, and of setting themselves, and achieving, higher and higher aims. With each generation, labor itself became different, more perfect, more diversified. Agriculture was added to hunting and cattle-breeding, then spinning, weaving, metal-working, pottery, and navigation. Along with trade and industry, there appeared finally art and science. From tribes there developed nations and states. Law and politics arose, and with them the fantastic reflection of human things in the human mind: religion.[1] In the face of all these creations, which appeared in the first place to be products of the mind, and which seemed to dominate human society, the more modest productions of the working hand retreated into the background, the more so since the mind that plans the labor process already at a very early stage of development of society (e.g., already in the simple family), was able to have the labor that had been planned carried out by other hands than its own.[2] All merit for the swift advance of civilization was ascribed to the mind, to the development and activity of the brain. Men became accustomed to explain their actions from their thoughts, instead of from their needs—(which in any case are reflected and come to consciousness in the mind)—and so there arose in the course of time that idealistic outlook on the world which, especially since the decline of the ancient world, has dominated men's minds.[3] It still rules them to such a degree that even the most materialistic natural scientists of the Darwinian school are still unable to form any clear idea of the origin of man, because under this ideological influence they do not recognize the part that has been played therein by labor.[4]

Animals, as already indicated, change external nature by their activities just as man does, if not to the same extent, and these changes made by them in their environment, as we have seen, in turn react upon and change their originators. For in nature nothing takes place in isolation. Everything affects every other thing and vice versa, and it is usually because this many-sided motion and interaction is forgotten that our natural scientists are prevented from clearly seeing the simplest things. We have seen how goats have prevented the regeneration of forest in Greece; on the island of St. Helena, goats and pigs brought by the first arrivals have succeeded in exterminating almost completely the old vegetation of the island, and so have prepared the soil for the spreading of plants brought by later sailors and colonists. But if animals exert a lasting effect on their environment, it happens unintentionally, and, as far as the animals themselves are concerned, it is an accident. The further men become removed from animals, however, the more their effect on nature assumes the character of a premeditated, planned action directed towards definite ends known in advance. The animal destroys the vegetation of a locality without realizing what it is doing. Man destroys it in order to sow field crops on the soil thus released, or to plant trees or vines which he knows will yield many times the amount sown. He transfers useful plants and domestic animals from one country to another and thus changes the flora and fauna of whole continents. More than this. Under artificial cultivation, both plants and animals are so changed by the hand of man that they become unrecognizable. The wild plants from which our grain varieties originated are still being sought in vain. The question of the wild animal from which our dogs are descended, the dogs themselves being so different from one another, or our equally numerous breeds of horses, is still under dispute.

In any case, of course, we have no intention of disputing the ability of animals to act in a planned and premeditated fashion. On the contrary, a planned mode of action exists in embryo wherever protoplasm, living protein, exists and reacts, i.e., carries out definite, even if extremely simple, movements as a result of definite external stimuli. Such reaction takes place even where there is as yet no cell at all, far less a nerve cell. The manner in which insectivorous plants capture their prey appears likewise in a certain respect as a planned action, although performed quite unconsciously. In animals the capacity for conscious, planned action develops side by side with the development of the nervous system and among mammals it attains quite a high level. While fox hunting in England, one can daily observe how unerringly the fox knows how to make use of its excellent knowledge of the locality in order to escape from its pursuers, and how well it knows and turns to account all favorable features of the ground that cause the scent to be interrupted. Among our domestic animals, more highly developed thanks to association with man, every day one can note acts of cunning on exactly the same level as those of children. For, just as the developmental history of the human embryo in the mother's womb is only an abbreviated version of the history, extending over millions of years, of the bodily evolution of our animal ancestors, beginning from the worm, so the mental development of the human child is only a still more abbreviated repetition of the intellectual development of these same ancestors, at least of the later ones. But all the planned action of all animals has never resulted in impressing the stamp of their will upon nature. For that, man was required.

In short, the animal merely *uses* external nature, and brings about changes in it simply by his presence; man by its changes makes it serve his ends, *masters* it. This is the final, essential distinction between man and the other animals, and once again it is labor that brings about this distinction.[5]

Let us not, however, flatter ourselves overmuch on account of our human conquest over nature. For each such conquest takes its revenge on us. Each of them, it is true, has in the first place the consequences on which we counted, but in the second and third places it has quite different, unforeseen effects which only too often cancel out the first. The people who, in Mesopotamia, Greece, Asia Minor, and elsewhere, destroyed the forests to obtain cultivable land, never dreamed that they were laying the basis for the present devastated condition of these countries, by removing along with the forests the collecting centers and reservoirs of moisture. When, on the southern slopes of the mountains, the Italians of the Alps used up the pine forests so carefully cherished on the northern slopes, they had no inkling that by doing so they were cutting at the roots of the dairy industry in their region; they had still less inkling that they were thereby depriving their mountain springs of water for the greater part of the year, with the effect that these would be able to pour still more furious flood torrents on the plains during the rainy seasons. Those who spread the potato in Europe were not aware that they were at the same time spreading the disease of scrofula.[6] Thus at every step we are reminded that we by no means rule over nature like a conqueror over a foreign people, like someone standing outside nature—but that we, with flesh, blood, and brain, belong to nature, and exist in its midst, and that all our mastery of it consists in the fact that we have the advantage over all other beings of being able to know and correctly apply its laws.

And, in fact, with every day that passes we are learning to understand these laws more correctly, and getting to know both the more immediate and the more remote consequences of our interference with the traditional course of nature. In particular, after the mighty advances of natural science in the present century, we are more and more getting to know, and hence to control, even the more remote natural consequences at least of our more ordinary productive activities. But the more this happens, the more will men not only feel, but also know, their unity with nature, and thus the more impossible will become the senseless and antinatural contradiction between mind and matter, man and nature, soul and body, such as arose in Europe after the decline of classic antiquity and which obtained its highest elaboration in Christianity.[7]

But if it has already required the labor of thousands of years for us to learn to some extent to calculate the more remote *natural* consequences of our actions aiming at production, it has been still more difficult in regard to the more remote *social* consequences of these actions. ...

The men who in the seventeenth and eighteenth centuries labored to create the steam engine had no idea that they were preparing the instrument which more than any other was to revolutionize social conditions throughout the world.[8] Especially in Europe, by concentrating wealth in the hands of a minority, the huge majority being rendered propertyless, this instrument was destined at first to give social and political domination to the bourgeoisie,[9] and then, however, to give rise to a class struggle between bourgeoisie and proletariat, which can end only in the overthrow of the bourgeoisie and the abolition of all class contradictions. But even in this sphere, by long and often cruel experience and by collecting and analyzing the historical material, we are gradually learning to get a clear view of the indirect, more remote, social effects of our productive activity, and so the possibility is afforded us of mastering and controlling these effects as well.

To carry out this control requires something more than mere knowledge. It requires a complete revolution in our hitherto existing mode of production, and with it of our whole contemporary social order.

All hitherto existing modes of production have aimed merely at achieving the most immediately and directly useful effect of labor. The further consequences, which only appear later on and become effective through gradual repetition and accumulation, were totally neglected. Primitive communal ownership of land corresponded, on the one hand, to a level of development of human beings in which their horizon was restricted in general to what lay immediately at hand, and presupposed, on the other hand, a certain surplus of available land, allowing a certain latitude for correcting any possible bad results of this primitive forest type of economy. When this surplus land was exhausted, communal ownership also declined. All higher forms of production, however, proceeded in their development to the division of the population into different classes and thereby to the contradiction of ruling and oppressed classes.[10] But thanks to this, the interest of the ruling class became the driving factor of production, in so far as the latter was not restricted to the barest means of subsistence of the oppressed people. This has been carried through most completely in the capitalist mode of production prevailing today in Western Europe. The individual capitalists, who dominate production and exchange, are able to concern themselves only with the most immediate useful effect of their actions. Indeed, even this useful effect—in as much as it is a question of the usefulness of the commodity that is produced or exchanged—retreats right into the background, and the sole incentive becomes the profit to be gained on selling.[11]

The social science of the bourgeoisie, classical political economy, is predominantly occupied only with the directly intended social effects of human actions connected with production and exchange. This fully corresponds to the social organization of which it is the theoretical expression. When individual capitalists are engaged in production and exchange for the sake of the immediate profit, only the nearest, most immediate results can be taken into account in the first place. When an individual manufacturer or merchant sells a manufactured or purchased commodity with only the usual small profit, he is satisfied, and he is not concerned as to what becomes of the commodity afterwards or who are its purchasers. The same thing applies to the natural effects of the same actions. What did the Spanish planters in Cuba, who burned down forests on the slopes of the mountains and obtained from the ashes sufficient fertiliser for one generation of very highly profitable coffee trees, care that the tropical rainfall afterwards washed away the now unprotected upper stratum of the soil, leaving behind only bare rock? In relation to nature, as to society, the present mode of production is predominantly concerned only about the first, tangible success; and then surprise is expressed that the more remote effects of actions directed to this end turn out to be of quite a different, mainly even of quite an opposite, character; that the harmony of demand and supply becomes transformed into their polar opposites, as shown by the course of each ten years' industrial cycle, and of which even Germany has experienced a little preliminary in the "crash"; that private ownership based on individual labor necessarily develops into the propertylessness of the workers, while all wealth becomes more and more concentrated in the hands of nonworkers; that - - -[12]

Notes

1 As materialist philosophers, Marx and Engels took all religions to be fundamentally false. They thought that religious beliefs and institutions kept people from achieving the freedom of which they were capable, because they trapped believers into false beliefs concerning higher powers. These beliefs serve to perpetuate the economic structures that oppress workers.

2 Engels is pointing to the origin of class structure in society. There came a time in the development of the human species when the people who decided what labor was to be done were different from the ones who actually performed the labor.

3 For our purposes, we can consider an idealistic philosophy as one that takes thought and choice to be processes that are not solely material in nature.

4 Darwin explained the development of the human species as he explained the development of any species: random variation and natural selection. Engels suggests that human labor and the economic and historical changes that it brings about can lead to a development of human beings that is of a different order.

5 Engels, like Porphyry, points to examples of animal intelligence in order to argue against any metaphysical distinction between the nature of human and nonhuman beings. For

Engels, intelligence is a wholly material characteristic, whose essence can be found in any life form, insofar as it responds to its environment in a teleological way. The crucial difference between human beings and all other beings is that only the former is capable of labor, by which nature is changed as one wills it. But Engels does not think that there is in human beings a "free will" that has its basis in some immaterial aspect of the human person. Labor and will remain material through and through.

6   Scrofula, a form of tuberculosis, is found among malnourished people, and those who eat only potatoes are malnourished. But the disease is not directly caused by a diet of potatoes, as Engels believed.

7   Engels has in mind distinctions between the mind as immaterial and the body as material, as can be seen in the philosophy of Plato, Aristotle, St. Augustine, St. Thomas Aquinas, and Descartes.

8   We have just seen Engels discuss how changes in human labor can have unintended effects on the natural environment, and how greater scientific knowledge will enable these effects to be foreseen and controlled. Engels is now making the same point in the social sphere. Changes in the means of production, such as the rapid industrialization of Europe, necessarily lead to changes in the structure of society. Engels asserts that with enough knowledge, these effects, too, can be foreseen and controlled.

9   The bourgeoisie make up the commercial class of a capitalist economy. They own and control the means of production. The labor exerted by working people enriches the bourgeoisie, while the workers suffer.

10   For Marx and Engels, an industrial capitalist economy can come about only by means of having a few people own and control the factories, the means by which the working people do their labor. This necessitates severe class distinctions between the haves and the have-nots. On the Marxist account of history, these class distinctions are necessarily temporary. A capitalist economy must be followed by a revolution in which the workers themselves own and control the means of production.

11   Because a capitalist economy is driven by the desire for profit alone, the means of production are employed not for the sake of what will truly better people's lives, but only for what will sell.

12   The manuscript of this unfinished essay ends here.

VI

Living with Nature

CHAPTER 25

Jean Jacques Rousseau

JEAN JACQUES ROUSSEAU (1712–1778), French political philosopher, writer, botanist, and musician, helped to initiate Romanticism, an intellectual movement that emphasizes the importance of emotions over the intellect. Romantics tended to blame personal and social ills on the pressures that civilization brings to bear on human beings; for the Romantics, the free, spontaneous, and "natural" reactions of human beings are often a better guide to a healthy, happy life—for both individuals and groups—than the rules laid down by society. One can best become aware of these natural feelings and reactions, and can best avoid the negative influence of society, by taking refuge in natural, uninhabited surroundings.

Many of the Romantics were interested in biology. They took the spontaneous growth of plants to be a more appropriate object of study for a soul seeking pleasure and beauty than the physics of inorganic matter.

Traces of each of these aspects of Romanticism can be found in the ecological movement of today, and each can be discerned in Rousseau's final work, *The Reveries of a Solitary Walker*. This is a continuation of Rousseau's autobiography, the *Confessions*. Among other things, the *Confessions* documents how a sense of persecution by personal enemies increasingly dominated Rousseau's thinking. In the *Reveries*, Rousseau points to the peace from such troubles that he found in living a rural life, close to the natural world. He also celebrates the study of botany for its own sake, rather than for the sake of discovering medicines and other profitable goods produced from plants, or for the sake of career-building and the admiration of society.

JEAN JACQUES ROUSSEAU
The Reveries of a Solitary Walker
TR. JOHN GOULD FLETCHER, REV. PATRICIA KILROE

"Fifth Promenade"

… [I]f there is a state where the soul finds a position sufficiently solid to repose thereon, and to gather together all its being, without having need for recalling the past, nor to encroach upon the future; where time counts for nothing, where the present lasts forever, without marking its duration in any way, and without any trace of succession, without any other feeling of deprivation or enjoyment, of pleasure or pain, of desire or of fear, than that alone of our existence, and which this feeling alone can fill entirely; so long as this state lasts, he who finds himself in it may be called happy, not with an imperfect happiness, scanty and relative, such as that which one finds in the pleasures of life, but with a sufficient happiness, perfect and full, which does not leave in the soul any void which it feels the need of filling. Such is the state in which I often found myself on the island of St. Peter,[1] in my solitary reveries, either lying in my boat which I let drift at the will of the water, or seated on the banks of the turbulent lake, or elsewhere at the edge of a beautiful river, or of a brook murmuring on the sand.

... Without movement, life is only lethargy. If the movement is unequal or too strong it awakens; in recalling us to surrounding objects, it destroys the charm of the reverie and pulls us out of ourselves, to put us instantly back under the yoke of chance and mankind and to bring us back to the feeling of our unhappiness. An absolute silence leads to sadness; it offers an image of death. Thus the help of a cheerful imagination is necessary and occurs naturally in those whom heaven has bestowed with it. Movement which does not come from without, then, is made within us. The repose is less, it is true; but it is also more pleasant when light and gentle ideas, without stirring the depths of the soul, do nothing but skim its surface. There is needed only enough of them to remember oneself while forgetting all one's troubles. This sort of reverie can be tasted everywhere where one can be still; and I have often thought that at the Bastille, and even in a cell where no object would strike my sight, I still could have dreamed agreeably.

But it must be admitted that this was done better and more favorably on a fertile and solitary island, naturally circumscribed and separated from the rest of the world, where nothing was offered to me but cheerful images, where nothing recalled sad memories, where the society of the small number of inhabitants was affable and sweet, without being interesting to the point of occupying me incessantly, where I could finally surrender myself all day long, without obstacles and without cares, to the pursuits of my liking or to the most luxurious idleness. The opportunity without a doubt was excellent for a dreamer, who, knowing how to nourish himself with pleasant fantasies in the midst of the most unpleasant objects, could take his fill of them at his leisure while adding to them everything which actually struck his senses. On emerging from a long and sweet reverie, seeing myself surrounded with verdure, flowers, birds, and letting my eyes wander far and wide over romantic banks which bordered a vast extent of clear and crystalline water, I assimilated all these fine objects to my fictions; and finding myself brought back by degrees to myself and to what surrounded me, I could not distinguish the point of separation between fiction and reality, so much did all concur equally to render dear the solitary and contemplative life that I led in this fair dwelling. If it could only come again! If I could only go and end my days in this dear island, without ever leaving it, or ever seeing any inhabitant of the continent who would recall to me the memory of the calamities of every sort which they have been pleased to heap upon me for so many years! They would be soon forgotten for ever;

without a doubt they would not forget me in the same way; but what would this matter to me, provided that they had no way to come there and disturb my repose? Delivered from all the earthly passions to which the tumult of social life gives rise, my soul would frequently soar above this atmosphere and have converse beforehand with the celestial intellects, of which it hopes to augment the number in a short time. ...

"Seventh Promenade"

... All of a sudden, at age sixty-five plus, deprived of the little memory I had, and of the strength which remained to me to roam the fields, without a guide, without books, without a garden, without an herbal, I have returned to this folly, but with even more ardor than I had in yielding myself to it for the first time:[2] now I am seriously busied with the wise project of learning by heart the whole of Murray's "Vegetable Kingdom," becoming acquainted with all the known plants on earth. Not being able to afford to buy botany books again, I have undertaken to copy out those that have been lent to me; and, resolved to remake an herbal more copious than the first. Until I can put in it all the plants of the sea and the Alps, and all the trees of India, I begin at small cost with chickweed, chervil, borage, and groundsel; I learnedly botanize in my birdcage, and at every new blade of grass that I encounter, I say with satisfaction: Here is yet another plant.

... I had even to fear, in my reveries, that my imagination, disturbed by my misfortunes, would turn its activity in that direction only, and that the continual feeling of my woes, gradually tightening around my heart, would finally overwhelm me with their weight. In this state, an instinct which is natural to me, making me flee from every sorrowful idea, imposed silence upon my imagination, and, fixing my attention upon the objects which surrounded me, made me, for the first time, absorb in detail the spectacle of nature, which I had scarcely contemplated except as a mass and as a whole.

Trees, shrubs, and plants are the clothing and finery of the earth. Nothing is so sad as the look of a bald and naked country, which displays to the eye nothing but stones, silt, and sands. But, invigorated by nature and adorned with its wedding gown in the midst of streams and the song of the birds, the earth offers to man, in the harmony of its three kingdoms, a spectacle full of life, interest and charm, the one spectacle in the world of which his eyes and his heart never grow weary.

The more a contemplator has a sensitive soul, the more he yields himself to the ecstasies which this harmony excites in him. A profound and pleasing reverie then gets hold of his senses, and he loses himself with a delicious intoxication in the immensity of the beautiful system with which he feels identified. Then all particular objects escape him; he does not see and does not feel anything but in the whole. It is necessary that some particular circumstance should collect his ideas and limit his imagination, in order for him to observe the parts of this universe which he was struggling to embrace.

This happened to me naturally when my heart, bound by distress, brought together and concentrated all its movements on itself in order to preserve the remains of ardor which were ready to evaporate and to disappear, in the despondency into which I was gradually falling. I wandered aimlessly through the woods and the mountains, not daring to think for fear of stirring up my anguish. My imagination, which resists painful objects, let my senses yield to the light but sweet impressions of surrounding objects. My eyes wandered ceaselessly from one to another, and it was not possible that amidst such great variety there weren't some objects which would capture their attention, and hold it longer.

I acquired a taste for this recreation of the eyes, which in misfortune reposes, amuses, and distracts the mind and suspends the feeling of misery. The nature of the objects greatly aids this diversion, and renders it more seductive. Delicate odors, strong colors, and the most elegant forms seem to contend for the right to hold one's attention. It is only necessary to love pleasure in order to yield to sensations so sweet; and, if this effect does not occur in all those who are affected by them, it is, in some, due to a lack of natural sensibility, and, in most, because their mind is too much occupied by other ideas and does not yield except surreptitiously to the objects which strike their senses.

Another thing contributes to avert the attention of people of taste from the vegetable kingdom: the habit of seeking in plants nothing but drugs and remedies. Theophrastus[3] took to it for a different reason, and this philosopher may be looked upon as the sole botanist of antiquity; consequently he is scarcely known among us. But thanks to a certain Dioscorides[4]—a great compiler of recipes—and to his commentators, medicine took possession of plants in the form of simples to such an extent that people only see in them what is not there to see—that is to say, the supposed virtues which it pleases three-quarters of mankind to attribute to them. They cannot understand that the structure of plants should merit some attention for its own sake; people who spend their lives in learnedly arranging a few shells ridicule botany as a useless study when it is not supplemented, as they say, by that of the properties; that is to say, when one does not abandon the observation of nature, which does not lie and says nothing to us about all this, in order to yield oneself solely to the authority of men (who are liars and who assert many things which must be believed upon their word), which is itself founded most frequently upon the authority of another. Pause in a flowering plain and examine successively the flowers with which it glows; those who will see you doing this, taking you for a quacksalver, will ask for herbs to heal the itch of children, the scabies of men, or the glanders of horses. This disgusting prejudice has been done away with in part in other countries, and especially in England, thanks to Linnaeus, who has taken botany a little away from schools of pharmacy to return it to natural history and to economic use; but in France, where this study has least penetrated among any people in the world, people have remained so barbarous in this respect that a clever man from Paris, seeing in London a connoisseur's garden, full of trees and rare plants, exclaimed in praise, "There is a fine garden for an apothecary." In that case, the first apothecary was Adam, for it is not easy to imagine a garden better furnished with plants than that of Eden.

These medicinal ideas are assuredly hardly suitable for rendering the study of botany pleasant; they spoil the glory of the meadows, the luster of flowers, dry up the freshness of the woods, and make the greenery and the shade insipid and disgusting: all these charming and gracious structures interest very little anyone who only wants to bray them in a mortar, and no one will go seeking garlands for shepherdesses among herbs for enemas.

None of this pharmacology sullied my rustic imagery; nothing was further from my mind than infusions and plasters. I have often thought, when looking closely upon the fields, the orchards, the woods and their numerous inhabitants, that the vegetable kingdom was a storehouse of food given by nature to men and beasts; but it never entered my mind to look for drugs or remedies there. I do not see anything in this diverse produce which indicates for me such a usage; and nature would have shown us the way to choose, if she had prescribed it for us, as she has done for edibles. I even feel that the pleasure I take in walking about the groves would be poisoned by the sentiment of human infirmities, if it allowed me to think of fever, stones, gout, and epilepsy. Moreover, I do not deny to plants the great virtues which are attributed to them; I will only say that in supposing these virtues to be real, it is pure malice for sick people to continue to be so; because among all the illnesses which people ascribe to themselves, there is not a single one which twenty sorts of herbs do not completely heal.

These tendencies of the mind, which always bring everything back to our material interests, which make us seek profit or remedies everywhere, and which would make us regard with indifference the whole of nature if we were always well, have never been mine. I feel myself of a contrary opinion to other people on that subject: everything which concerns my needs saddens and spoils my thoughts, and never have I found true charm in the pleasures of the mind save by completely losing sight of interest in my body. Thus, even if I myself believed in medicine, and even if its remedies were pleasant, I should never find, in occupying myself with it, those delights which pure and disinterested contemplation provides, and my soul could not be exalted and soar above nature, so long as I felt it held back by the shackles of my body. ...

No, nothing personal, nothing which concerns the interest of my body, can truly occupy my soul. I never meditate, never dream more delightfully than when I forget myself. I feel ecstasy, inexpressible rapture, in dissolving myself, so to speak, in the system of beings, in identifying myself with the whole of nature. So long as men were my brothers, I made projects of earthly happiness; these projects being always relative to the whole, I could not be happy except in a public happiness, and never has the idea of private happiness touched my heart except when I have seen my brothers seeking theirs in my misery. Then, in order not to hate them, it was necessary to flee from them; so, taking refuge in the common mother, I have sought in her arms to escape the attacks of her children. I have become solitary, or, as they say, unsociable and misanthropic, because the wildest solitude appears to me preferable to the society of the wicked, which feeds only upon betrayal and hatred. ...

Fleeing from men, seeking solitude, no longer imagining, thinking even less, yet still endowed with a lively temperament, which keeps me far from languid and melancholy apathy, I began to interest myself in all that surrounded me, and by a very natural instinct I gave preference to the most pleasant objects. The mineral kingdom has nothing in itself either desirable or attractive; its riches, enclosed in the bosom of the earth, seem to have been removed from the gaze of men in order not to tempt their cupidity. They are there like a reserve to serve one day as a supplement to the true wealth which is more within his reach, and for which he loses taste according to the extent of his corruption. Then he is compelled to call in industry, to toil, and to labor to alleviate his misery. He ransacks the entrails of the earth; he goes searching at its center, at the risk of his life and at the expense of his health, for imaginary goods in place of the real goods which the earth offered of itself when he knew how to enjoy them. He flees the sun and the day, which he is no longer worthy to see; he buries himself alive, and does well, no longer being worthy of living in the light of day. There quarries, pits, forges, furnaces, a battery of anvils, hammers, smoke and fire, succeed the fair images of his rustic labors. The wan faces of the unhappy people who languish in the foul vapors of mines, of black forgemen, of hideous cyclopes, are the spectacle which the working of the mines substitute, in the bosom of the earth, for that of greenery and flowers, the azure sky, amorous shepherds and robust laborers upon its surface.

It is easy, I admit, to go gathering sand and stones, to fill one's pockets and one's study with them, and to give oneself the airs of a naturalist; but those who attach themselves and limit themselves to these sorts of collections are, ordinarily, ignorant rich people who seek only the pleasure of display. To profit from the study of minerals, it is necessary to be a chemist and a physicist; it is necessary to make difficult and costly experiments, to work in laboratories, to expend much money and time with charcoal, crucibles, furnaces, retorts, in stifling smoke and vapors, always at the risk of one's life, and often at the expense of one's health. From all this dreary and fatiguing labor comes, ordinarily, much less knowledge than pride; and where is the most mediocre chemist who does not believe that he has penetrated all the great operations of nature because he has found, perhaps by chance, a few little combinations of the art?

The animal kingdom is more within our reach and certainly deserves even more to be studied; but after all, has not this study also its difficulties, its encumbrances, its disgusts and its worries? Above all for a solitary who has not, either in his play or his work, any hope of assistance from anyone? How to observe, dissect, study, understand the birds in the air, the fish in the water, the quadrupeds swifter than the wind, stronger than man, and which are not more inclined to come and offer themselves to my research than I am to run after them in order to make them submit to it by force? I might have recourse to snails, worms, and flies, and I might spend my life getting out of breath by running after butterflies, and impale poor insects, dissect mice when I could catch them, or the carrion of beasts I happened to find dead. The study of animals is nothing without anatomy; it is by this that one learns to classify and to distinguish the genera, the species. To study them for their behavior, their character, it would be necessary to have aviaries, fish ponds, menageries; it would be necessary to constrain them, by whatever means possible, so they would remain assembled near me; I have neither the taste nor the means to retain them in captivity, nor the agility necessary to follow them at their pace when they are at liberty. I should be compelled then to study them dead, to tear them up, to bone them, to grope at leisure in their palpitating entrails! What a frightful apparatus an anatomical amphitheater is! Stinking corpses, swollen and livid flesh, blood, disgusting entrails, frightful skeletons, pestilential vapors! Upon my word, it is not there that Jean Jacques will go looking for entertainment.

Brilliant flowers, glossy meadows, fresh shade, rivulets, groves, verdure, come and purify my imagination defiled by all these hideous objects. My soul, dead to all great movements, can no longer be moved by anything but sensible objects; I have only sensations, and it is through them alone that pain and pleasure can reach me here below. Attracted by the cheerful objects which surround me, I consider them, contemplate them, compare them, and end up learning to classify them, and there I am, suddenly as much a botanist as anyone needs to be who does not wish to study nature except to perpetually find new reasons for loving it!

I do not seek to instruct myself; it is too late. Besides, I have never noticed that so much science ever contributed to happiness in life. But I seek to provide myself with sweet and simple amusements, which I can enjoy without effort and which distract me from my misfortunes. I have neither to spend money nor take trouble to wander aimlessly from herb to herb, from plant to plant, in order to examine them, to compare their diverse characters, to note their similarities and their differences, in short to observe plant organization so as to follow the course and the workings of these living machines, to seek, with success sometimes, their general laws, the reason for and the end of their diverse structures, and to yield myself to the charm of grateful admiration for the hand which allows me to enjoy all of it. ...

... Botany is the study of an idle and lazy solitary; a sharp point and a magnifying glass are all the apparatus he needs to observe plants. He walks about, he wanders freely from one object to another; he examines each flower with interest and curiosity; and as soon as he begins to grasp the laws of their structure, he tastes an easy pleasure in observing them, as keen as if it cost him much. There is in this idle occupation a charm which is only felt when the passions are calmed, but which alone suffices to make life happy and sweet. But as soon as a motive of interest or vanity is mingled with it, either to fill empty seats or to turn out books, as soon as we only wish to learn in order to teach, only gather specimens to become an author or professor, all this sweet charm evaporates; we no longer see in plants anything but the instruments of our passions, we no longer find any true pleasure in their study, we no longer wish to know but to show that we know. And in the woods we are only on the world stage, preoccupied with getting admiration. Or else—limiting ourselves to the botany of the study and the garden at the most—instead of observing plants in nature, we concern ourselves only with systems and methods, an eternal matter for dispute which does not make one plant any better known and does not throw any true light upon natural history or the vegetable kingdom. Hence the hatred and jealousy which the competition for celebrity excites among botanical authors as much or more than among other scholars. In distorting this amiable study, they transplant it into the midst of cities and academies, where it degenerates no less than the exotic plants in the gardens of the connoisseurs.

Very different inclinations have made of this study a sort of passion for me which fills the void left by all those which I no longer have. I climb the rocks and the mountains, I bury myself in vales and in woods, to conceal myself, as far as is possible, from the memory of men and the reach of wicked people. It seems to me that in the shade of a forest I am forgotten, free, and peaceful, as if I had no more enemies, or as if the foliage of the woods would guard me from their reach just as it distances them from my memory; and in my foolishness I imagine that, by not thinking of them, they will not think of me. I find so great a sweetness in this illusion, that I would yield myself to it entirely if my situation, my weakness, and my needs would permit it. The more profound the solitude in which I live, then, the more it is necessary for some object to fill the void; and those which my imagination withholds from me or my memory rejects are made up for by the spontaneous products that the earth, not forced by men, offers to my eyes on all sides. The pleasure of going into a wilderness to search for new plants overlays that of escaping from my persecutors; and having arrived in places where I do not see any trace of men, I breathe more easily, as if in a sanctuary where their hatred no longer pursues me. ...

Notes

1 St. Peter is an island in Lake Biel, Switzerland.

2 Rousseau has just related how he had given up the study of botany, a passion of his younger days. He expresses surprise in his renewed enthusiasm for this study in his last years.

3 On Theophrastus, see Porphyry, *On Abstaining from Animals* (in this volume), 3.25 and n. 39.

4 Dioscorides, a first century AD Greek doctor, was a specialist in things botanical and the author of *On Medical Matters*.

CHAPTER 26

Ralph Waldo Emerson

RALPH WALDO EMERSON (1803–1882) was one of the most notable American poets and essayists of the nineteenth century. Like many literary figures of his time, Emerson looked to philosophical theories to give conceptual grounding to his work and world view. Like Rousseau, Emerson found in the natural world solace from the cares imposed by human society. He also shared the Romantic tendency to reflect on the inner life of human beings within the nonhuman world. Like Kant, Emerson took the physical world to be phenomenal, emerging only in the meeting between the human mind and things as they really are, which, as Kant taught, will always be hidden from us. Unlike Kant, however, Emerson thought that careful attention paid to the natural world would reveal truths about the deepest reality that underlies both the human mind and the natural world as it appears to us, truths that would otherwise be hidden from rational thought.

These ideas are all found in the essay "Nature," excerpted below. This essay had a significant influence on such writers as Henry David Thoreau and John Muir.

RALPH WALDO EMERSON
"Nature"

Introduction

... Philosophically considered, the universe is composed of Nature and the Soul. Strictly speaking, therefore, all that is separate from us, all which Philosophy distinguishes as the NOT ME, that is, both nature and art, all other men and my own body, must be ranked under this name, NATURE. In enumerating the values of nature and casting up their sum, I shall use the word in both senses; — in its common and in its philosophical import. In inquiries so general as our present one, the inaccuracy is not material; no confusion of thought will occur. *Nature*, in the common sense, refers to essences unchanged by man; space, the air, the river, the leaf. *Art* is applied to the mixture of his will with the same things, as in a house, a canal, a statue, a picture. But his operations taken together are so insignificant, a little chipping, baking, patching, and washing, that in an impression so grand as that of the world on the human mind, they do not vary the result.

Chapter 1: Nature

... Nature never wears a mean appearance. Neither does the wisest man extort her secret, and lose his curiosity by finding out all her perfection. Nature never became a toy to a wise spirit. The flowers, the animals, the mountains, reflected the wisdom of his best hour, as much as they had delighted the simplicity of his childhood.

When we speak of nature in this manner, we have a distinct but most poetical sense in the mind. We mean the integrity of impression made by manifold natural objects. It is this which distinguishes the stick of timber of the wood-cutter, from the tree of the poet. The charming landscape which I saw this morning, is indubitably made up of some twenty or thirty farms. Miller owns this field, Locke that, and Manning the woodland beyond. But none of them owns the landscape. There is a property in the horizon which no man has but he whose eye can integrate all the parts, that is, the poet. This is the best part of these men's farms, yet to this their warranty-deeds give no title.

... In the woods, is perpetual youth. Within these plantations of God, a decorum and sanctity reign, a perennial festival is dressed, and the guest sees not how he should tire of them in a thousand years. In the woods, we return to reason and faith. There I feel that nothing can befall me in life—no disgrace, no calamity (leaving me my eyes) which nature cannot repair. Standing on the bare ground—my head bathed by the blithe air, and uplifted into infinite space—all mean egotism vanishes. I become a transparent eye-ball; I am nothing; I see all; the currents of the Universal Being circulate through me; I am part or particle of God. The name of the nearest friend sounds then foreign and accidental: to be brothers, to be acquaintances,—master or servant, is then a trifle and a disturbance. I am the lover of uncontained and immortal beauty. In the wilderness, I find something more dear and connate than in streets or villages. In the tranquil landscape, and especially in the distant line of the horizon, man beholds somewhat as beautiful as his own nature.

The greatest delight which the fields and woods minister, is the suggestion of an occult relation between man and the vegetable. I am not alone and unacknowledged. They nod to me, and I to them. The waving of the boughs in the storm, is new to me and old. It takes me by surprise, and yet is not unknown. Its effect is like that of a higher thought or a better emotion coming over me, when I deemed I was thinking justly or doing right.

Yet it is certain that the power to produce this delight, does not reside in nature, but in man, or in a harmony of both.[1] It is necessary to use these pleasures with great temperance. For, nature is not always tricked in holiday attire, but the same scene which yesterday breathed perfume and glittered as for the frolic of the nymphs, is overspread with melancholy today. Nature always wears the colors of the spirit. To a man laboring under calamity, the heat of his own fire hath sadness in it. Then, there is a kind of contempt of the landscape felt by him who has just lost by death a dear friend. The sky is less grand as it shuts down over less worth in the population.

Chapter 2: Commodity

Whoever considers the final cause of the world, will discern a multitude of uses that result. They all admit of being thrown into one of the following classes; Commodity; Beauty; Language; and Discipline.[2] ...

Chapter 3: Beauty

A nobler want of man is served by nature, namely, the love of Beauty.

The ancient Greeks called the world *kosmos*, beauty. Such is the constitution of all things, or such the plastic power of the human eye, that the primary forms, as the sky, the mountain, the tree, the animal, give us a delight *in and for themselves*, a pleasure arising from outline, color, motion, and grouping. ... For better consideration, we may distribute the aspects of Beauty in a threefold manner.[3]

1. First, the simple perception of natural forms is a delight. ...

2. The presence of a higher, namely, of the spiritual element is essential to its perfection. The high and divine beauty which can be loved without effeminacy, is that which is found in combination with the human will. Beauty is the mark God sets upon virtue. Every natural action is graceful. Every heroic act is also decent, and causes the place and the bystanders to shine. We are taught by great actions that the universe is the property of every individual in it. Every rational creature has all nature for his dowry and estate. It is his, if he will. He may divest himself of it; he may creep into a corner, and abdicate his kingdom, as most men do, but he is entitled to the world by his constitution. In proportion to the energy of his thought and will, he takes up the world into himself. ...

3. There is still another aspect under which the beauty of the world may be viewed, namely, as it becomes an object of the intellect. Beside the relation of things to virtue, they have a relation to thought. The intellect searches out the absolute order of things as they stand in the mind of God, and without the colors of affection. The intellectual and the active powers seem to succeed each other, and the exclusive activity of the one, generates the exclusive activity of the other. There is something unfriendly in each to the other, but they are like the alternate periods of feeding and working in animals; each prepares and will be followed by the other. Therefore does beauty, which, in relation to actions, as we have seen, comes unsought, and comes because it is unsought, remain for the apprehension and pursuit of the intellect; and then again, in its turn, of the active power. Nothing divine dies. All good is eternally reproductive. The beauty of nature reforms itself in the mind, and not for barren contemplation, but for new creation. ...

The world thus exists to the soul to satisfy the desire of beauty. This element I call an ultimate end. No reason can be asked or given why the soul seeks beauty. Beauty, in its largest and profoundest sense, is one expression for the universe. God is the all-fair. Truth, and goodness, and beauty, are but different faces of the same All. But beauty in nature is not ultimate. It is the herald of inward and eternal beauty, and is not alone a solid and satisfactory good. It must stand as a part, and not as yet the last or highest expression of the final cause of Nature.

Chapter 4: Language

Language is a third use which Nature subserves to man. Nature is the vehicle of thought, and in a simple, double, and threefold degree.

1. Words are signs of natural facts.
2. Particular natural facts are symbols of particular spiritual facts.
3. Nature is the symbol of spirit.

1. Words are signs of natural facts. The use of natural history is to give us aid in supernatural history: the use of the outer creation, to give us language for the beings and changes of the inward creation. Every word which is used to express a moral or intellectual fact, if traced to its root, is found to be borrowed from some material appearance. *Right* means *straight; wrong* means *twisted. Spirit* primarily means *wind; transgression,* the crossing of a *line; supercilious,* the *raising of the eyebrow.* We say the *heart* to express emotion, the *head* to denote thought; and *thought* and *emotion* are words borrowed from sensible things, and now appropriated to spiritual nature. Most of the process by which this transformation is made, is hidden from us in the remote time when language was framed; but the same tendency may be daily observed in children. Children and savages use only nouns or names of things, which they convert into verbs, and apply to analogous mental acts.

2. But this origin of all words that convey a spiritual import,—so conspicuous a fact in the history of language—is our least debt to nature. It is not words only that are emblematic; it is things which are emblematic. Every natural fact is a symbol of some spiritual fact. Every appearance in nature corresponds to some state of the mind, and that state of the mind can only be described by presenting that natural appearance as its picture. An enraged man is a lion, a cunning man is a fox, a firm man is a rock, a learned man is a torch. A lamb is innocence; a snake is subtle spite; flowers express to us the delicate affections. Light and darkness are our familiar expression for knowledge and ignorance; and heat for love. Visible distance behind and before us, is respectively our image of memory and hope.

Who looks upon a river in a meditative hour, and is not reminded of the flux of all things? Throw a stone into the stream, and the circles that propagate themselves are the beautiful type of all influence. Man is conscious of a universal soul within or behind his individual life, wherein, as in a firmament, the natures of Justice, Truth, Love, Freedom, arise and shine. This universal soul, he calls Reason: it is not mine, or thine, or his, but we are its; we are its property and men. And the blue sky in which the private earth is buried, the sky with its eternal calm, and full of everlasting orbs, is the type of Reason. That which, intellectually considered, we call Reason, considered in relation to nature, we call Spirit. Spirit is the Creator. Spirit hath life in itself. And man in all ages and countries, embodies it in his language, as the FATHER.

It is easily seen that there is nothing lucky or capricious in these analogies, but that they are constant, and pervade nature. These are not the dreams of a few poets, here and there, but man is an analogist, and studies relations in all objects. He is placed in the centre of beings, and a ray of relation passes from every other being to him. And neither can man be understood without these objects, nor these objects without man. All the facts in natural history taken by themselves, have no value, but are barren, like a single sex. But marry it to human history, and it is full of life. Whole Floras, all Linnaeus' and Buffon's volumes, are dry catalogues of facts; but the most trivial of these facts, the habit of a plant, the organs, or work, or noise of an insect, applied to the illustration of a fact in intellectual philosophy, or, in any way associated to human nature, affects us in the most lively and agreeable manner. The seed of a plant,—to what affecting analogies in the nature of man, is that little fruit made use of, in all discourse, up to the voice of Paul, who calls the human corpse a seed,—"It is sown a natural body;[4] it is raised a spiritual body." The motion of the earth round its axis, and round the sun, makes the day, and the year. These are certain amounts of brute light and heat. But is there no intent of an analogy between man's life and the seasons? And do the seasons gain no grandeur or pathos from that analogy? The instincts of the ant are very unimportant, considered as the ant's; but the moment a ray of relation is seen to extend from it to man, and the little drudge is seen to be a monitor, a little body with a mighty heart, then all its habits, even that said to be recently observed, that it never sleeps, become sublime. ...

We know more from nature than we can at will communicate. Its light flows into the mind evermore, and we forget its presence. The poet, the orator, bred in the woods, whose senses have been nourished by their fair and appeasing changes, year after year, without design and without heed, — shall not lose their lesson altogether, in the roar of cities or the broil of politics. Long hereafter, amidst agitation and terror in national councils, — in the hour of revolution, — these solemn images shall reappear in their morning lustre, as fit symbols and words of the thoughts which the passing events shall awaken. At the call of a noble sentiment, again the woods wave, the pines murmur, the river rolls and shines, and the cattle low upon the mountains, as he saw and heard them in his infancy. And with these forms, the spells of persuasion, the keys of power are put into his hands.

3. We are thus assisted by natural objects in the expression of particular meanings. But how great a language to convey such pepper-corn informations! Did it need such noble races of creatures, this profusion of forms, this host of orbs in heaven, to furnish man with the dictionary and grammar of his municipal speech? Whilst we

use this grand cipher to expedite the affairs of our pot and kettle, we feel that we have not yet put it to its use, neither are able. We are like travellers using the cinders of a volcano to roast their eggs. Whilst we see that it always stands ready to clothe what we would say, we cannot avoid the question, whether the characters are not significant of themselves. Have mountains, and waves, and skies, no significance but what we consciously give them, when we employ them as emblems of our thoughts? The world is emblematic. Parts of speech are metaphors, because the whole of nature is a metaphor of the human mind. The laws of moral nature answer to those of matter as face to face in a glass. "The visible world and the relation of its parts, is the dial plate of the invisible."[5] The axioms of physics translate the laws of ethics. Thus, "the whole is greater than its part"; "reaction is equal to action"; "the smallest weight may be made to lift the greatest, the difference of weight being compensated by time"; and many the like propositions, which have an ethical as well as physical sense. These propositions have a much more extensive and universal sense when applied to human life, than when confined to technical use.

In like manner, the memorable words of history, and the proverbs of nations, consist usually of a natural fact, selected as a picture or parable of a moral truth. Thus; A rolling stone gathers no moss; A bird in the hand is worth two in the bush; A cripple in the right way, will beat a racer in the wrong; Make hay while the sun shines; 'Tis hard to carry a full cup even; Vinegar is the son of wine; The last ounce broke the camel's back; Long-lived trees make roots first;—and the like. In their primary sense these are trivial facts, but we repeat them for the value of their analogical import. What is true of proverbs, is true of all fables, parables, and allegories.

This relation between the mind and matter is not fancied by some poet, but stands in the will of God, and so is free to be known by all men. It appears to men, or it does not appear. ... It is the standing problem which has exercised the wonder and the study of every fine genius since the world began; from the era of the Egyptians and the Brahmins, to that of Pythagoras, of Plato, of Bacon, of Leibnitz, of Swedenborg. There sits the Sphinx at the road-side, and from age to age, as each prophet comes by, he tries his fortune at reading her riddle. There seems to be a necessity in spirit to manifest itself in material forms; and day and night, river and storm, beast and bird, acid and alkali, preexist in necessary Ideas in the mind of God, and are what they are by virtue of preceding affections, in the world of spirit.[6] A Fact is the end or last issue of spirit. The visible creation is the terminus or the circumference of the invisible world. ...

... A life in harmony with nature, the love of truth and of virtue, will purge the eyes to understand her text. By degrees we may come to know the primitive sense of the permanent objects of nature, so that the world shall be to us an open book, and every form significant of its hidden life and final cause.

A new interest surprises us, whilst, under the view now suggested, we contemplate the fearful extent and multitude of objects; since "every object rightly seen, unlocks a new faculty of the soul."[7] That which was unconscious truth, becomes, when interpreted and defined in an object, a part of the domain of knowledge, — a new weapon in the magazine of power.

Chapter 5: Discipline

... Space, time, society, labor, climate, food, locomotion, the animals, the mechanical forces, give us sincerest lessons, day by day, whose meaning is unlimited. They educate both the Understanding and the Reason.[8] ...

1. Nature is a discipline of the understanding in intellectual truths.[9] ...

2. Sensible objects conform to the premonitions of Reason and reflect the conscience. All things are moral; and in their boundless changes have an unceasing reference to spiritual nature. Therefore is nature glorious with form, color, and motion, that every globe in the remotest heaven; every chemical change from the rudest crystal up to the laws of life; every change of vegetation from the first principle of growth in the eye of a leaf, to the tropical forest and antediluvian coal-mine; every animal function from the sponge up to Hercules, shall hint or thunder to man the laws of right and wrong, and echo the Ten Commandments. Therefore is nature ever the ally of Religion: lends all her pomp and riches to the religious sentiment. Prophet and priest, David, Isaiah, Jesus, have drawn deeply from this source. This ethical character so penetrates the bone and marrow of nature, as to seem the end for which it was made. Whatever private purpose is answered by any member or part, this is its public and universal function, and is never omitted. Nothing in nature is exhausted in its first use. When a thing has served an end to the uttermost, it is wholly new for an ulterior service. In God, every end is converted into a new means. Thus the use of commodity, regarded by itself, is mean and squalid. But it is to the mind an education in the doctrine of Use, namely, that a thing is good only so far as it serves; that a conspiring of parts and efforts to the production of an end, is essential to any being. The first and gross manifestation of this truth, is our inevitable and hated training in values and wants, in corn and meat.

It has already been illustrated, that every natural process is a version of a moral sentence. The moral law lies at the centre of nature and radiates to the circumference. It is the pith and marrow of every substance, every relation, and every process. All things with which we deal, preach to us. ...

Chapter 6: Idealism

Thus is the unspeakable but intelligible and practicable meaning of the world conveyed to man, the immortal pupil, in every object of sense. To this one end of Discipline, all parts of nature conspire.

A noble doubt perpetually suggests itself, whether this end be not the Final Cause of the Universe; and whether nature outwardly exists.[10] ...

Finally, religion and ethics, which may be fitly called,—the practice of ideas, or the introduction of ideas into life,—have an analogous effect with all lower culture, in degrading nature and suggesting its dependence on spirit. Ethics and religion differ herein; that the one is the system of human duties commencing from man; the other, from God. Religion includes the personality of God; Ethics does not. They are one to our present design. They both put nature under foot. The first and last lesson of religion is, "The things that are seen, are temporal; the things that are unseen, are eternal."[11] It puts an affront upon nature. It does that for the unschooled, which philosophy does for Berkeley[12] and Viasa.[13] The uniform language that may be heard in the churches of the most ignorant sects, is,—"Contemn the unsubstantial shows of the world; they are vanities, dreams, shadows, unrealities; seek the realities of religion." The devotee flouts nature. Some theosophists have arrived at a certain hostility and indignation towards matter, as the Manichean and Plotinus.[14] They distrusted in themselves any looking back to these flesh-pots of Egypt. Plotinus was ashamed of his body. In short, they might all say of matter, what Michelangelo said of external beauty, "it is the frail and weary weed, in which God dresses the soul, which he has called into time."

It appears that motion, poetry, physical and intellectual science, and religion, all tend to affect our convictions of the reality of the external world. But I own there is something ungrateful in expanding too curiously the particulars of the general proposition, that all culture tends to imbue us with idealism. I have no hostility to nature, but a child's love to it. I expand and live in the warm day like corn and melons. Let us speak her fair. I do not wish to fling stones at my beautiful mother, nor soil my gentle nest. I only wish to indicate the true position of nature in regard to man, wherein to establish man, all right education tends; as the ground which to attain is the object of human life, that is, of man's connection with nature. Culture inverts the vulgar views of nature, and brings the mind to call that apparent, which it uses to call real, and that real, which it uses to call visionary. Children, it is true, believe in the external world. The belief that it appears only, is an afterthought, but with culture, this faith will as surely arise on the mind as did the first. ...

Chapter 7: Spirit

It is essential to a true theory of nature and of man, that it should contain somewhat progressive. Uses that are exhausted or that may be, and facts that end in the statement, cannot be all that is true of this brave lodging wherein man is harbored, and wherein all his faculties find appropriate and endless exercise. And all the uses of nature admit of being summed in one, which yields the activity of man an infinite scope. Through all its kingdoms, to the suburbs and outskirts of things, it is faithful to the cause whence it had its origin. It always speaks of Spirit. It suggests the absolute. It is a perpetual effect. It is a great shadow pointing always to the sun behind us. ...

... [W]hen, following the invisible steps of thought, we come to inquire, Whence is matter? and Whereto? many truths arise to us out of the recesses of consciousness. We learn that the highest is present to the soul of man, that the dread universal essence, which is not wisdom, or love, or beauty, or power, but all in one, and each entirely, is that for which all things exist, and that by which they are; that spirit creates; that behind nature, throughout nature, spirit is present; one and not compound, it does not act upon us from without, that is, in space and time, but spiritually, or through ourselves: therefore, that spirit, that is, the Supreme Being, does not build up nature around us, but puts it forth through us, as the life of the tree puts forth new branches and leaves through the pores of the old. As a plant upon the earth, so a man rests upon the bosom of God; he is nourished by unfailing fountains, and draws, at his need, inexhaustible power. Who can set bounds to the possibilities of man? Once inhale the upper air, being admitted to behold the absolute natures of justice and truth, and we learn that man has access to the entire mind of the Creator, is himself the creator in the finite. This view, which admonishes me where the sources of wisdom and power lie, and points to virtue as to

> "The golden key
> Which opes the palace of eternity,"[15]

carries upon its face the highest certificate of truth, because it animates me to create my own world through the purification of my soul.

The world proceeds from the same spirit as the body of man. It is a remoter and inferior incarnation of God, a projection of God in the unconscious. But it differs from the body in one important respect. It is not, like that, now subjected to the human will. Its serene order is inviolable by us. It is, therefore, to us, the present expositor of the divine mind. It is a fixed point whereby we may measure our departure. As we degenerate, the contrast between us and our house is more evident. We are as much strangers in nature, as we are aliens from God. We do not understand the notes of birds. The fox and the deer run away from us; the bear and tiger rend us. We do not know the uses of more than a few plants, as corn and the apple, the potato and the vine. Is not the landscape, every glimpse of which hath a grandeur, a face of him? Yet this may show us what discord is between man and nature, for you cannot freely admire a noble landscape, if laborers are digging in the field hard by. The poet finds something ridiculous in his delight, until he is out of the sight of men.

Chapter 8: Prospects

In inquiries respecting the laws of the world and the frame of things, the highest reason is always the truest. That which seems faintly possible—it is so refined, is often faint and dim because it is deepest seated in the mind among the eternal verities. Empirical science is apt to cloud the sight, and, by the very knowledge of functions and processes, to bereave the student of the manly contemplation of the whole. The savant becomes unpoetic. But the best read naturalist who lends an entire and devout attention to truth, will see that there remains much to learn of his relation to the world, and that it is not to be learned by any addition or subtraction or other comparison of known quantities, but is arrived at by untaught sallies of the spirit, by a continual self-recovery, and by entire humility. He will perceive that there are far more excellent qualities in the student than preciseness and infallibility; that a guess is often more fruitful than an indisputable affirmation, and that a dream may let us deeper into the secret of nature than a hundred concerted experiments.

For, the problems to be solved are precisely those which the physiologist and the naturalist omit to state. It is not so pertinent to man to know all the individuals of the animal kingdom, as it is to know whence and whereto is this tyrannizing unity in his constitution, which evermore separates and classifies things, endeavoring to reduce the most diverse to one form. When I behold a rich landscape, it is less to my purpose to recite correctly the order and superposition of the strata, than to know why all thought of multitude is lost in a tranquil sense of unity. I cannot greatly honor minuteness in details, so long as there is no hint to explain the relation between things and thoughts; no ray upon the *metaphysics* of conchology, of botany, of the arts, to show the relation of the forms of flowers, shells, animals, architecture, to the mind, and build science upon ideas. In a cabinet of natural history, we become sensible of a certain occult recognition and sympathy in regard to the most unwieldly and eccentric forms of beast, fish, and insect. The American who has been confined, in his own country, to the sight of buildings designed after foreign models, is surprised on entering York Minster or St. Peter's at Rome, by the feeling that these structures are imitations also—faint copies of an invisible archetype. Nor has science sufficient humanity, so long as the naturalist overlooks that wonderful congruity which subsists between man and the world; of which he is lord, not because he is the most subtile inhabitant, but because he is its head and heart, and finds something of himself in every great and small thing, in every mountain stratum, in every new law of color, fact of astronomy, or atmospheric influence which observation or analysis lay open. ...

... A wise writer will feel that the ends of study and composition are best answered by announcing undiscovered regions of thought, and so communicating, through hope, new activity to the torpid spirit.

I shall therefore conclude this essay with some traditions of man and nature, which a certain poet sang to me; and which, as they have always been in the world, and perhaps reappear to every bard, may be both history and prophecy.

"The foundations of man are not in matter, but in spirit. But the element of spirit is eternity. To it, therefore, the longest series of events, the oldest chronologies are young

and recent. In the cycle of the universal man, from whom the known individuals proceed, centuries are points, and all history is but the epoch of one degradation.

"We distrust and deny inwardly our sympathy with nature. We own and disown
our relation to it, by turns. We are, like Nebuchadnezzar, dethroned, bereft of reason,
and eating grass like an ox.[16] But who can set limits to the remedial force of spirit?

"A man is a god in ruins. ...

"Man is the dwarf of himself. Once he was permeated and dissolved by spirit.
He filled nature with his overflowing currents. Out from him sprang the sun and
moon; from man, the sun; from woman, the moon. The laws of his mind, the periods of his actions externized themselves into day and night, into the year and the
seasons. But, having made for himself this huge shell, his waters retired; he no longer
fills the veins and veinlets; he is shrunk to a drop. He sees, that the structure still fits
him, but fits him colossally. Say, rather, once it fitted him, now it corresponds to him
from far and on high. He adores timidly his own work. Now is man the follower of
the sun, and woman the follower of the moon. Yet sometimes he starts in his slum-
ber, and wonders at himself and his house, and muses strangely at the resemblance
betwixt him and it. He perceives that if his law is still paramount, if still he have
elemental power, if his word is sterling yet in nature, it is not conscious power, it is
not inferior but superior to his will. It is Instinct." Thus my Orphic poet sang.

At present, man applies to nature but half his force. He works on the world with
his understanding alone. He lives in it, and masters it by a penny-wisdom; and he that
works most in it, is but a half-man, and whilst his arms are strong and his digestion
good, his mind is imbruted, and he is a selfish savage. His relation to nature, his power
over it, is through the understanding; as by manure; the economic use of fire, wind,
water, and the mariner's needle; steam, coal, chemical agriculture; the repairs of the
human body by the dentist and the surgeon. This is such a resumption of power, as if a
banished king should buy his territories inch by inch, instead of vaulting at once into
his throne. Meantime, in the thick darkness, there are not wanting gleams of a better
light—occasional examples of the action of man upon nature with his entire force,—
with reason as well as understanding. Such examples are; the traditions of miracles in
the earliest antiquity of all nations; the history of Jesus Christ; the achievements of a
principle, as in religious and political revolutions, and in the abolition of the Slave-trade;
the miracles of enthusiasm, as those reported of Swedenborg, Hohenlohe, and the Shak-
ers; many obscure and yet contested facts, now arranged under the name of Animal
Magnetism; prayer; eloquence; self-healing; and the wisdom of children. These are examples of Reason's momentary grasp of the sceptre; the exertions of a power which exists not in time or space, but an instantaneous in-streaming causing power. The
difference between the actual and the ideal force of man is happily figured by the
schoolmen, in saying, that the knowledge of man is an evening knowledge, *vespertina
cognitio*, but that of God is a morning knowledge, *matutina cognitio*.

The problem of restoring to the world original and eternal beauty, is solved by the redemption of the soul.[17] ...

So shall we come to look at the world with new eyes. It shall answer the endless inquiry of the intellect,—What is truth? and of the affections—What is good? by yielding itself passive to the educated Will. Then shall come to pass what my poet said; "Nature is not fixed but fluid. Spirit alters, molds, makes it. The immobility or bruteness of nature, is the absence of spirit; to pure spirit, it is fluid, it is volatile, it is obedient. Every spirit builds itself a house; and beyond its house a world; and beyond its world, a heaven. Know then, that the world exists for you. For you is the phenomenon perfect. What we are, that only can we see. All that Adam had, all that Caesar could, you have and can do. Adam called his house, heaven and earth; Caesar called his house, Rome; you perhaps call yours, a cobbler's trade; a hundred acres of ploughed land; or a scholar's garret. Yet line for line and point for point, your dominion is as great as theirs, though without fine names. Build, therefore, your own world. As fast as you conform your life to the pure idea in your mind, that will unfold its great proportions. A correspondent revolution in things will attend the influx of the spirit. So fast will disagreeable appearances, swine, spiders, snakes, pests, madhouses, prisons, enemies, vanish; they are temporary and shall be no more seen. The sordor and filths of nature, the sun shall dry up, and the wind exhale. As when the summer comes from the south; the snow-banks melt, and the face of the earth becomes green before it, so shall the advancing spirit create its ornaments along its path, and carry with it the beauty it visits, and the song which enchants it; it shall draw beautiful faces, warm hearts, wise discourse, and heroic acts, around its way, until evil is no more seen. The kingdom of man over nature, which cometh not with observation,— a dominion such as now is beyond his dream of God,—he shall enter without more wonder than the blind man feels who is gradually restored to perfect sight."

Notes

1 Emerson is making the quasi-Kantian point that the natural world does not directly disclose to us certain truths that are in some sense already present in the natural world prior to its being experienced. Rather, its teachings come about only through the mutual interface of the mind and the external world.

2 These are the titles of Chapters 2–5, referring to the different sorts of goods afforded to human beings by the natural world. "Commodity" refers to the various physical goods that human beings find of use in pursuing their goals.

3 Emerson distinguishes three kinds of beauty found in the natural world. First is the beauty of form in which the senses take pleasure. Second is the beauty of the natural world when it serves as a kind of frame for the ethical deeds of human beings. Third is the beauty of the internal structure of the natural world, which reveals itself to the intellect when studied by science.

4 I Cor. 15:44.

5 This quotation is from Emanuel Swedenborg (1688–1772), Swedish theologian, who wrote a number of mystical works that were favorites of Emerson.

6 Emerson accepts a variety of neoplatonic metaphysics, according to which all truths pre-exist in a more basic form within the mind of God.

7 The quotation is from S. T. Coleridge.

8 The distinction between Understanding and Reason is borrowed from the English poet S. T. Coleridge, and has a predecessor in a similar distinction in Kant. Put simply, "Understanding" is the end-point of scientific, inferential thinking. "Reason" is more intuitive, and allows one to arrive at higher truths, including those of ethics.

9 Emerson's point is that many basic lessons about the constitution and behavior of the physical world are learned by direct study and experience of the nonhuman world. This aids the development of what Emerson calls "Understanding."

10 According to the neoplatonic metaphysics that Emerson accepts, the physical world is less real than the mental world. (Compare how in the *Timaeus* of Plato the physical world is a mere image of immaterial Forms.) This is for two reasons. First, the physical world is what it is only on account of the mind of God; it thus derives all of the reality it possesses from the mental life of God. Second, as Kant argued, the physical world is as it is only insofar as our own minds are constrained to interpret it according to the laws of our own thought.

11 II Cor. 4:18.

12 George Berkeley (1685–1753), one of the great British empiricists, held that the physical world is, at bottom, an ordered sequence of perceptions directly projected into human consciousness by the mind of God.

13 Viasa is a legendary figure said to have authored the *Vedas*, the oldest Hindu sacred text.

14 Plotinus (205–269/70) was the greatest neoplatonic philosopher, and was the teacher of Porphyry.

15 Milton, *Comus*, 13–14.

16 Nebuchadnezzar II was the king of Babylonia who defeated the kingdom of Judea and sent the Jews into captivity in Babylonia. Daniel 4. 25, 32–33 tells of his spells of madness, in which he ate grass in the fields like an ox.

17 Emerson holds high hopes for the future of the human species. By means of a spiritual rebirth, human beings will have a new relationship with nature. Emerson suggests that this will result in human power over the nonhuman world that surpasses that of known technology; Emerson mentions the sorts of human influence over events that are often classed as occult. More importantly, Emerson foresees a general improvement in the moral and spiritual life of human beings, which, as the following passage makes clear, will in itself radically transform the natural world, transforming it into a new Eden.

CHAPTER 27

Henry David Thoreau

Best remembered as an essayist and philosopher, Henry David Thoreau (1817–1862) was also a painstaking naturalist, whose studies of the biota of his native New England show a keen understanding of species' mutual interdependence within a given habitat.

Like his friend Emerson, Thoreau looked upon time spent in the natural world as a remedy for the stultifying effects human society could have on the human mind, leading it to preoccupation with trivialities and turning it away from attention to the development of the spirit. This theme takes center stage in Thoreau's writings, which extol the untrammeled wilderness, both for its own value and for its nourishment of human life and ambition. In this, Thoreau goes farther than Emerson in finding spiritual value in wildness; as such, he stands at the beginning of a tradition of Americans of European descent, defending the quickly vanishing wild lands.

Emerson valued experience in the natural world insofar as it purifies the human mind, leading it to a higher level of rationality. This strand is present in Thoreau's thought as well, but there is also a celebration of the wild, undisciplined aspect of the human soul, nourished through living close to nature, which Thoreau takes to be the root of individual genius as well as of a society's greatness. For Thoreau, the Western frontier was a symbol of the wildness to which human beings should aspire.

Thoreau went much farther than Emerson in advocating a rejection of the norms of conventional life in the service of attaining such spiritual growth. His most famous work, *Walden*, relates a time in his life in which he pursued this goal by living in utmost simplicity, close to nature. Later, he returned to Concord, but took long aimless walks through the woods. These walks form the backdrop of the following selection, which clearly presents the main themes of Thoreau's thought on the importance of Nature to human well-being.

HENRY DAVID THOREAU
"Walking"

I wish to speak a word for Nature, for absolute freedom and wildness, as contrasted with a freedom and culture merely civil—to regard man as an inhabitant, or a part and parcel of Nature, rather than a member of society. I wish to make an extreme statement, if so I may make an emphatic one, for there are enough champions of civilization: the minister and the school committee and every one of you will take care of that. …

I think that I cannot preserve my health and spirits, unless I spend four hours a day at least—and it is commonly more than that—sauntering through the woods and over the hills and fields, absolutely free from all worldly engagements. You may safely say, A penny for your thoughts, or a thousand pounds. When sometimes I am reminded that the mechanics and shopkeepers stay in their shops not only all the forenoon, but all the afternoon too, sitting with crossed legs, so many of them,—as if the legs were made to sit upon, and not to stand or walk upon,—I think that they deserve some credit for not having all committed suicide long ago. ...

At present, in this vicinity, the best part of the land is not private property; the landscape is not owned, and the walker enjoys comparative freedom. But possibly the day will come when it will be partitioned off into so-called pleasure-grounds, in which a few will take a narrow and exclusive pleasure only, — when fences shall be multiplied, and man-traps and other engines invented to confine men to the *public* road, and walking over the surface of God's earth shall be construed to mean trespassing on some gentleman's grounds. To enjoy a thing exclusively is commonly to exclude yourself from the true enjoyment of it. Let us improve our opportunities, then, before the evil days come. ...

We go eastward to realize history and study the works of art and literature, retracing the steps of the race; we go westward as into the future, with a spirit of enterprise and adventure. ...

The West of which I speak is but another name for the Wild; and what I have been preparing to say is, that in Wildness is the preservation of the World. Every tree sends its fibres forth in search of the Wild. The cities import it at any price. Men plow and sail for it. From the forest and wilderness come the tonics and barks which brace mankind. Our ancestors were savages. The story of Romulus and Remus being suckled by a wolf is not a meaningless fable.[1] The founders of every state which has risen to eminence have drawn their nourishment and vigor from a similar wild source. It was because the children of the Empire were not suckled by the wolf that they were conquered and displaced by the children of the northern forests who were.

I believe in the forest, and in the meadow, and in the night in which the corn grows. We require an infusion of hemlock spruce or arbor-vitae in our tea. There is a difference between eating and drinking for strength and from mere gluttony. The Hottentots eagerly devour the marrow of the koodoo and other antelopes raw, as a matter of course. Some of our northern Indians eat raw the marrow of the Arctic reindeer, as well as various other parts, including the summits of the antlers, as long as they are soft. And herein, perchance, they have stolen a march on the cooks of Paris. They get what usually goes to feed the fire. This is probably better than stall-fed beef and slaughter-house pork to make a man of. Give me a wildness whose glance no civilization can endure,—as if we lived on the marrow of koodoos devoured raw.

There are some intervals which border the strain of the wood thrush, to which I would migrate,—wild lands where no settler has squatted; to which, methinks, I am already acclimated.

The African hunter Cummings tells us that the skin of the eland, as well as that of most other antelopes just killed, emits the most delicious perfume of trees and grass. I would have every man so much like a wild antelope, so much a part and parcel of nature, that his very person should thus sweetly advertise our senses of his presence, and remind us of those parts of nature which he most haunts. I feel no disposition to be satirical, when the trapper's coat emits the odor of musquash even; it is a sweeter scent to me than that which commonly exhales from the merchant's or the scholar's garments. When I go into their wardrobes and handle their vestments, I am reminded of no grassy plains and flowery meads which they have frequented, but of dusty merchants' exchanges and libraries rather. ...

... Life consists with wildness. The most alive is the wildest. Not yet subdued to man, its presence refreshes him. One who pressed forward incessantly and never rested from his labors, who grew fast and made infinite demands on life, would always find himself in a new country or wilderness, and surrounded by the raw material of life. He would be climbing over the prostrate stems of primitive forest-trees.

Hope and the future for me are not in lawns and cultivated fields, not in towns and cities, but in the impervious and quaking swamps. When, formerly, I have analyzed my partiality for some farm which I had contemplated purchasing, I have frequently found that I was attracted solely by a few square rods of impermeable and unfathomable bog—a natural sink in one corner of it. That was the jewel which dazzled me. I derive more of my subsistence from the swamps which surround my native town than from the cultivated gardens in the village. There are no richer parterres to my eyes than the dense beds of dwarf andromeda (*Cassandra calyculata*) which cover these tender places on the earth's surface. Botany cannot go farther than tell me the names of the shrubs which grow there—the high blueberry, panicled andromeda, lambkill, azalea, and rhodora—all standing in the quaking sphagnum. I often think that I should like to have my house front on this mass of dull red bushes, omitting other flower plots and borders, transplanted spruce and trim box, even graveled walks— to have this fertile spot under my windows, not a few imported barrowfuls of soil only to cover the sand which was thrown out in digging the cellar. Why not put my house, my parlor, behind this plot, instead of behind that meagre assemblage of curiosities, that poor apology for a Nature and Art, which I call my front yard? It is an effort to clear up and make a decent appearance when the carpenter and mason have departed, though done as much for the passer-by as the dweller within. The most tasteful front-yard fence was never an agreeable object of study to me; the most elaborate ornaments, acorn tops, or what not, soon wearied and disgusted me. Bring your sills up to the very edge of the swamp, then (though it may not be the best place for a dry cellar), so that there be no access on that side to citizens. Front yards are not made to walk in, but, at most, through, and you could go in the back way.

Yes, though you may think me perverse, if it were proposed to me to dwell in the neighborhood of the most beautiful garden that ever human art contrived, or else of a Dismal Swamp, I should certainly decide for the swamp. How vain, then, have been all your labors, citizens, for me!

My spirits infallibly rise in proportion to the outward dreariness. Give me the ocean, the desert, or the wilderness! In the desert, pure air and solitude compensate for want of moisture and fertility. The traveler Burton says of it: "Your *morale* improves; you become frank and cordial, hospitable and single-minded. ... In the desert, spirituous liquors excite only disgust. There is a keen enjoyment in a mere animal existence." They who have been traveling long on the steppes of Tartary say, "On reentering cultivated lands, the agitation, perplexity, and turmoil of civilization oppressed and suffocated us; the air seemed to fail us, and we felt every moment as if about to die of asphyxia." When I would recreate myself, I seek the darkest wood, the thickest and most interminable and, to the citizen, most dismal, swamp. I enter a swamp as a sacred place, a *sanctum sanctorum.* There is the strength, the marrow, of Nature. The wildwood covers the virgin mould, and the same soil is good for men and for trees. A man's health requires as many acres of meadow to his prospect as his farm does loads of muck. There are the strong meats on which he feeds. A town is saved, not more by the righteous men in it than by the woods and swamps that surround it. A township where one primitive forest waves above while another primitive forest rots below, such a town is fitted to raise not only corn and potatoes, but poets and philosophers for the coming ages. In such a soil grew Homer and Confucius and the rest, and out of such a wilderness comes the Reformer eating locusts and wild honey.

To preserve wild animals implies generally the creation of a forest for them to dwell in or resort to. So it is with man. A hundred years ago they sold bark in our streets peeled from our own woods. In the very aspect of those primitive and rugged trees there was, methinks, a tanning principle which hardened and consolidated the fibres of men's thoughts. Ah! already I shudder for these comparatively degenerate days of my native village, when you cannot collect a load of bark of good thickness, and we no longer produce tar and turpentine.

The civilized nations—Greece, Rome, England—have been sustained by the primitive forests which anciently rotted where they stand. They survive as long as the soil is not exhausted. Alas for human culture! Little is to be expected of a nation, when the vegetable mould is exhausted, and it is compelled to make manure of the bones of its fathers. There the poet sustains himself merely by his own superfluous fat, and the philosopher comes down on his marrow-bones. ...

In short, all good things are wild and free. There is something in a strain of music, whether produced by an instrument or by the human voice,—take the sound of a bugle in a summer night, for instance,—which by its wildness, to speak without satire, reminds me of the cries emitted by wild beasts in their native forests. It is so much of their wildness as I can understand. Give me for my friends and neighbors wild men, not tame ones. The wildness of the savage is but a faint symbol of the awful ferity with which good men and lovers meet.

I love even to see the domestic animals reassert their native rights,—any evidence that they have not wholly lost their original wild habits and vigor; as when my neighbor's cow breaks out of her pasture early in the spring and boldly swims the river, a cold, gray tide, twenty-five or thirty rods wide, swollen by the melted snow. It is the buffalo crossing the Mississippi. This exploit confers some dignity on the herd in my eyes,—already dignified. The seeds of instinct are preserved under the thick hides of cattle and horses, like seeds in the bowels of the earth, an indefinite period. ...

While almost all men feel an attraction drawing them to society, few are attracted strongly to Nature. In their reaction to Nature men appear to me for the most part, notwithstanding their arts, lower than the animals. It is not often a beautiful relation, as in the case of the animals. How little appreciation of the beauty of the landscape there is among us! We have to be told that the Greeks called the world *kosmos*, Beauty, or Order, but we do not see clearly why they did so, and we esteem it at best only a curious philological fact.

For my part, I feel that with regard to Nature I live a sort of border life, on the confines of a world into which I make occasional and transient forays only, and my patriotism and allegiance to the state into whose territories I seem to retreat are those of a moss-trooper.[2] Unto a life which I call natural I would gladly follow even a will-o'-the-wisp through bogs and sloughs unimaginable, but no moon nor firefly has shown me the causeway to it. Nature is a personality so vast and universal that we have never seen one of her features. The walker in the familiar fields which stretch around my native town sometimes finds himself in another land than is described in their owners' deeds, as it were in some faraway field on the confines of the actual Concord, where her jurisdiction ceases, and the idea which the word Concord suggests ceases to be suggested. These farms which I have myself surveyed, these bounds which I have set up, appear dimly still as through a mist; but they have no chemistry to fix them; they fade from the surface of the glass, and the picture which the painter painted stands out dimly from beneath. The world with which we are commonly acquainted leaves no trace, and it will have no anniversary. ...

Above all, we cannot afford not to live in the present. He is blessed over all mortals who loses no moment of the passing life in remembering the past. Unless our philosophy hears the cock crow in every barn-yard within our horizon, it is belated.

That sound commonly reminds us that we are growing rusty and antique in our employments and habits of thought. His philosophy comes down to a more recent time than ours. There is something suggested by it that is a newer testament—the gospel according to this moment. He has not fallen astern; he has got up early and kept up early, and to be where he is is to be in season, in the foremost rank of time. It is an expression of the health and soundness of Nature, a brag for all the world— healthiness as of a spring burst forth, a new fountain of the Muses, to celebrate this last instant of time. Where he lives no fugitive slave laws are passed. Who has not betrayed his master many times since last he heard that note?

The merit of this bird's strain is in its freedom from all plaintiveness. The singer can easily move us to tears or to laughter, but where is he who can excite in us a pure morning joy? When, in doleful dumps, breaking the awful stillness of our wooden sidewalk on a Sunday, or, perchance, a watcher in the house of mourning, I hear a cockerel crow far or near, I think to myself, "There is one of us well, at any rate,"— and with a sudden gush return to my senses.

We had a remarkable sunset one day last November. I was walking in a meadow, the source of a small brook, when the sun at last, just before setting, after a cold, gray day, reached a clear stratum in the horizon, and the softest, brightest morning sunlight fell on the dry grass and on the stems of the trees in the opposite horizon and on the leaves of the shrub oaks on the hillside, while our shadows stretched long over the meadow eastward, as if we were the only motes in its beams. It was such a light as we could not have imagined a moment before, and the air also was so warm and serene that nothing was wanting to make a paradise of that meadow. When we reflected that this was not a solitary phenomenon, never to happen again, but that it would happen forever and ever, an infinite number of evenings, and cheer and reassure the latest child that walked there, it was more glorious still.

The sun sets on some retired meadow, where no house is visible, with all the glory and splendor that it lavishes on cities, and perchance as it has never set before, — where there is but a solitary marsh hawk to have his wings gilded by it, or only a musquash looks out from his cabin, and there is some little black-veined brook in the midst of the marsh, just beginning to meander, winding slowly round a decaying stump. We walked in so pure and bright a light, gilding the withered grass and leaves, so softly and serenely bright, I thought I had never bathed in such a golden flood, without a ripple or a murmur to it. The west side of every wood and rising ground gleamed like the boundary of Elysium and the sun on our backs seemed like a gentle herdsman driving us home at evening.

So we saunter toward the Holy Land, till one day the sun shall shine more brightly than ever he has done, shall perchance shine into our minds and hearts, and light up our whole lives with a great awakening light, as warm and serene and golden as on a banquet in autumn.

Notes

1 According to Roman mythology, the brothers Romulus and Remus were the founders of Rome.

2 The moss-troopers were bands of criminals who preyed on travelers in the English and Scottish bogs during the seventeenth century.